Putting God on the Map

Putting God on the Map

Theology and Conceptual Mapping

Edited by
Erin Kidd and
Jakob Karl Rinderknecht

Foreword by Robert Masson

LEXINGTON BOOKS/FORTRESS ACADEMIC
Lanham • Boulder • New York • London

Published by Lexington Books/Fortress Academic

Lexington Books is an imprint of The Rowman & Littlefield Publishing Group, Inc.
4501 Forbes Boulevard, Suite 200, Lanham, Maryland 20706
www.rowman.com

Unit A, Whitacre Mews, 26-34 Stannary Street, London SE11 4AB

British Library Cataloguing in Publication Information Available

Library of Congress Cataloging-in-Publication Data

Names: Kidd, Erin, editor.
Title: Putting God on the map : theology and conceptual mapping / edited by Erin Kidd and Jakob Karl Rinderknecht ; foreword by Robert Masson.
Description: Lanham : Lexington Books-Fortress Academic, 2018. | Includes bibliographical references and index.
Identifiers: LCCN 2018025734 (print) | LCCN 2018032121 (ebook) | ISBN 9781978703971 (Electronic) | ISBN 9781978703964 (cloth : alk. paper)
Subjects: LCSH: Theology. | Information visualization. | Concept mapping.
Classification: LCC BR118 (ebook) | LCC BR118 .P88 2018 (print) | DDC 230.01—dc23
LC record available at https://lccn.loc.gov/2018025734

∞™ The paper used in this publication meets the minimum requirements of American National Standard for Information Sciences—Permanence of Paper for Printed Library Materials, ANSI/NISO Z39.48-1992.

Printed in the United States of America

Many thanks to all those who supported this project,
particularly Bob Masson,
who introduced us to this new terrain
and equipped us to explore it.

Contents

Figures

Foreword

Robert Masson

The chapters in this book graphically illustrate how the cognitive sciences' explorations of neural and conceptual mapping offer theology new tools for charting our fractured religious landscape. Like a handy theological atlas, the book provides "easy-to-read" explanations of the terminology and background for these innovative roadmaps. So, no introduction of that sort is required of me. Nonetheless, I am glad for the opportunity to offer as an initial orientation some reflections on the aptness of the volume's guiding metaphor.[1]

Asking where we put God on our conceptual map captures a serious challenge posed by the pluralism and polarization that is reshaping our religious and cultural landscape. It is difficult to get accurate bearings on God, if we do not agree on what count as coordinates. Agreement of that sort is becoming more difficult to find within religions traditions, not to speak of between them. Part of the difficulty has to do with the seemingly huge fissures between different levels and contexts of understanding:

- gaps between the average person's world of understanding and academic theology's;
- disconnects between the type of thinking, argumentation, and presuppositions in theology and the methods of other academic disciplines;
- the chasm which has emerged between the academic and ecclesial settings;
- ruptures between divided churches, opposed schools of thought, and polarized subgroups within churches and schools of thought; and, finally,
- the gulf between the secular imaginary and the ways believers and religious authorities imagine things.

A further aspect of the difficulty has to do with the growing recognition that the pluralism of our religious, philosophical, and cultural perspectives is irreducible, at least as a matter of fact, if not in principle. None of our traditional theological maps accurately cover the whole terrain. Conflict between the maps undermines confidence that any of them truthfully depict the landscape. Fully and accurately charting the diversity of our religious topography calls for new kinds of theological mapping just as advances in medicine have required new ways of imaging and mapping the human body.

Herein lies the special aptness of the mapping metaphor: conceptual mapping is a central notion in contemporary cognitive linguistics that suggests a new way of thinking about religion and theology. As readers will discover in the book, if they did not already know, much of the research in cognitive linguistics upends the conventional notion that literal meaning is foundational. In this research, neural mapping is the fundamental model for thought, reasoning, conceptualization, and imagination. In the early stages in the 1980s and 1990s, cognitive linguists, particularly George Lakoff and a number of collaborators, sought to understand how meanings are mapped from "source domains," which are more familiar and concrete, to less familiar and more abstract "target domains."[2] This research has been extremely effective at clarifying a range of conceptual and grammatical issues that had previously resisted satisfactory theoretical explanation, such as how categorization works or how prepositions work across languages. According to this research, reasoning and concepts are not literal, abstract, and disembodied. Rather our conceptual systems and inferences arise from, use, and are crucially shaped by the perceptual and motor systems of our bodies and the neural systems of our brains. Hence, metaphorical mappings are not secondary and illustrative. Reasoning is guided by metaphorical mappings derived from our embodiment. This metaphorical mapping is a fundamental and pervasive feature of human thought and language. Physical motion, for example, provides the underlying conceptual mapping that guides much of our thinking about time, change, and actions. We conceptualize time as "flying," as "ahead" of us, as "behind" us, as "stopping," or as "going on" forever. We "move" through time. Time "passes" us by.

Lakoff and his followers concluded from their research that the imaginative aspects of cognition—metonymy, metaphor, framing, image schemas, and mental images—are crucial and primary, not derivative and secondary. From this perspective, objectivity, precision, and stability in cognition are possible, but literal meaning is not the default position or foundation. It is just the opposite. Words prompt for meaning rather than capture it. Language is an underspecified tip of a giant iceberg of underlying and mostly unconscious cognitive processes of categorization and metaphorical mapping.

Recent research in cognitive linguistics, particularly by Gilles Fauconnier and Mark Turner, argues that conceptualization and inference is much more complex than the earlier metaphorical model suggested.[3] Conceptualization and inference are hardly ever the result of a single unidirectional mapping between a source domain and a target domain. Rather conceptualization and reasoning typically involve mappings that blend inputs in multiple and complex ways to create larger networks of meaning. Both our everyday and our theoretical worlds of meanings are built up over generations through the cobbling and sculpting of these networks of meanings. Fauconnier and Turner describe the most sophisticated kind of blend as a bi-directional mapping between multiple source frames. Their research makes a compelling case that this capacity for double-scope mapping generated human evolution's "cultural big bang" in art, religion, and technology 30,000 to 60,000 years ago. They contend that double-scope conceptual mapping continues to drive humanity's amazing potential for developing new understandings and new methods of discovery.

Blending theory provides a theoretical framework for explaining the largely unconscious cognitive processes underlying these conceptual mappings and networks of meanings. I leave it to the chapters which follow to describe in more detail how this mapping works and the implications for theology, mindful that *reading* maps and *comprehending their logic* is different than any *talking about* the maps on my part here in the Foreword. By way of anticipation, however, it is important to emphasize that mapping is not a univocal process and that some mapping is tectonic. The technological and medical revolution in imaging the body (x-ray, CT, MRI, PET, etc.) illustrates how there are many ways of mapping that often entail very different logics for their charting and interpretation. Mary Gerhart and Allan Russell's investigations of metaphor and the logic of discovery brought to attention the tectonic character of the kind of conceptual mapping that accounts for creativity in the arts, discovery in science, and the disclosure of revelatory possibilities in religion.[4]

What do Gerhart and Russell mean by tectonic? The most significant developments in science, technology, the arts, and religion emerge as the manifestation of dramatic and revelatory shifts in human conceptualization and inference. Such shifts yield brand-new ways of understanding, not merely new data or knowledge. Consider an example from science. There are significant differences between the discovery of a new planet, a black hole, and the theory of general relativity. In the first case, the discovery of a planet, new data is added to our understanding, but our way of understanding the constituents of the universe is not altered. In the case of black holes, there is a metaphorical mapping and imaginative extension of the category of cosmic entities to include something in addition to planets and empty space. In this case, it is not just a matter of new data. Here we have added a new category, not just a new constituent of the prior categories. So, we have expanded our knowledge of the constituents of the universe. But a far more fundamental shift in understanding is brought about by Einstein's theoretical "discoveries." His theoretical discoveries made it possible to think about the cosmos in altogether new ways and consequently opened up, for the first time, conceptual space in which the idea of black holes was conceivable at all. Here we are talking about a brand-new way of understanding, rather than new data, or an expansion of knowledge.

God-talk emerges as the manifestation of this sort of dramatic and revelatory shift in human conceptualization and inference. The study of religion and theology has as much to do with clarifying such shifts in understanding as it does with the acquisition of new information. Religion can be understood as living with the disclosure of a particular tectonic understanding and mapping. The scriptures narrate the tectonic understanding and its origins. Doctrine conceptualizes the tectonic understanding as various beliefs. Commandments and other prescribed behaviors spell out the implications of the tectonic understanding for our comportment. Rituals, dance, song, and other arts are symbolic expressions of the tectonic understanding. Catechisms outline the basics or parameters of the tectonic understanding. Theology can be thought of as the effort to make sense of the revelatory understanding in terms of its tectonic and novel mapping, rather than in terms of something else, such as psychology, sociology, history, or philosophy, which is the task of religious studies.

Considerable confusion about God-talk, objections to its validity, and disagreement between faiths and schools of thought can be clarified by more carefully attending to the conceptual mapping of our religious discourse and theological argumentation. It would be quixotic to imagine that the insights and tools of cognitive linguistics by themselves will transform how God is put on the map or resolve the challenges posed by the pluralism and polarization that is reshaping our religious and cultural landscape. But the approach nevertheless has significant potential. Let me give some examples. Earlier I mentioned the gaps between the average person's world of understanding and academic theology's and between the secular imaginary and the ways believers and religious authorities imagine things. A crucial factor in both is an eclipse of tectonic understanding. Instead we have the pervasive notion that understanding is either literal or figurative. This binary choice does not indicate a complete loss of metaphorical, symbolic, and analogical thinking. Rather it conceals the legitimate claims of tectonic understanding by diminishing it as an entirely subjective, relative, and "merely" figurative way of making sense of the world and expressing truth about it. The average person has little background or patience for traditional metaphysical explanations, such as the doctrine of analogy, or for theological discourses on religious epistemology. Nor is the average person much influenced by the authority or pronouncements of philosophers, theologians, and religious leaders on such matters. Moreover, there are a good number of the latter who also frame theological arguments as true either literally or figuratively without entertaining the possibility of a conceptual mapping that is semantically proper, logically warranted, and factually the case, but neither literal nor figurative in the narrower conventional senses.[5] The average person, however, does give some credit, whether for good or bad, to the findings of the sciences. George Lakoff and collaborators such as Fauconnier and Turner have shown that it is possible to reach relatively broad audiences with their research. So, it is not unreasonable to hope that theological appropriations of blending theory's insights focused on concrete and familiar illustrations could help address the eclipse of tectonic understanding. The chapters in this book help to move that project forward.

Likewise, conceptual mapping has exceptional potential for clarifying the ruptures between divided churches and opposed schools of thought. Two groundbreaking examples of this potential have been demonstrated in Jakob Rinderknecht's analysis of "differentiated consensus" in the 1999 *Joint Declaration on the Doctrine of Justification*, and Stephen Shaver's dissertation on the neuralgic ecumenical issue of Eucharistic presence.[6] Both have contributed essays to this volume.

Finally, an examination of theology and conceptual mapping can play a significant role in addressing the gap between theology and other academic disciplines. In making this claim I agree in part with Edward Slingerland's argument in *What Science Offers the Humanities*[7] that conceptual mapping provides objective analytical tools for making sense of religious conceptions and the logic of theological inferences. I also agree that while these tools are exceptionally helpful in clarifying the meaning and inferential logic of religious discourse, these means cannot settle issues about their truth, for which other kinds of argumentation are necessary. I take strong exception, however, to Slingerland's Darwinist rejection of meaningful God-talk. Slingerland fails to credit blending theory's account of how new tectonic understanding emerges in religion as well as in the sciences.[8] In any case, conceptual mapping provides common ground for significant engagement between theology and the sciences as several chapters in this book also illustrate.

In sum, "putting God on the map" is no simple matter today because there are so many seemingly conflicting theological "maps" and religious "territories" before us. This volume is a wonderfully accessible introduction to some of the ways blending theory, and cognitive science more generally, can help us to more clearly think about what we are doing when we think about God and religion. In doing so, it will hopefully help foster a better conversation about the God who is charted by this richness of maps.

NOTES

1. My comments anticipate notions that the contributors more fully explain, nuance, illustrate, and document in the chapters that follow and for which I have provided more detailed arguments in my own publications.

2. The chapters which follow will provide citations for key books by Lakoff and colleagues and introductions to their main ideas, as well as references to the overviews provided in John Sanders's book and mine.

3. The key work is Gilles Fauconnier and Mark Turner, *The Way We Think: Conceptual Blending and the Mind's Hidden Complexities* (New York: Basic Books, 2002).

4. Mary Gerhart and Allan Melvin Russell, *Metaphoric Process: The Creation of Scientific and Religious Understanding* (Fort Worth, TX: Texas Christian University Press, 1984); *New Maps for Old: Explorations in Science and Religion* (New York: Continuum, 2001).

5. For more on this see my "Conceiving God: Literal and Figurative Prompt for a More Tectonic Distinction," *Open Theology* 4, no. 1 (2018).

6. Jakob Karl Rinderknecht, *Mapping the Differentiated Consensus of the Joint Declaration* (New York: Palgrave Macmillan, 2016), and Stephen Shaver, "Metaphors of Eucharistic Presence: A Cognitive Linguistics Approach to an Ecumenical Theology of Bread, Wine, and the Body and Blood of Christ" (PhD diss., Graduate Theological Union Berkeley, 2017).

7. Edward Slingerland, *What Science Offers the Humanities*, (New York: Cambridge University Press, 2008).

8. See my "What a Theological Appropriation of Cognitive Linguistics' Blending Theory Brings to a Scientific Understanding of the Evolution of Religion," in *The Evolution of Religion: How Biology, Psychology, Theology and Culture Interact*, ed. Jay R. Feierman and Lluis Oviedo (Routledge, forthcoming).

BIBLIOGRAPHY

Fauconnier, Gilles and Mark Turner. *The Way We Think: Conceptual Blending and the Mind's Hidden Complexities.* New York: Basic Books, 2002.

Gerhart, Mary, and Allan Russell. *Metaphoric Process: The Creation of Scientific and Religious Understanding*. Fort Worth: Texas Christian University Press, 1984.

———. *New Maps for Old: Explorations in Science and Religion*. New York: Continuum, 2001.

Masson, Robert. "Conceiving God: Literal and Figurative Prompt for a More Tectonic Distinction." *Open Theology* 4, no. 1 (2018): 136–57.

———. "What a Theological Appropriation of Cognitive Linguistics' Blending Theory Brings to a Scientific Understanding of the Evolution of Religion." In *The Evolution of Religion: How Biology, Psychology, Theology and Culture Interact.* Edited by Jay R. Feierman and Lluis Oviedo. Routledge, forthcoming.

Rinderknecht, Jakob Karl. *Mapping the Differentiated Consensus of the Joint Declaration.* New York: Palgrave, 2016.

Shaver, Stephen. "Metaphors of Eucharistic Presence: A Cognitive Linguistics Approach to an Ecumenical Theology of Bread, Wine, and the Body and Blood of Christ." PhD dissertation, Graduate Theological Union Berkeley, 2017. ProQuest (10741782).

Slingerland, Edward. *What Science Offers the Humanities.* New York: Cambridge University Press, 2008.

Chapter One

An Introduction to Conceptual Mapping

Erin Kidd and Jakob Rinderknecht

Since the middle of the last century, the emergence and development of fields as diverse as artificial intelligence, evolutionary science, cognitive linguistics, and neuroscience have led to a greater understanding of how humans think. Gone are the models of a disembodied mind performing calculations on abstract symbols. In their stead is a growing consensus that meaning emerges from the body's interaction with the world. These insights have revolutionized the way in which scientists and philosophers think about the mind/body problem, the formation and function of language, the evolution of human being, and even the development of scientific progress itself. Until recently, however, this research has gone largely unnoticed within Christian theology. But this revolution in understanding human cognition calls for broader and richer engagement with theology and religious studies: How does this new insight into human meaning-making bear on our understanding of religious meaning-making? And how might Christian theology interpret and respond to this new understanding of the development of human thought?

CONCEPTUAL MAPPING

This book focuses particularly on what is referred to as *conceptual mapping*—the mind's ability to create new meaning by making connections between previously disparate domains of thought.[1] The most basic of these connections arise from our simple motor and sensory experience. These in turn serve as the building blocks for more complicated and creative meaning-making. The theory of conceptual mapping therefore roots higher-order human thinking in the physicality of the human body, offering resources for thinking about how we think and speak and also for understanding how these capacities have evolved.

This research begins with the work of George Lakoff and Mark Johnson. In their 1980 *Metaphors We Live By*, Lakoff and Johnson argue that metaphor characterizes our most basic ways of interacting with and thinking about the world. The mind creates meaning through what they call *conceptual metaphor*—that is, "understanding and experiencing one kind of thing in terms of another."[2] Through conceptual metaphor, we make sense of what is complex or ambiguous in terms of what is more clear and distinct.[3] Consider the language we use to talk about arguments: "Your claims are *indefensible*," "He *attacked every weak point* in my argument," "I *demolished* his argument."[4] Here we are talking about argumentation in terms of war. Lakoff and Johnson identify this as the ARGUMENT IS WAR conceptual metaphor, where the rules and methods of warfare (the source domain) structure our experience of arguing (the target domain).

These metaphors are not merely rhetorical flourishes but fundamentally structure our ways of interacting with the world. As Lakoff and Johnson write,

> We don't just *talk* about arguments in terms of war. We can actually win or lose arguments. We see the person we are arguing with as an opponent. We attack his positions and we defend our own. We gain and lose ground. We plan and use strategies. If we find a position indefensible, we can abandon it and take a new line of attack. Many of the things we *do* in arguing are partially structured by the concept of war.[5]

In other words, warfare not only helps us make sense of arguments but actively structures our understanding and participation in them. According to conceptual metaphor theory, much of our experience is characterized by this "understanding and experiencing one kind of thing in terms of another."[6] In short, human thinking and activity is metaphorical all the way down.

The particular metaphors we use arise from our embodied interaction with the world. We think not as logical machines or as disembodied intellects but as human beings. We are upright bipedal mammals and therefore inescapably experience the world in this way. Many of our most basic metaphors (MORE IS UP, EQUALITY IS BALANCE, AFFECTION IS WARMTH) are predicated on the kind of creatures that we are and the kind of world we live in.[7]

Culture also contributes to what metaphors structure our experience of the world. Consider the conceptual metaphor TIME IS MONEY. This metaphor enables us to think of time as something that can be spent, saved, or wasted. Its structuring goes deep—we do not merely speak poetically of "lost time" but experience it as an economic reality. And yet this structuring is completely culture dependent. Not all cultures conceive of time this way. In fact, Lakoff and Johnson suggest that it is particularly localized to industrial cultures.[8]

Thus, conceptual metaphor theory recognizes that meaning-making is a co-constitutive process between mind, body, and world. The particularities of human embodiment and cultural context ground the metaphors we live by. In turn, these conceptual metaphors deeply shape our experience of the world.

While fundamental to the development of contemporary cognitive linguistics, Lakoff and Johnson's work has been complicated in many respects by theories that draw attention to the multidirectional and complex mappings of the mind. In *The Way We Think*, Gilles Fauconnier and Mark Turner describe a process they call *conceptual blending* in which the mind, often unconsciously, maps input from two different domains into one new blended space. According to Fauconnier and Turner, conceptual blending is the source of "the human power to construct meanings."[9] Our capacity for conceptual blending is the basis of human language, art, religion, and science.[10]

While Lakoff and Johnson's conceptual metaphor theory is unidirectional—with a target and a source—conceptual blending allows for more complicated relationships between mental spaces. In fact, what Lakoff and Johnson identify as conceptual metaphors are really just a set of simple blends that Fauconnier and Turner identify as *single-scope*, in which one field of meaning is mapped onto another. In the most complex blends, which they refer to as *double-scope*, two fields of meaning collide to produce a third, whose emergent structure makes new and unpredictable meaning possible.

A mundane example is the contemporary computer desktop. According to Fauconnier and Turner, it represents a unique blend between two previously disparate domains: a desk and a computer. The computer desktop represents a genuinely novel construction—a new logic in which throwing something in the trash is equivalent to ejecting a drive. This new space allows users who understand the rules of an office space—that documents go in files, for instance—to interact with a computer. If this were all the blend did, however, it would be single-scope, similar to Lakoff and Johnson's experiencing one thing in terms of another. Rather, in the new blended space, the user moves seamlessly through traditional computer commands (print, save, delete, run program) and digital forms of traditional office tasks (file, copy, trash).[11] The computer desktop becomes a third space, drawing—and changing—meanings from both of these areas.

Physicist Allan Russell and religious scholar Mary Gerhart have attended to similar phenomena of how scientific and religious ideas progress under the rubric of *metaphoric process*.[12] A classical case for them is the general theory of relativity. According to Gerhart and Russell, Einstein came to this theory by drawing connections between two disparate—even contradictory—fields of meaning. On the one hand was the principle of classical mechanics that all motion is relative. Physical laws operate without respect to a frame of reference. In other words, perfectly consistent descriptions of the world can arise whether I take the earth or the sun to be the center of the galaxy, but the physical laws will be the same. On the other hand, in electrodynamics, the frame of reference does matter. It makes an important difference whether a magnet is rotated around a conductor or whether a conductor is rotated around a magnet—despite these activities being equivalent given different frames of reference.[13]

By drawing an equivalence between the two fields, Einstein forced "distortions of our epistemic field . . . [that] are so extraordinary that they would not be accepted within the public world of meanings were it not for a substantial number of experimental observations that are in agreement with the relativity theory."[14] Einstein's revelatory synthesis of classical mechanics and electrodynamics offered a way of consolidating and formally expressing what had seemed at the time to be disparate and contradictory evidence—for instance, the constant speed of light in a vacuum and the failure of accelerometers to register free fall. His synthesis of these two domains of thought not only revolutionized each of them—that is, how we now understand classical mechanics and electrodynamics—but also created a new theoretical space. In other words, this new theory not only made intelligible the experimental results scientists had already achieved but also made possible new scientific questions and, therefore, new experiments.[15] Gerhart and Russell call the specific metaphoric expansion that occurs when "two concepts [that are] both firmly or rigidly embedded in a field of meanings" are equated, *tectonic*.[16]

Gerhart and Russell are interested in metaphoric processes like these because, as they argue, such processes occur within both the fields of scientific and religious reflection—recognition of which could serve as a way of expanding dialogue between science and religion.[17] But while their work focuses on the creation of new meaning within the fields of science and religion (and the dialogue between them) the processes at work in Einstein's theorizing is not qualitatively different from the more mundane ability to use a computer desktop. The cognitive mechanism behind Einstein's theory of relativity is the same blending that occurs in our everyday interactions with the world.[18]

Following Fauconnier and Turner, we use the term *conceptual mapping* to refer to research on metaphor theory and blending theory as a whole. And following Robert Masson, we understand Gerhart and Russell's metaphoric process as being made possible by the mind's conceptual mapping.[19] Together, these theories offer an understanding of the human being as a creature with the capacity for higher thought that arises in and through her concrete interactions with the environment, made manifest by the mind's ability to make increasingly complex connections across disparate domains of thought.

IMPLICATIONS OF CONCEPTUAL MAPPING

This research has broad implications for philosophical and theological reflection. As Lakoff and Johnson argue in *Metaphors We Live By*, recognition that we think in conceptual metaphors requires reevaluating how we define both *truth* and *meaning*—focusing more on the coherence of a statement within a particular framework.[20] It also fundamentally challenges any simple dichotomy between objectivity and subjectivity.[21] Lakoff and Johnson argue instead for "an experientialist synthesis"[22] in which "truth is relative to our conceptual system, which is grounded in, and constantly tested by, our experiences and those of other members of our culture in our daily interactions with other people and with our physical and cultural environments."[23]

They develop these ideas further in their 1999 *Philosophy in the Flesh*, arguing that understanding human thought requires rethinking many of our philosophical assumptions: "The mind is inherently embodied. Thought is mostly unconscious. Abstract concepts are largely metaphorical. . . . Because of these discoveries, philosophy can never be the same again."[24] As Lakoff and Johnson go on to demonstrate, these three major findings of cognitive science not only revolutionize our understandings of how humans think but have broader philosophical implications in epistemology, metaphysics, and morality. Lakoff and Johnson therefore offer what they call a *philosophy in the flesh*.

They argue that many traditional philosophical antinomies (soul/body, subject/self, person/nature, subject/object) make sense only if one assumes human reason is disembodied, conscious, and nonmetaphorical. Within a philosophy in the flesh, these antinomies disappear. Consider, for example, how their embodied realism posits the relationship between subject and object—and therefore subjectivity and objectivity. Lakoff and Johnson appeal to color to explain their theory. They argue that even a brief consideration of color vision undercuts both metaphysical realism and subjectivism.

Traditional correspondence theories of truth and objectivity fail to describe our experience of color. Our vision of red is not an inner mental state that corresponds to an external reality. There is no such thing as "red" in the world.[25] Our perception of an object's color is the result of a complex set of interactions between (1) lighting conditions, (2) wavelengths of light, (3) the structure of our eyes, and (4) the interpretation of the signals sent by our eyes to our brain.[26] Each of these interactions contributes to the seemingly simple experience we call "sight." Things become more complicated the more closely we look. Consider, for example, the relationship between lighting conditions and wavelengths of light. While both the sky and an object may appear to us as blue, the first does so because of the wavelengths it scatters, and the second does so as a result of a surface reflecting light.[27] Furthermore, the object may be reflecting this wavelength of light because its pigmentation absorbs other wavelengths of light, or because of microstructures on its surface (as in the case of butterflies or peacock feathers).[28] Even in the case of simple pigment reflection, the object will appear blue only under certain lighting conditions.[29] In other words, one cannot know from the perception of the color itself what kind of interaction created it. Nor is there a consistent relationship between wavelength and color—both the oppositions of colors on the color wheel and the way colors blend are features of our neural processing, not of wavelengths. There is no one-to-one translation between our perception of color and the world out there.

Neither is color vision merely subjective. The experience that is mediated through so many interactions is still an experience of a reality outside of ourselves. These interactions truly tell humans something about the world. "Green" is a result of a real transaction between our biology and the environment. A radical subjectivism "fails to explain color. . . . This is not to say that color does not differ in its significance from culture to culture. It clearly does. Rather, color is a function of the world and our biology interacting."[30] In other words, "green" is neither a property inherent to the grass nor a descriptor imposed arbitrarily by the subject. It is a characteristic that arises from the interaction between the body and the world.

Correspondence theory of truth is simply not adequate to statements about color. Color cannot be explained without reference to both the world and the body. A statement about the color of an object is therefore a statement about the interaction between the world and the human person. This implies an "embodied realism, a form of interactionism that is neither purely objective nor purely subjective."[31] The realism here is a matter not of correspondence but of function. Evolutionarily speaking, we have developed the ability to see color as a way of successfully navigating the world.[32]

For Lakoff and Johnson, color is not unique in this respect. All of our basic ways of knowing and interacting with the world are similarly mediated. Consider, for instance, what they refer to as *basic-level categories*. These categories are often in the middle of hierarchies: the category *chair* in the hierarchy furniture—chair—Windsor chair and the category *dog* in the hierarchy mammal—dog—komondor, for example. What is interesting about these categories is that they are the ones our minds are best able to handle. If I ask you to picture a chair, you most likely can. But go any higher up in the hierarchy and we run into problems: what is the shape of a piece of furniture? Likewise, go further down and many of us have trouble for different reasons. We can successfully live our lives without knowing what a komondor is. This is because most of our knowledge is organized at the level of basic categories, with only experts knowing much about the lower-level categories.[33] The point is that there are certain mid-level categories that are basic insofar as they have "cognitive priority."[34] This cognitive priority seems to be based on the fact that this is the level we most often interact with. We think on a human scale. As Lakoff and Johnson write, "The properties of categories are mediated by the body."[35] Like color, our categories are interactional, arising from the structure of our brains and bodies, from our histories, and "from our evolved capacity for basic-level categorization—a level at which we optimally interact with the world."[36]

We do not form mental pictures of the world "as it is," but neither are we deceived by our senses. We successfully interact with the real world in distinctly human ways. For Lakoff and Johnson, such mediation does not distance us from the world but puts us in contact with it.[37] There is no "ontological chasm" between subject and object; as "embodied, imaginative creatures, *we never were separated or divorced from reality in the first place*."[38]

THEOLOGY AND THE COGNITIVE SCIENCES

This development in understanding human knowledge has only begun to be applied to theological understanding. Indeed, for Lakoff and Johnson, embodied realism precludes any belief in a transcendent God, the idea of which they argue arose only because of a tendency of the mind to make false metaphysical abstractions. Other theorists working in the Cognitive Science of Religion (CSR) have understood religion to be a by-product of evolutionary pressures, especially the bias toward detecting agency.[39]

A number of theologians, biblical scholars, and scholars of religion have begun to explore the potential this work has for theology. Biblical scholars in particular have used the tools of conceptual mapping to describe the development of particular metaphors across biblical texts. In doing so, they have argued that these changes led to the possibility of thinking new things and allowed the development of theological understanding.[40] More recently, Robert Masson and John Sanders have begun to note its importance for systematic theology, especially in nuancing the ways that theology describes how we as embodied creatures speak of ourselves and of the transcendent God.

In his 2014 *Without Metaphor, No Saving God*, Masson demonstrates the immense theological potential of engaging with the cognitive sciences.

Drawing together the work of Lakoff and Johnson, Fauconnier and Turner, and Gerhart and Russell, Masson argues that an understanding of conceptual mapping is critical to any theology today that seeks to articulate how God saves.[41] It is our failure as Christians to understand how this idea is conceptualized that is "at the root of substantive misunderstandings and confusions in academic theology as well as in popular theology, within the church as well as between churches and between religions, and in our spiritual quests, just as much as in our religious practices and institutions."[42] Masson therefore uses resources in conceptual mapping to provide a robust account of the structure of theological reasoning.

In *Theology in the Flesh*, Sanders argues that cognitive linguistic approaches help to understand how "embodied cognition produces a constrained pluralism."[43] The embodiment that humans share places constraints on all human reasoning and therefore constrains human reasoning about God. But there is also a wide diversity of cultural means of reasoning—conceptual mappings differ between communities. This diversity exists between interlocutors across history; between different communities separated by space, language, or other divides; or even between a single way of thought before and after a genuinely new insight. Because meaning is instantiated in conceptual mappings of the world, these differences matter, but they need not be insurmountable. Christian theologians therefore need to be aware of their own social location and the ways in which the normative sources of Christian revelation, including the Bible, are culturally located. This way of thinking underlines Sanders's argument that the Bible requires interpretation and that deciding "which biblical teachings [to] accept, which ones [to] revise, and which ones [to] set aside" is an important and indeed unavoidable task for Christian communities.[44]

Together Masson's and Sanders's work demonstrate the immense potential of interdisciplinary research in theology and cognitive science, particularly its ability to illuminate theological method and debate. The editors of this volume propose that there are at least three distinct ways in which this recent research on conceptual mapping can—and ought to—deepen theological reflection today.

I. Conceptual mapping enriches theological anthropology.

Along with the other cognitive sciences, conceptual mapping informs not merely how we think and speak but who we are as human beings. Reflection on human being is a critical and central task for Christian theology, which proclaims that human being has been created by God and assumed by the Word. Since the twentieth century, theological anthropology has emerged as a distinct subfield in its own right, bringing the best of the natural and social sciences and humanities to bear on theological understandings of human being. Attending to the work of cognitive scientists and cognitive linguists provides new tools to extend this work. It allows us to theorize about the subject without falling into the antinomies Lakoff and Johnson argue plague theological and philosophical reflection. The subject underlying conceptual mapping is an embodied whole who makes meaning through her engagement with the world. A theological anthropology informed by research in conceptual mapping is better able to recognize that our spirituality is embodied, that humans encounter the transcendent in and through the material world. That our minds are embodied gives new insight into understanding our need for sacraments and rituals. It also deepens our understanding of the Incarnation, and what it meant for the Word to assume flesh.

II. An empirically informed theological anthropology is an essential and primary step to theology.

Theology engages anthropology not merely in its own right but also as a necessary moment in theological method. Who we are as human beings grounds who we are as knowers and lovers of God. Theological reflection demands that we attend to the nature of the human person and her knowledge of God. As the Thomistic adage has it, *quidquid recipitur ad modum recipientis recepitur*, "whatsoever is received is received according to the mode of the receiver."[45] We cannot understand what we profess about the divine without attending to the human "receivers" who have received that divine revelation as human beings. Anthropology is therefore essential to any theology.

This results in two related assertions: *First*, research in cognitive science supports the Thomist adage by showing just how substantially what kinds of beings we are can determine what kinds of things we know. As Robert Masson writes,

> There is no escaping the constitutive role of embodied mind in cognition and language. There is no "stepping outside" our bodily, socially, and culturally constituted conceptual frameworks to gain a God's-eye view of reality independent from metaphorical and figurative conceptualization.[46]

This requires, as Masson argues, wrestling with how embodied beings, lacking any disembodied mind with access to universal and metaphysical truths, are capable of speaking about God. As he notes, this challenge is eerily similar to that which Thomas faced regarding the claim that all knowledge is rooted in the senses.[47]

Second, it provides concrete data for *how* that structuring occurs, which better enables us to think, know, and speak about both the human and the divine. Cognitive science tells us, for instance, that we are prone to thinking about human and divine transcendence in dualistic ways on account of how our conceptual mapping develops.[48] It can also help us analyze the cultural basis of different blends—how, for example, an idea like white supremacy can be transmitted.[49] Understanding the mind's mapping thus better enables us to be aware of—and if necessary work against—our cognitive habits.

III. Recognition of the embodied and contextual nature of theological reflection is useful in exploring differences across theological reflection, including between communities and across time.

Many philosophers and theologians have followed Ricoeur in understanding that metaphors create rather than describe meaning.[50] Extending this insight in terms of the present project, we can add that, without the processes that compose conceptual mapping, many of our interactions with the world, including much of our theology, would literally be unthinkable. Paying attention to how this ability is present in our thinking allows us to see how the human capacity for thinking about our world is both deeply enmeshed in particular times and places, and capable of recognizing and accounting for difference. As John Sanders has argued, "It is quite legitimate to form theological models, yet Christian communities need to be aware that they are doing so based on particular metaphorical concepts and this should lead to greater humility when making claims to possess 'the' Christian understanding on a topic."[51] In other words, different communities have different maps for God. Theology must therefore attend not only to the fact that we map God but that we map God *differently*. Doing so requires considering the structures of our own theologies more seriously.

Consider, for instance, the way that Robert Masson develops Gerhart and Russell's notion of *tectonic equivalence*, which he identifies as describing how an important subset of double-scope blends create meaning.[52] Masson identifies tectonic equivalences as an important subset of double-scope blends, where the new meaning created has a dramatic effect—think Einstein's theory of relativity as opposed to our computer desktop. For Masson, not only do such blends dramatically alter the field of meaning, "creating the possibility for new knowledge and new understanding that otherwise would be unavailable,"[53] but recognizing their operation also calls for rethinking the very categories of *metaphorical*, *literal*, and *figurative*.[54] As Masson argues, such tectonic thinking can be found throughout theological history, from the insistence of classical theism that the one God is not a thing in the world, through the claim that Jesus is the Messiah and the conciliar definitions about the Trinity and the Incarnation, to James Cone's equation of Jesus's cross and the lynching tree. Our present field of theology has been shaped by a history of tectonic activity. Recognizing this fact and beginning to deal with its repercussions has itself been a recent quake.

Attending to tectonic moments in theology therefore makes us better able to understand differences in how people conceptualize God. Masson uses the tools of conceptual mapping to analyze the rhetoric of four controversies in contemporary Christian theology. Consider his analysis of the United States Conference of Catholic Bishops' Committee on Doctrine's censure of Elizabeth Johnson's 2011 *Quest for the Living God*, particularly her claim that all God-talk is metaphorical. The Committee understands Johnson's claim that all God-talk is metaphorical as implying that one cannot speak properly of God; they neglect to see how *metaphor* can also be used to describe the robust sense of analogy they support themselves.

But neither does Masson side completely with Johnson. Engaging her image of language about God being like a finger pointing to the moon, he argues that Johnson's depiction of metaphoric speech may not give enough credence to the ways in which human language (which cannot be univocally true about God) nevertheless can be meaningful:

> The finger analogy does not capture the tectonic character of analogous usage and the ways in which such analogous usage can be considered literal in the second sense, what Aquinas calls *proprie* (semantically proper, logically warranted, and factually the case). Nor does the finger illustration distinguish clearly between the everyday sense of analogy as a comparison between partially similar realities and the sort of tectonic conceptual mapping required to speak of God. This opens the door, against Johnson's intention, for interpreting the image as a denial of any positive knowledge of God.[55]

According to Masson, neither the Bishops' Committee on Doctrine nor Johnson adequately accounts for the tectonic logic of Thomas's understanding of analogy, in which he radically configures how we understand language to apply to God.[56] The Catholic tradition, Masson argues, simultaneously insists on the possibility that human speech can speak properly about God while denying that that language is what we usually call *literal.* Understanding what is happening in such speech itself requires a kind of tectonic engagement with language that moves beyond our habitual uses of the categories of *literal*, *figurative*, and *metaphoric.* Attention to the tectonic aspect of Thomas's theology allows Masson to gain perspective on just how Johnson and the Committee can disagree so strongly while both laying claim to Thomas's theological legacy.

Conceptual mapping can also facilitate and better illuminate ecumenical and interfaith dialogue. For example, in his book *Mapping the Differentiated Consensus of the Joint Declaration*, Jakob Rinderknecht uses conceptual mapping to analyze how consensus can be reached across denominational differences. As he argues, attention to the presence of tectonic shifts in meaning can help us understand how dialogue has led Lutherans and Catholics to find real consensus between what had—for hundreds of years—seemed to be contradictory positions.[57] Thus conceptual mapping allows us to better understand what differences are "church-dividing" and to grapple with the very history of division.[58] Theological engagement with conceptual mapping provides tools for understanding, and potentially overcoming, theological differences without erasing them.

There are no universal theologies.[59] Attending to difference in this way is therefore critical across the theological disciplines: for understanding theological debates, engaging in ecumenical and interfaith dialogue, respecting cultural differences, and interpreting historical texts. Because every theology is culturally and temporally located, but the practice of theology and religious studies is ever more global, these issues become ever more important.

PUTTING GOD ON THE MAP

Directly engaging with the metaphoric structure of our thought provides a new horizon for theology in the modern era. We offer this volume as a map for this new land. The following essays chart out new directions in theology and cognitive science. Together they demonstrate how "putting God on the map" both requires and provides new ways of thinking.

The first set of chapters places conceptual mapping in dialogue with Christian theological questions and ideas about the human person. In chapter 2, Erin Kidd provides a more in-depth introduction to the work of Lakoff and Johnson, focusing particularly on the embodiment of conceptual metaphors, and investigates what this aspect of human thought and language has to say about God-talk. Julia Feder further situates theological thinking not only within the embodiment of the individual but as a cooperative enterprise rooted in communities. She draws on Edward Schillebeeckx's description of sacramentality to show how this symbolic imagination mediates the divine-human engagement. In chapter 4, Jason Roberts identifies conceptual blending—and the ability to think symbolically—within the history of human evolution. He argues that conceptual integration theory provides a plausible explanation of how *Homo sapiens* evolved to become a species capable of self-definition. This means that this human capacity for double-scope blending changes the ways we speak of human distinctiveness and the *imago dei*. Conceptual integration theory not only describes the human evolution of language but changes how humans understand themselves and God.

The second set of chapters demonstrates the breadth of applications of conceptual mapping. Each of these three chapters shows how the tools of conceptual mapping can help address perennial debates in theology. In chapter 5, Christopher Hadley argues that the logic of chapters 2 and 3 of the Epistle to the Philippians constitutes a complex blend inviting the reader to imitate Christ in a self-emptying that is simultaneously a striving to fulfill the divine call. Stephen Shaver then examines two different Eucharistic spiritualities, arguing that they express two different scriptural metaphors. In chapter 7, Jakob Rinderknecht examines the fraught process of receiving ecumenical dialogue texts and argues that it can be fostered by using the tools of conceptual mapping to help people understand the differences between churches and the solutions proposed by the dialogues more clearly.

Finally, the third set of chapters demonstrates how interdisciplinary work in theology and conceptual mapping can impact how we theorize about ethical and political issues. Adam Willows argues in chapter 8 that Thomas Aquinas's ethics are predicated on a tectonic blend equating the Good with God and that this blend can helpfully reframe the contemporary evolutionary arguments about the evolutionary basis of altruism. In chapter 9, Kathryn Lilla Cox examines the problem of frozen fertilized human embryos, named "insoluble" by the Congregation for the Doctrine of the Faith, and argues that we are in a period of development in which the ways that we conceive of these embryos is not yet fixed. The metaphors we use to conceive of them greatly shape the conclusions that we draw. While recognizing the ongoing developments that need to be made, she lays out some characteristics of what will be a successful metaphoric integration.

It is our hope that this book helps to expand the conversation around conceptual mapping in theological circles. The processes that we describe are universally found throughout human thought, including in all attempts to come to grips with the self-revelation of a transcendent God in history. Paying direct attention to the means by which we consider these mysteries can only help us reason better about them together. The goal of the present volume is not only to develop the exchange between theology and cognitive science—showing how this interdisciplinary work can be useful for many distinct questions in theology—but to do so clearly and accessibly for those who are new to the field. Much of this territory remains uncharted, and it calls for a new generation of scholars committed to putting God on the map.

NOTES

1. Gilles Fauconnier and Mark Turner, "Rethinking Metaphor," in *The Cambridge Handbook of Metaphor and Thought*, ed. Raymond W. Gibbs Jr. (New York: Cambridge University Press, 2008), 53–66.

2. George Lakoff and Mark Johnson, *Metaphors We Live By* (Chicago: University of Chicago, 1980), 5.

3. Lakoff and Johnson, *Metaphors We Live By*, 6.
4. Ibid., 4.
5. Ibid.
6. Ibid., 5.
7. Ibid., chapter 4.
8. Ibid., chapter 24.
9. Gilles Fauconnier and Mark Turner, *The Way We Think: Conceptual Blending and the Mind's Hidden Complexities* (New York: Basic Books, 2002), 6.
10. Fauconnier and Turner, *The Way We Think*, 180–82.
11. Fauconnier and Turner, *The Way We Think*, 131.
12. Mary Gerhart and Allan Russell, *Metaphoric Process: The Creation of Scientific and Religious Understanding* (Fort Worth: Texas Christian University Press, 1984), 135–37. Gerhart and Russell have described their understanding of the difference between their work and that of cognitive linguists, including Lakoff and Johnson, in "Changing Worldviews: Responding to Betty Birner and Robert Masson," *Zygon* 39, no. 1 (March 2004): 63–75. We have not found any direct interactions between Gerhart and Russell and the work of Fauconnier and Turner. They read Lakoff, and cognitive linguists generally, to be more focused on linguistic process, while they themselves attend to the process by which new meaning develops. One of the things that we hope will be clear to the reader is how entangled and inseparable we believe these approaches to be.
13. Albert Einstein, "On the Electrodynamics of Moving Bodies," prepared by John Walker, based on the English translation available in *The Principle of Relativity*, trans. W. Perrett and G. B. Jeffery (London: Methuen and Company, 1923), last accessed March 8, 2018, http://www.fourmilab.ch/etexts/einstein/specrel/www/.
14. Gerhart and Russell, *Metaphoric Process*, 137.
15. As Gerhart and Russell point out, there was experimental evidence for Einstein's claim at the time of his experiment, although these do not seem to have been directly involved in his reasoning. The growing experimental research, however, over time overcame the "outrage" caused by this epistemic distortion. Gerhart and Russell, *Metaphoric Process*, 138–39.
16. Mary Gerhart and Allan Russell, *New Maps for Old: Explorations in Science and Religion* (New York: Continuum, 2001), 52. They had introduced this language in "Metaphoric Process as the Tectonic Reformation of Worlds of Meanings in Theology and Natural Science," *CTNS Bulletin* 13, no. 2 (1993): 7–13.
17. We are indebted to the work of Robert Masson in connecting Gerhart and Russell's "metaphoric process" with Fauconnier and Turner's "double-scope blending" in *Without Metaphor, No Saving God: Theology after Cognitive Linguistics* (Leuven: Peeters, 2014), 106–9. See also the symposium between Gerhart and Russell, Masson, and Betty Birner, in *Zygon* 39, no 1 (2004): 5–75.
18. Fauconnier and Turner, *The Way We Think*, 6.
19. See, for example, Fauconnier and Turner, "Rethinking Metaphor," 53–66; Masson, *Without Metaphor*, 4–5, 106–9.
20. Lakoff and Johnson, *Metaphors We Live By*, chapter 2. Theologian George Lindbeck has made similar arguments about the nature of truth claims. He famously

makes a distinction between a statement's "ontological" and "intra-systematic" truth and predicates the possibility of ontological truth on the intra-systematic. Thus, the crusader's cry of "Jesus is Lord" loses its truth value when it is used to justify the killing of non-Christians. See *The Nature of Doctrine: Religion and Theology in a Postliberal Age* (Louisville: Westminster John Knox, 1984), 65. For an examination of Lindbeck's proposal and its connection to the conceptual mapping proposal of this book, see Jakob Rinderknecht, *Mapping the Differentiated Consensus of the Joint Declaration* (New York: Palgrave, 2016), 87–143.

21. Lakoff and Johnson, *Metaphors We Live By*, chapter 25.
22. Ibid., 192.
23. Ibid., 193.
24. George Lakoff and Mark Johnson, *Philosophy in the Flesh: The Embodied Mind and Its Challenge to Western Thought* (New York: Basic Books, 1999), 3.
25. Lakoff and Johnson, *Philosophy in the Flesh*, 25.
26. Ibid., 23–24.
27. Ibid., 25.
28. Cristina Luigi, "Color from Structure," *The Scientist* (February 1, 2013), http://www.the-scientist.com/?articles.view/articleNo/34200/title/Color-from-Structure/.
29. Many people are familiar with the phenomenon of fabrics that look different under florescent lights and in daylight. The different wavelengths of light reflect off of the pigments in a different way. A further complication is caused by the ways in which our brains attempt to correct for this kind of distortion in terms of background and perceived lighting conditions. In February of 2015, a picture of a dress briefly became an internet sensation for precisely this reason. The picture was strangely lit and could be interpreted by the brain as either being a picture of a blue and black dress (which it was) or of a white and gold dress. Wired Magazine reporter Adam Rogers reported on the phenomenon and the underlying science in "The Science of Why No One Agrees on the Color of This Dress," *Wired* (February 26, 2015), https://www.wired.com/2015/02/science-one-agrees-color-dress/.
30. Lakoff and Johnson, *Philosophy in the Flesh*, 25.
31. Ibid.
32. Ibid.
33. Ibid., 27–28.
34. Ibid., 27.
35. Ibid., 28.
36. Ibid., 30.
37. Ibid., 44.
38. Ibid., 93.
39. For a representative set of engagements on this topic, see Harvey Whitehouse and James Laidlaw, eds., *Religion, Anthropology and Cognitive Science* (Durham: Carolina Academic Press, 2007). For a directly theological response to these arguments, see Jonathan Jong, Christopher Kavanagh, and Aku Visala, "Born Idolaters: The Limits of the Philosophical Implications of the Cognitive Science of Religion," *Neue Zeitschrift für Systematische Theologie und Religionsphilosophie* 57, no. 2 (2015): 244–66.

40. Some representative examples include Gary A. Anderson, *Sin: A History* (New Haven: Yale University Press, 2009); Elizabeth Hayes, *The Pragmatics of Perception and Cognition in MT Jeremiah 1:1–6:30* (Boston: Brill, 2011); P. J. P. van Hecke, "Shepherds and Linguists: A Cognitive-Linguistic Approach to the Metaphor 'God Is Shepherd' in Gen 48:15 and Context," in *Studies in the Book of Genesis: Literature, Redaction and History*, ed. André Wénin (Leuven: Peeters, 2001), 479–95; Bonnie Howe and Joel B. Green, eds., *Cognitive Linguistic Explorations in Biblical Studies* (Berlin: de Gruyter, 2014); Peter Daniel Myers, "Cognitive Linguistics and the Tripartite Division of the Law," *Westminster Theological Journal* 74, no. 2 (2012): 387–415; Danilo Verde, "War-Games in the Song of Songs: A Reading of Song 2,4 in Light of Cognitive Linguistics," *SJOT* 30 no. 2 (2016): 185–97.

41. Masson, *Without Metaphor*, 7.

42. Ibid., 7–8.

43. John Sanders, *Theology in the Flesh: How Embodiment and Culture Shape the Way We Think about Truth, Morality, and God* (Minneapolis: Fortress Press, 2016), 280.

44. Ibid., 281.

45. cf. Thomas Aquinas, *Summa Theologicae*, 1a q.75 a.5; 3a q.5; 1a q.12, a4.

46. Masson, *Without Metaphor*, 55.

47. Ibid., 15.

48. See chapter 2 in this volume.

49. See Erin Kidd, "The Subject of Conceptual Mapping: Theological Anthropology across Brain, Body, and World," *Open Theology* 4, no. 1 (2018): 117–35.

50. For Paul Ricoeur, metaphors are events in which the tension in the juxtaposition of terms creates new meaning and, therefore, a new vision of the world. See *Interpretation Theory: Discourse and the Surplus of Meaning* (Fort Worth: Texas Christian Press, 1976), 49–52, 68. See also *The Rule of Metaphor: Multi-Disciplinary Studies in the Creation of Meaning in Language*, trans. Robert Czerny with Kathleen McLaughling and John Costello (London: Routledge, 1978), 79–83, 92–93. For the impact of this insight on theology, see, for example, Sallie McFague, *Metaphorical Theology: Models of God in Religious Language* (Philadelphia: Fortress Press, 1982) and *Speaking in Parables* (Philadelphia: Fortress Press, 1975), and Elizabeth Johnson, *She Who Is: The Mystery of God in Feminist Theological Discourse*, 10th Anniversary Edition (New York: Crossroad, 2002).

51. Sanders, *Theology in the Flesh*, 278.

52. See Masson, *Without Metaphor*, 66 and 106–9 for how he is interpreting "tectonic." See also his "Conceiving God: Literal and Figurative Prompt for a More Tectonic Distinction," *Open Theology* 4, no. 1 (2018), 136–57.

53. Masson, *Without Metaphor*, 8.

54. Ibid., 5–6.

55. Ibid., 202–3.

56. Ibid., 190.

57. Jakob Karl Rinderknecht, *Mapping the Differentiated Consensus of the Joint Declaration* (New York: Palgrave, 2016).

58. Since the history of division itself colors how particular differences are understood, this becomes a complex judgment. For example, definitions of the term *church*

are deeply shaped by the history of Christian division. Any analysis of how one group of Christians recognizes other Christians as forming a church (or not) must reckon with the history of this development, so as not to merely reproduce the division that gave rise to the definitions. See Jakob Karl Rinderknecht, "CHURCH, Category, and Speciation," *Open Theology* 4, no. 1 (2018): 46–59.

59. This is true even for thinkers who have served as supposedly universal centers for their own traditions, like Thomas Aquinas, who is sometimes referred to as the "universal doctor." But, as David Turnbloom has recently argued, Thomas cannot truly be a conversation partner with other theologies unless his own tradition and history are taken seriously. Turnbloom thus argues that in the contemporary world Thomas's theology requires a kind of *ressourcement* approach, of which "the defining characteristic of true *ressourcement* is maintaining the object of study as a source to be translated, as a source from which to progressively develop a meaningful theology." David Farina Turnbloom, *Speaking with Aquinas: A Conversation about Grace, Virtue, and the Eucharist* (Collegeville, MN: Liturgical Press, 2017), xxix.

BIBLIOGRAPHY

Anderson, Gary A. *Sin: A History*. New Haven: Yale University Press, 2009.

Einstein, Albert. "On the Electrodynamics of Moving Bodies." Prepared by John Walker, based on the English translation available in *The Principle of Relativity*, translated by W. Perrett and G. B. Jeffery. London: Methuen and Company, 1923. Last accessed March 8, 2018. http://www.fourmilab.ch/etexts/einstein/specrel/www/. Translation of "Zur Elektrodynamik bewegten Körper." *Annalen der Physik* 322 (1905): 891–921.

Fauconnier, Gilles, and Mark Turner. *The Way We Think: Conceptual Blending and the Mind's Hidden Complexities*. New York: Basic Books, 2002.

———. "Rethinking Metaphor." In *The Cambridge Handbook of Metaphor and Thought*, edited by Raymond W. Gibbs Jr., 53–66. New York: Cambridge University Press, 2008.

Gerhart, Mary, and Allan Russell. *Metaphoric Process: The Creation of Scientific and Religious Understanding*. Fort Worth: Texas Christian University Press, 1984.

———. "Metaphoric Process as the Tectonic Reformation of Worlds of Meanings in Theology and Natural Science." *CTNS Bulletin* 13, no. 2 (1993): 7–13.

———. *New Maps for Old: Explorations in Science and Religion*. New York: Continuum, 2001.

———. "Symposium: Metaphor as a Space for Religion/Science Engagement." *Zygon* 39, no. 1 (March 2004): 5–75.

Hayes, Elizabeth. *The Pragmatics of Perception and Cognition in MT Jeremiah 1:1–6:30*. Boston: Brill, 2011.

van Hecke, P. J. P. "Shepherds and Linguists: A Cognitive-Linguistic Approach to the Metaphor 'God Is Shepherd' in Gen 48:15 and Context." In *Studies in the Book of Genesis: Literature, Redaction and History*, edited by André Wénin, 479–95. Leuven: Peeters, 2001.

Johnson, Elizabeth. *She Who Is: The Mystery of God in Feminist Theological Discourse.* 10th Anniversary Edition. New York: Crossroad, 2002.

Jong, Jonathan, Christopher Kavanagh, and Aku Visala. "Born Idolaters: The Limits of the Philosophical Implications of the Cognitive Science of Religion." *Neue Zeitschrift für Systematische Theologie und Religionsphilosophie* 57, no. 2 (2015): 244–66.

Kidd, Erin. "The Subject of Conceptual Mapping: Theological Anthropology across Brain, Body, and World." *Open Theology* 4, no. 1 (2018): 117–35.

Lakoff, George, and Mark Johnson. *Metaphors We Live By.* Chicago: University of Chicago Press, 1980.

———. *Philosophy in the Flesh: The Embodied Mind and Its Challenge to Western Thought.* New York: Basic Books, 1999.

Lindbeck, George A. *The Nature of Doctrine: Religion and Theology in a Postliberal Age*. Louisville: Westminster John Knox, 1984.

Luigi, Cristina. "Color from Structure." *The Scientist* (February 1, 2013). http://www.the-scientist.com/?articles.view/articleNo/34200/title/Color-from-Structure/.

Masson, Robert. *Without Metaphor, No Saving God: Theology after Cognitive Linguistics.* Leuven: Peeters, 2014.

———. "Conceiving God: Literal and Figurative Prompt for a More Tectonic Distinction." *Open Theology* 4, no. 1 (2018): 136–57.

McFague, Sallie. *Metaphorical Theology: Models of God in Religious Language*. Philadelphia: Fortress Press, 1982.

———. *Speaking in Parables*. Philadelphia: Fortress Press, 1975.

Myers, Peter Daniel. "Cognitive Linguistics and the Tripartite Division of the Law." *Westminster Theological Journal* 74, no. 2 (2012): 387–415.

Ricoeur, Paul. *Interpretation Theory: Discourse and the Surplus of Meaning.* Fort Worth: Texas Christian University Press, 1976.

———. *The Rule of Metaphor: Multi-Disciplinary Studies in the Creation of Meaning in Language*. Translated by Robert Czerny with Kathleen McLaughlin and John Costello. London: Routledge, 1978.

Rinderknecht, Jakob Karl. *Mapping the Differentiated Consensus of the Joint Declaration.* New York: Palgrave, 2016.

———. "CHURCH, Category, and Speciation." *Open Theology* 4, no. 1 (2018): 46–59.

Rogers, Adam. "The Science of Why No One Agrees on the Color of This Dress." *Wired* (February 26, 2015). https://www.wired.com/2015/02/science-one-agrees-color-dress/.

Sanders, John. *Theology in the Flesh: How Embodiment and Culture Shape the Way We Think about Truth, Morality, and God*. Minneapolis: Fortress Press, 2016.

Turnbloom, David Farina. *Speaking with Aquinas: A Conversation about Grace, Virtue, and the Eucharist*. Collegeville, MN: Liturgical Press, 2017.

Verde, Danilo. "War-Games in the Song of Songs: A Reading of Song 2, 4 in Light of Cognitive Linguistics." *Scandanavian Journal of the Old Testament* 30, no. 2 (2016): 185–97.

Whitehouse, Harvey, and James Laidlaw, eds. *Religion, Anthropology and Cognitive Science*. Durham: Carolina Academic Press, 2007.

Chapter Two

The Embodied Mind and How to Pray with One

Erin Kidd

The mind is embodied. The conceptual mapping that shapes our understanding of the world is itself structured by the particularities of human embodiment. Our thoughts are distinctively human. This means too that our theology is distinctively human. Reflection on human cognition is therefore a critical moment in the task of theology. But awareness of how the human body constrains theological reasoning raises the question of whether theology is possible at all. How can we speak of the transcendent God?

Because cognitive science grounds human meaning-making in the very structure and activity of human bodies, it can explain complicated human processes without appeal to anthropological dualism. It can also explain just why dualism is so compelling to us. The wheels of our mind turn in ruts that guide us toward conceiving ourselves as split—with our agency, spirituality, and intellect on one side, and our embodiment and finitude on the other. Imagining ourselves as over against the world, we are likewise pulled toward conceptions of God as "above us" or "out there."

For George Lakoff and Mark Johnson, this genealogy of divine transcendence is proof of its falsehood; the embodied mind precludes talk of a transcendent God. However, I argue that not only is an embodied theology possible, but that research in the embodied mind provides resources for thinking about what language is best-suited for speaking of the mystery of God. Lakoff and Johnson's critique is based on an error in conceptualizing Christian models of the God-world relationship. This genealogy does not preclude language of transcendence, but rather illuminates how it can go awry. In fact, it can inform us on how best to avoid—or hop out of—the ruts that cross our way.

What is necessary is an embodied theology that speaks of a divine transcendence not opposed to human embodiment. As I will argue in this chapter, conceiving of the human-divine relationship in terms of touch—as both

Mayra Rivera and Linn Marie Tonstad do—may better counter our cognitive tendencies, protecting our understanding of the mystery of God and embodied human being.

THE EMBODIED MIND CALLS FOR AN EMBODIED THEOLOGY

Within the disciplines that make up the cognitive sciences—neuroscience, computer science, robotics, and linguistics—the dominant assumption until the latter part of the last century was that human intelligence consisted of the ability to manipulate abstract symbols.[1] In this conception of human being, the body's activity is reduced to providing sensory input to the mind and executing its commands. But contemporary cognitive science has largely rejected this model, recognizing instead the integral role of the body in human thought.

As we will see, this means we cannot understand the patterns of human thought without first understanding the patterns of human movement in the world. These movements are distinct to creatures who walk upright on land, and so too are the patterns of thought that arise from them. It is not merely that we think about God from the perspective of finitude, embodiment, or socio-cultural location—all aspects that have been given considerable attention in theological anthropology and theological method. But the very shape and movement of our distinctively human bodies determines our thought. We think in terms of the body.

Thinking in Terms of the Body

Consider the way that the mind's metaphors are embodied. In their groundbreaking research on metaphor, George Lakoff and Mark Johnson argue that what they call *conceptual metaphors* characterize our most basic ways of interacting with and thinking about the world. They define conceptual metaphors as "understanding and experiencing one kind of thing in terms of another."[2] These conceptual metaphors facilitate understanding by allowing us to grab ahold of unwieldy concepts via what is more clearly delineated to us. A concrete source domain structures our understanding of a more abstract target domain.[3] Ultimately, Lakoff and Johnson argue, almost all of our normal language belies a deeply metaphorical conceptual structure.[4]

These metaphors in turn arise from our embodied experience of the world.[5] Consider what Lakoff and Johnson call *primary metaphors*, which structure subjective experiences in terms of sensorimotor experience.[6] An example is AFFECTION IS WARMTH. As children, experiences like being held prompt us to conflate affection with warmth, the traces of which we can see when we describe someone as "cold" because they are emotionally unavailable.[7] As Lakoff and Johnson argue, this conflation is not just phenomenological or linguistic but neurologically hardwired. The acquisition of such metaphors is automatic, unconscious, and pervasive due to the common nature of the experiences they are based on. The result is that we cannot help but think in them.[8]

Primary metaphors serve as the building blocks for more complex conceptual metaphors.[9] Consider the primary metaphor MORE IS UP where quantity is understood in terms of verticality. In their early interactions with the world, human beings recognize that a pile of objects becomes higher if more objects are added. We learn this without the use of propositions, but in the context of manipulating objects in our world. This pattern of interacting with the world, in which quantity and height are linked, becomes the basis of conceptual metaphors like MORE IS UP.[10] Such a metaphor can in turn be extended to speak of rather abstract ideas. To speak of the stock market falling, for example, is to conceive of a decrease in value as a downward movement.

A subset of primary metaphors called *orientational metaphors* are organized in a system of concepts. The primary metaphor MORE IS UP for instance, exists in relationship to a host of other metaphors using up-down spatialization, such as GOOD IS UP, HAPPY IS UP, and HEALTHY IS UP. These metaphors are referred to as orientational precisely because they are often grounded in the basic orientation of the body in the world: "up-down, in-out, front-back, on-off, deep-shallow, central-peripheral. These orientations arise from the fact that we have bodies of the sort we have and that they function as they do in our physical environment."[11] These metaphors not only employ the same source domain to understand different subjective experiences, but also tend to operate coherently according to general rules. In UP-DOWN metaphors for instance, the positive value is keyed as UP unless it contradicts MORE IS UP, such as in the phrase "inflation is rising."[12] The pervasiveness of orientational metaphors lead Lakoff and Johnson to state, "no metaphor can ever be comprehended or even adequately represented independently of its experiential basis."[13] In fact, Lakoff and Johnson note that some of our concepts are so rooted in orientational metaphors that it is difficult to think them otherwise.[14] Indeed, they are forced to identify the way in which status is conflated with as verticality through a redundant use of UP-DOWN language: "HIGH STATUS IS UP; LOW STATUS IS DOWN."[15] UP and DOWN structure our understanding of class and status so consistently that they cannot find words outside the orientational metaphor to describe high and low status.

Underlying conceptual metaphors are image schemata. As Johnson defines them, image schemata are "basic structures of sensory-motor experience by which we encounter a world that we can understand and act within."[16] While not images in any conventional sense of the word, these schemata are non-propositional patterns of interacting with the world that fundamentally structure our experience of it.[17] For instance, an orientational metaphor like MORE IS UP depends upon the VERTICALITY image schema—a pattern of interacting in the world in terms of UP-DOWN. This pattern emerges naturally from the fact that human beings walk erect in a world with gravity and in turn structures our understanding of and ability to move in that world.[18] Consider how significantly the VERTICALITY image schema shapes not only our ability to move in the world, but our conception of values (e.g., GOOD IS UP). Even seemingly direct terms like *high-energy particles* and *high-quality work* depend on this schema.[19]

The VERTICALITY image schema is one of many schemata involved in balancing, which Johnson collectively refers to as the BALANCE schemata. In his 1987 solo work, *The Body in the Mind*, Johnson appeals to these schemata to show "how it is possible for metaphorical projections to play a constitutive role in the structuring of our experience."[20] For human beings, learning to balance is an early activity. Many young children lurch and fumble as they begin to walk. As Johnson argues, the knowledge of how to keep one's balance is not propositional: "It is crucially important to see that balancing is an *activity we learn with our bodies* and not by grasping a set of rules or concepts. First and foremost, balancing is something we *do*."[21] In other words, it is not analogous to a list of rules or lines of code. There is no reason to think that children who have learned to walk have mastered a list of formula, like a pilot might run through a checklist. Such a model is needlessly complicated and cannot explain the ways in which a child adapts her sense of balance for new situations—rocky terrain, a slippery surface—without beginning anew. Rather, Johnson suggests that imagining various axes—a vertical one such as when one is upright, a horizontal one with arms outstretched—is what allows for mastery of the complicated muscle movements required in an activity such as walking. Such axes serve as image schemata by which an upright being learns to walk.[22]

In turn, such schemata ground our higher-level meaning-making. Kandinsky's theory and use of color demonstrate that our perception of artwork requires the BALANCE schemata.[23] Johnson even argues that such image schemata structure our most abstract and symbolic forms of rationality—like the laws governing mathematics and logic. For example, from the experience of balancing alone, the human mind develops a notion of equality. One recognizes that carrying a weight in one hand involves a corresponding shift in one's posture. Through this one learns that given two weights or forces, A is balanced by B only if B is balanced by A. One can even develop an understanding of the transitive property by recognizing that if C is balanced by B, it will also be balanced by A.[24] The BALANCE schemata are basic patterns of sensorimotor experience that structure some of the fundamental rules of logic and mathematics. Thus the patterns of our thought, our ability even to reason symbolically, emerge from the distinctive ways in which human bodies move in the world. Perception of the balance of a Kandinsky, reference to God as the "Most High," and conception of upper and lower classes, are each possible because we are upright, bilaterally symmetrical beings who move in a world with gravity.

Metaphors like these diffuse throughout a culture. As Lakoff and Johnson write, even if you have no experience of war, "you still conceive of arguments, and execute them, according to the ARGUMENT IS WAR metaphor because the metaphor is built into the conceptual system of the culture in which you live."[25] According to Andy Clark, the depths and heights of human thought are made possible in part because we are able to offload our cognition onto the world: "our behavior is often sculpted and sequenced by a special class of complex external structures: the linguistic and cultural artifact that structure modern life, including maps, texts, and written plans."[26] Consider for instance how GOOD IS UP becomes encoded in many Christian churches: in the height of the podium, the altar, and the building itself; the communal practice of kneeling and rising; the singing of "Hosannah in the highest!"; and the recitation of the creed in which Jesus "came down from heaven," and "rose again on the third day" and "ascended into heaven."[27] These structures and patterns of activity distribute a conceptual metaphor throughout a community, so that an individual subject need not walk upright to conceive of GOOD as UP.[28]

Our conceptual metaphors both structure and are structured by our physical and social environment. The operations of the mind are therefore not independent of body or culture. There is no moment in the human life where we interact with a world that is not already shaped by the patterns of human thought. Our thinking therefore cannot be understood in isolation. In Johnson's words, we understand the world with "*our whole being*—our bodily capacities and skills, our values, our moods and attitudes, our entire cultural tradition, the way in which we are bound up with a linguistic community, our aesthetic sensibilities, and so forth." [29]

Thinking Otherwise: The Hermit Ant and the Orb

The VERTICALITY schema and UP-DOWN orientation metaphors emerge because we walk upright. See how the GOOD IS UP metaphor is turned upside down in Ursula K. Le Guin's short story "The Author of the Acacia Seeds."[30] In it D'Arbay and Bardol, two therolinguistics professors, propose a new interpretation of an ancient ant manuscript. The manuscript, chewed on to a series of acacia seeds by a hermit ant, reads simply, "Eat the eggs. Up with the Queen." While the text had long been interpreted as praise for the monarchy (despite the quite graphic command to "eat the eggs"), D'Arbay and Bardol's new reading hinges on a revolutionary insight into the embodiment of ant metaphors. Previous translators, our therolinguists argue, had operated from an "ethnocentric interpretation of the word 'up'"[31]; they assumed that *up* has positive connotations and *down* negative connotations. But for ants *down* would indicate going down into the anthill and therefore connote warmth and safety. Meanwhile *up*—that is, out of the anthill—there is danger. In other words, life in an ant colony would prompt for GOOD IS DOWN. The text is not praise, but treason. A phrase like "Down with the Queen!" might not immediately appear as metaphorical. Recognizing how this language would function in a colony of intelligent ants however reminds us just how much our interpretive worlds are shaped by the particularities of human embodiment.

Similarly, Lakoff and Johnson ask us to imagine "a spherical being living outside any gravitational field, with no knowledge or imagination of any other kind of experience. What could *up* possibly mean to such a being? The answer to this question would depend, not only on the physiology of this spherical being, but also on its culture."[32] What would it take to communicate with such a creature? It would not be a mere matter of removing superfluous metaphors, avoiding idioms that appeal to VERTICALITY or other image schemata. Even our mathematical notation is shaped by our existence as upright beings; no doubt our marine creature's thinking is structured by her experience as a free-floating orb.

In his 1991 *Reading Minds*, Mark Turner makes use of a similar thought experiment to show the impact of the symmetry of the human body on literature. He notes that organisms that float are often spherical—there is no evolutionary advantage to developing a front or back and an intelligent creature of this sort would not have these categories. Organisms that are stationary, such as plants, often have a distinct top and bottom in response to gravity's effects, but are symmetrical when rotated around the z-axis. Without front or back, trees widen relatively evenly, the rings of the tree demonstrating this radial symmetry. Human beings however, are self-propelled and subject to gravity. To navigate the world successfully we need to be able to distinguish where we are coming from where we are going. In general however, equal opportunities and constraints make bilateral symmetry an effective adaptation.[33] Turner's point is not merely that our bodies exhibit bilateral symmetry, but that "we have a felt, schematic, embodied understanding of bilateral symmetry."[34] Such a schema—which he identifies as part of Johnson's BALANCE schemata—structures our interaction with the world and makes possible palindromes, copulas, and chiasmi.

In reflecting on these sorts of species differences, John Sanders writes that "our knowledge of things in the world is not a perspective-free or neutral position. Rather, it is grounded in our species-specific interaction with entities. There is a real world that exists independently of us, but our understanding of it is shaped by our embodied minds."[35] Human intelligence is fundamentally human. We do not access or participate in some objective, universal rationality, but reason as human beings in distinctively human ways. Our physical interaction with the world, governed in turn by the transaction between our physiology and our environment, is the ground out of which all our most complicated thoughts emerge.[36]

Thinking of God

We think in distinctively human ways. The human mind is an embodied mind, whose processes are determined by our bodily interaction with the physical world. For Lakoff and Johnson this entails rethinking the assumptions of both continental and analytic philosophy to develop a philosophy in the flesh.[37] But this means that we also think about God in distinctively human ways. What does this mean for a *theology* in the flesh?

To begin with, all theology is *human*. Recall our intelligent ants and floating orbs. Neither of them would have any ability to understand the conception GOD IS UP which structures many Christian beliefs, rituals, and practices (e.g., praying to the "the most high," bowing while proclaiming that Jesus "came down from heaven," and building churches with vaulted ceilings all conceptualize the divine as UP).[38] An ant might find such ideas and practices terrifying; the orb would have no idea which way was up (or perhaps of there being discrete ways at all!).

Recognition that we think with our bodies adds an additional layer in thinking about the possibility and propriety of God-talk. It is not merely that God is mystery *in se*; nor that we are finite beings; nor that we learn through our senses; nor that we are affected by sin. Our very way of thinking about the world, our experience of it, our ability to navigate in it, is distinctively human. Recognition of the human character of even our most symbolic and rational thinking raises the question of whether we are constrained to make God in our image. The simple answer to this question is yes. There is no magical formula by which we escape the limits of human understanding to understand God *in se*. As John Sanders writes, "we have no other choice than to use the mental tools available to us to think about God. Our human conceptual structures are all we have to understand anything, including God. The real debate is not whether we should use human categories and concepts to understand God, but which ones we deem appropriate for God."[39] Cognitive science gives us better tools for accomplishing this work. It allows us to reflect on how our bodies give rise to God-talk, and what implications this has for understanding both human being and God. The embodied mind calls for an embodied theology. As we will see in the next section, such an embodied theology does not preclude a classical account of divine transcendence, but rather corrects speech about the relationship between self, world, and God.

THE CASE FOR TRANSCENDENCE IN AN EMBODIED THEOLOGY

In *Philosophy in the Flesh*, George Lakoff and Mark Johnson argue that only a God understood as pure immanence is coherent with an empirical understanding of human being. For them, divine transcendence is a pernicious lie founded on our cognitive tendency to abstract from our embodied experience. Therefore, healing the divided self requires jettisoning belief in a transcendent God.

But their critique rests in turn on a misconception of *transcendence* and *immanence*. Contrary to their conclusions, a Christian theology may speak of both a transcendent God and the embodied mind without contradiction. In fact, overcoming the false dualism of the divided self strengthens our ability to speak of the God of classical theism.

The False Dualism of the Divided Self

As we have seen, human beings are embodied wholes who are capable of complex meaning-making precisely on account of their engagement with their environment. The loftiest human feelings and thoughts are extensions of our more basic and physical forms of being-in-the-world. Despite this fact of our embodiment, the ways in which we talk about ourselves demonstrate that we are all operating under the metaphor of a divided self.

In their cross-cultural studies of how people speak about the self, Lakoff and Johnson identify five major conceptual metaphors. Each of these metaphors uses the same overall SUBJECT-SELF schema. The subject is "that aspect of a person that is the experiencing consciousness and the locus of reason, will, and judgment, which, by its nature, exists only in the present,"[40] whereas they define the self as "that part of a person that is not picked out by the Subject . . . conceptualized metaphorically as either a person, an object or a location."[41] In other words, in my imagination I am a subject who acts as a free agent in the present tense. I conceive of other aspects of my person—for example, my body or my past—as some sort of secondary being, the self, with which I must contend.[42]

Lakoff and Johnson are not arguing merely that people speak as if they are divided. Nor are they arguing that people consciously conceptualize themselves in such a way. Rather, their research demonstrates that no matter the particular linguistic expression or belief about the self, a deep conceptual understanding of the human person as bifurcated shapes the way we think.

To show what they mean by this SUBJECT-SELF schema, I want to look at one particular conceptual metaphor: THE SELF IS AN OBJECT. As we develop in childhood, we learn how to manipulate objects and our own bodies at the same time. I develop motor skills that allow me to grasp a block. Lakoff and Johnson argue that this funds a conceptual understanding of the body as an object to be moved and controlled, of little difference to the objects we pick up. The Subject is an agent who moves her body, as if it were a separate object, to interact with the world. Consider the phrases "Raise your voice," "She can wiggle her toes," and "I dragged myself to work."[43] Lakoff and Johnson argue that they belie a deep conceptual structure, in which we experience the relationship between our subjectivity and our embodied existence much as a person operating a crane.

In order to imagine the body as an object that I move around in space, I cannot identify with it. Thus, at the same time that I posit my body as something other, I conceive of my agency and subjectivity as something that is essentially disembodied. In this way, Lakoff and Johnson argue that object manipulation ultimately prompts human beings to consider themselves in someway as split. In this schema it is the subject who acts upon her self as an object.

Use of these split-self metaphors is a cross-cultural phenomenon. As far as Lakoff and Johnson can tell, it is universal.[44] As they argue, the fact that all metaphors about inner life use the same overall SUBJECT-SELF schema, "reveals not only something deep about our conceptual systems but also something deep about our inner experience, mainly that we experience ourselves as split."[45] Therefore, they argue that such a metaphor is helpful at capturing aspects of human experience. That is, split-self metaphors do offer explanatory powers for certain aspects of inner life: "The fact that we can make true statements about our inner lives using these metaphors suggest that these metaphors conform in significant ways to the structure of our inner lives as we experience them phenomenologically. These metaphors capture the logic of much of inner experience and characterize how we reason about it."[46] Ultimately, however, Lakoff and Johnson question whether this is because the metaphor shapes our experience or vice versa. But taken ontologically, such a split is ultimately a falsehood. The way we conceive of ourselves is at odds with what we know about the human mind.[47] In other words, we do not think the way we think we think. Lakoff and Johnson thus challenge any understanding of human transcendence that depends upon anthropological dualism.

In his 2001 Gifford lectures, Lakoff engages in hypothesizing about the soul, should it exist. Since it is understood to endure after death, he assumes that the soul is something disembodied, and goes on to reason what disembodied cognition would be.[48] As he imagines, such a disembodied soul could not see color nor hear sound—it would not be able to perceive at all. It would likewise not be able to think or empathize. And so while Lakoff admits that his research cannot definitely prove that a soul does not exist, he argues that it does delimit how it could exist: "In short, the soul, if it exists: -cannot see, hear, or otherwise perceive; -cannot think using ordinary human concepts; -cannot empathize with human beings; -is not conscious; -is not the locus of anyone's personality or character."[49] While the existence of the soul may not be falsifiable, one wonders what relevance or value such a soul can have. In other words, the immortal soul that lives on after my death would not be me in any substantial sense.

Lakoff and Johnson's critique of human transcendence grounds their critique of divine transcendence. They identify two major Christian perspectives on the relationship between God and world: the "distant-God Christian tradition" and panentheism. Ultimately, they argue that views of God as transcendent—"out there," "above," or "other-worldly"—derive from an extension of understanding the subject as split:

> The tradition of the distant, monarchial God is centered around the idea that we are essentially disembodied Souls not of this world, that we are inhabiting our bodies only during an earthly sojourn, and that our ultimate purpose is to "dwell with God" elsewhere, in heaven, not on earth. In the distant-God Christian tradition, morality is tied to the disembodiment of the Soul. Christians are supposed to live a holy life focused on transcending all the things of this world—bodily desire, material possessions, fame, worldly success, and long life. This disembodied, otherworldly conception of spirituality and transcendence downplays one's relation to the world, the natural environment, and all other aspects of embodied existence.[50]

In their understanding of the distant-God Christian tradition, the same process through which we come to imagine ourselves as disembodied agents prompts us to imagine God as a disembodied figure wholly apart from the material world. In other words, divine transcendence is an extension of a false understanding of human transcendence.

Interestingly, Lakoff and Johnson themselves do not want to discourage spiritual practice. Rather, they want to imagine spirituality after the death of the transcendent God and the divided self. They suggest that we think of human transcendence in terms of empathy. Much of our development, including many of the dominant metaphors we use to understand our being-in-the-world, entails an imaginative process of understanding ourselves in the place of the other. We do so when we reason "If I were you . . ." or even when we employ simple statements of relationships. For example, I can refer to "Jose's mom" because I see in Jose an analog to myself and in his mother, my mother. But such empathic projection goes beyond the relationship to a concrete personal other. Lakoff and Johnson argue that it extends into nature itself. When we experience awe at an eagle soaring, they argue it is because our minds have developed to imagine ourselves as soaring as well. These imaginative projections are what Lakoff and Johnson identify as the source of many of the world's meditative traditions. In them, Lakoff and Johnson see resources for a spirituality in which one experiences a form of transcendence that does not pretend any sort of abstraction from, or negation of, one's embodied existence.[51]

It is important to note here that the relationship between self and world Lakoff and Johnson are describing is not merely in the mind of the one imagining. The imaginative process develops precisely because we are already in a permeable relationship with the world: "The environment is not an 'other' to us. It is not a collection of things that we encounter. Rather, it is part of our being. It is the locus of our existence and identity. We cannot and do not exist apart from it."[52] The concrete practices in which we develop our capacity for empathy are thus practices in which we develop greater insight about a relationship in which we already exist. They continue,

> It is through empathic projection that we come to know our environment, understand how we are part of it and how it is part of us. This is the bodily mechanism by which we can participate in nature, not just as hikers or climbers or swimmers, but as part of nature itself, part of a larger, all-encompassing whole. A mindful embodied spirituality is thus an ecological spirituality. . . . Embodied spirituality is more than spiritual experience. It is an ethical relationship to the physical world.[53]

Thus Lakoff and Johnson offer an understanding of human spirituality in which transcendence involves meditation upon and action on behalf of the world we live in. According to Lakoff and Johnson, such spirituality coheres with panentheism, which they describe as "an encounter with the divine in all things."[54]

In his Gifford lectures, George Lakoff reiterates that the only understandings of God that he finds reasonable are ones rooted in the conceptual metaphor GOD IS IMMANENT. If one understands that God is what exists, then one's spiritual activity is necessarily directed toward the world as it exists. One recognizes the sacrality of the material world.[55] Subjects who develop in transaction with the world, whose cognition is made possible through felt empathy with that world, are called to engage in the rigorous practice of developing right relationship with the other:

> What is sacred is the world. It has inherent and ultimate value. I take spiritual connection as empathy with the world (via mirror and canonical neurons), empathy with people, and with what David Abram calls 'the more than human world': plants, animals, soils, sea, clouds, geological formations, all of it, including the wonderful inventions of human minds. With it comes a way of life—a commitment to nurturant morality, that is, a commitment to empathy and responsibility. That includes a commitment to a practice, a quite demanding practice of rigorous thought, finding out about and trying to comprehend the world, meditation, exploration of self and others, appreciation, connection, giving, and experiencing fully the wonders of your own mind and body and the wonders of the Other—all kinds of Other.[56]

This sacred relationship to the other is what Johnson calls *horizontal transcendence*. As he argues, one does not need to seek an antidote to the bodily and material realm by positing a disembodied and immaterial one:

> If we are inescapably and gloriously embodied, then our spirituality cannot be grounded in otherworldliness. It must be grounded in our relation to the human and more-than-human world that we inhabit. It must involve a capacity for horizontal (as opposed to vertical) transcendence, namely, our ability both to transform experience and to be transformed ourselves by something that transcends us: the whole ongoing, ever-developing natural process for which we are a part.[57]

Such an embodied spirituality, Johnson argues, utterly opposes any spirituality satisfied only by the infinite—or more precisely, negation of the finite.

A False Dichotomy Does Not Overcome a False Dualism

Contra Lakoff and Johnson, I argue that such spirituality is compatible with a theology of both human and divine transcendence. We might first start by heeding Jonathan Jong, Christopher Kavanagh, and Aku Visala's caution about the relevance of cognitive science of religion for thinking about classical theism. As they argue, since classical theism in the Abrahamic traditions proclaims God's simplicity, cognitive accounts of concepts are ultimately irrelevant to the appropriateness of our beliefs about a God who is beyond concepts.[58] Tim Adamson has levied a similar charge against Lakoff and Johnson's move from the critique of the divided self to the critique of a transcendent God.[59] Robert Masson argues that Lakoff and Johnson take how humans arrive at concepts to be overly determinative of what concepts are reasonable.[60]

But in this particular case, the how and the what intersect. For Lakoff and Johnson the problem with divine transcendence is not merely that it posits a God beyond the human being's embodied transactions with the world, but that theories of divine transcendence depend upon the false metaphor of the divided self. As such talk about the transcendent God propagates lies about who we are as human beings. The urgent question here is whether that link is necessary. Can we conceive of divine transcendence in such a way that does not correspond to anthropological dualism?

As Lakoff and Johnson clarify, it is not the metaphor of the divided self per se that is a problem. As a model for understanding the inner life, it has immense explanatory power. Much of our embodied experience can be spoken of consistently and accurately within the conceptual metaphor of the subject-self schema. The problem is when the utility of this schema is taken as proof that a disembodied subject exists. This is how they understand the Christian conception of the soul.

Alternatively, they argue that an understanding of an "embodied soul" might capture the lived experience of bifurcation without falling into a dualism that denigrates the body and the earth:

> One might imagine a spiritual tradition in which such a Soul is fundamentally embodied—shaped in important ways by the body, located forever as part of the body, and dependent for its ongoing existence on the body. The results about the mind discussed throughout this book in no way rule out the existence of *that* kind of Soul, an embodied soul.[61]

While Lakoff and Johnson do not recognize it, this embodied Soul is not un-Christian. In fact, given the doctrines of the incarnation, the resurrection of the body, and certain Christian formations of hylomorphism, one could argue that it is profoundly Christian. For example, Karl Rahner—whose theological anthropology has influenced much of Catholic theology—argued that spirit does not have being proper to itself. Rather, it only becomes itself in space and over time through the materiality of the human body.[62]

If there is room in Lakoff and Johnson's philosophy in the flesh for an embodied soul, then might there be a similar space for a God who is not opposed to the world, but is rather "the whither of human [embodied] transcendence?"[63] According to Lakoff and Johnson, only a panentheistic understanding of God as wholly immanent suffices. Their argument depends however on a false dichotomy between the GOD IS TRANSCENDENT and GOD IS IMMANENT models. But as Masson notes, Lakoff and Johnson have a very unsophisticated grasp of theological concepts.[64] Their models of what transcendence and immanence look like are overly simplistic, as if God is either over against or completely identified with the world. Such a dichotomy obscures the sophisticated ways in which Christians have thought about the relationship between God and the world. For example, Masson points to Thomistic simplicity as a blend that defies either of Lakoff and Johnson's models.[65] Simplicity by definition eludes categorization. Thomas's use of it as a substantive for God indicates precisely that no predicates can be applied to God.[66] Thomas's reasoning therefore does not entail thinking about God as object and the world as a container—a set of constraints which forces one to think about God as either in or outside of the world.[67]

Ironically, Lakoff and Johnson's models of the God-world relationship are governed precisely by this CONTAINER schema. In following Marcus Borg's classification of Christian theology, they have reduced a rich and diverse set of traditions to a simple binary of whether an object (God) is in a container (the world). In their understanding, God is either that which is encountered in all things in the world, or God is that which is encountered when one somehow removes oneself from the world.

But if God is truly transcendent, then mapping God onto an object in space is an unnecessarily restrictive metaphor. God is not an object. Talk about God ought not to succeed or fail based on spatial reasoning no more than decisions about our affections ought to be governed according to the operations of heat. When Christians speak of divine transcendence what is being proposed is not that God is anti-world, but that God is the creator of the world and therefore not a being in it—or strictly speaking a being at all. The doctrine of divine simplicity—that God has neither parts nor predicates—means that God does not exist in a zero-sum game with creation. As D. Stephen Long argues, the doctrine thus preserves the biblical claim that God is love. It is because God is not an object in the world, and therefore not in competition with it, that God is able to truly love the world.[68]

Paradoxical as it may seem at first, in classical theism God's transcendence actually makes possible God's immanence—since God transcends the very simplistic opposition of transcendence and immanence imagined in the CONTAINER schema. Because of what Kathryn Tanner refers to as "a noncontrastive characterization of God's transcendence," God's presence to us does not come at the cost of transcendence.[69]

This paradoxical understanding of divine transcendence is made doubly so by the Chalcedonian proclamation that Jesus is fully divine and fully human. Here the God who transcends the difference between transcendence and immanence is, by that radical transcendence, capable of entering into history at a particular time and place, in a particular human body.[70] God suffers no loss of divinity when becoming incarnate. Rather, the unity of Jesus's two natures exists in such a way that, according to Karl Rahner, the human and the divine increase in direct proportion.[71]

In offering such a brief sketch of these Christian ideas, I do not mean to suggest that Christians are in unanimous agreement—either synchronously or diachronically—over the nature of Christ, divine transcendence, or the problem of God-talk. Only that thinking of Christian understandings of God in terms of two separate models—transcendence and immanence—is woefully inadequate. It neglects not only the complicated ways in which these two categories interpenetrate one another in Christian thought, but also the fact that the relationship between divine transcendence and immanence has itself been a major locus of theological reflection. Christianity offers more resources than Lakoff and Johnson realize for accomplishing a theology in the flesh that does not depend upon or perpetuate a false understanding of the self.

Still, their initial insight is critical to thinking through divine transcendence. Lakoff and Johnson want to disabuse us of thinking about God as other-worldly in such a way that God and world function dualistically, and thus one's devotion to God is in competition with one's concern for the world and one's own embodied existence. This in fact does not preclude a Christian understanding of God's transcendence, but corrects it—driving us away from any understanding of God at the top of a hierarchy of being or in competition with other beings, and toward an understanding of God whose otherness is not negation.

Christian language about divine transcendence is plagued by our cognitive tendencies, which nudge us toward idolatrous conceptions of God. We conceive of the divine in terms that are more clearly delineated to us—not merely in rhetorical flourish (e.g., "My God is a fortress"), but even in our most fundamental and abstract theological reflection (e.g., depending on the CONTAINER schema). Cognitive scientists of religion describe a process through which the habits of the mind tend—a tendency some have taken to calling the "god faculty"—to conceive of god as an agent in the world who operates within it. As a result, with respect to the Abrahamic traditions, the mind veers toward heresy: the god faculty "is perniciously theologically misleading, leading to persistent idolatrous ideas about God."[72] Theologians have long proclaimed that language fails to adequately describe God; cognitive science adds to this insight *how* it does so.

God is mystery. There is no language powerful or accurate enough to compensate for this. There is however, language that is better or worse at reminding us precisely *that* God is mystery. Conceptions of divine transcendence as God being "above" the world or "out there" exploit our natural tendency to think of ourselves as divided, transcendence as distance, and GOOD IS UP. This language belies a fundamental misunderstanding of ourselves and of God as objects. Instead we need language that embraces the mystery of human and divine being, and the value of the body and the material world.

THE TOUCH OF GOD: LANGUAGE FOR AN EMBODIED THEOLOGY

What language ought an embodied theology to use for a transcendent God? As Robert Masson, asks in his 2015 *Without Metaphor, No Saving God*:

> If the mind is inherently embodied and the very structure of reason itself comes from the details of our embodiment, right down to our neural systems, how is it possible to speak of God as one who cannot be perceived as others are perceived? How is it possible to speak of God, if God cannot be located in relation to our bodies as others are identified through our movement in our worlds?[73]

It is important to remember here that conceptual mapping does not fundamentally limit thought to the source domain. The fact that we conceive of affection in terms of warmth, for instance, does not mean that affection does not exist, or that what we experience as affection is only warmth. Rather, warmth is what provides the cognitive structure for our thoughts of something more abstract like affection. It roots—but does not reduce—experiences of love in the felt sense of the body. Likewise, talk of the divine will always be structured by our concrete engagement with the world. Here, precisely, is the challenge: what embodied experience ought to structure our understanding of the divine?

The body itself provides the vocabulary for a theology in the flesh. It offers its own transcendence, not abstracted from, but disclosed in, the sense of touch. Speaking of the *touch* of God may offer a corrective to a natural tendency to think of God in competition with the world.

In *A Touch of Transcendence*, Mayra Rivera documents the harm of thinking about divine transcendence as being over against the world. The root problem, she argues, is that transcendence is often understood as separation:

> Transcendence is often associated with hierarchical distance. Thus, the most common images and concepts that Christians have used to describe divine transcendence convey the idea that God's otherness entails separation from creation. This assumption has negative implications for our visions of God and the created world because it sets up real difference as antithetical to close relationships.[74]

To translate this into the framework we have been using, our conceptions of God make use of the primary metaphors MORE IS UP and SIMILARITY IS CLOSENESS in conceiving of God's transcendence as "up there" or "out there." Divine goodness and radical alterity are understood spatially. Unfortunately, this implies that God is an object in space, separated from the rest of creation.

Due to the primary metaphor INTIMACY IS CLOSENESS, such language also functions to imply that God does not care for creation.[75] We thus proclaim God's transcendence at the cost of God's love.

Our embodied minds thus have difficulty conceiving of difference as other than separation. This impoverishes not only our understanding of God, but also, according to Rivera, our relationships with human others as well. Drawing on both postcolonial and feminist thought, Rivera argues that conceiving of difference as separation has justified systems of domination in which those who are other are required to assimilate.[76] While many feminist theologians have, like Lakoff and Johnson propose, moved to a theology of immanence, Rivera argues that transcendence is necessary for any liberative theology. Drawing on the work of Homi Bhabha, Rivera argues that a sense of *beyond* is critical to identifying present injustices and hoping they may be overcome.[77] It is, per Derrida, totalizing systems that deny the beyond.[78] Right relationship—with God, other humans, and the created world—requires not denying differences but thinking *difference* differently.

In seeking new ways of speaking of God's transcendence, Rivera also proposes language of touch. Rivera writes that "God is irreducibly Other, always *beyond* our grasp. But not beyond our touch."[79] In developing this notion of the "touch of transcendence," Rivera employs Luce Irigary's sense of "touching upon:" which "means a 'touching which respects the other,' that never aims at appropriating or capturing."[80] In Irigary's work, the other remains a mystery even in the touch. In it, one comes into contact with another but the difference between them is irreducible.[81]

What kind of touch we imagine matters. As Linn Marie Tonstad demonstrates in *God and Difference*, the logic of human bodies already structures how we think about intra-human relationships, human-divine relationships, and the relationship between the divine persons. Unfortunately it is often the logic of reproductive sex, where bounded bodies unite through penetration. As she argues, theologies that offer an unfettered kenosis as virtue, for instance, do so because of a logic in which one must be penetrated by God because one's personal boundaries would otherwise keep God out: "This symbolic order spatializes kenosis by thinking it as a space-making in which the self must move aside to make room for the other, to be filled by the other, for self and other cannot be in the same place at the same time, as it were."[82] Such a logic is inimical to the gospel, which operates by a logic of plenitude and co-presence. Scarcity and competition no longer rule: there are bags of food left over when Jesus feeds people, and today Christ is present fully in each Eucharist.[83] The gospel is not a zero-sum game, and one does not need to negate oneself or the world to make more room for God.

Tonstad suggests "an economy of surface touch" to represent this new logic, which we can see in the stories of the resurrected Jesus:

> His body no longer competes with other bodies for the same space. His body and the wall or door can be in the same place at the same time without crashing into each other or shattering each other, yet his body has not become ethereal or vaporous—he eats and drinks, he can be touched. This transformation and intensification of materiality shows itself in other actions that Jesus performs after the resurrection. Jesus can walk through walls because his body has become most real: body without limit as threat, body as presence and particularity. Jesus' most intense encounters before and after the resurrection involve neither penetration nor internalization—when Mary rubs expensive ointment into his feet, that, too, is a surface touch rather than an invading touch.[84]

Tonstad's use of touch in this way offers language that keeps in mind both God's immanence and transcendence—"the skin's surface," she writes, both "reveals and hides"—and does so in ways that contribute as well to healthy ways of thinking about human bodies. [85]

Employing the language of touch for God-talk preserves divine transcendence without forsaking relationality. It better enables us to speak of a God who is simple *and* who is love. It follows the logic of the incarnation—as Rivera writes, "transcendence requires a stable"[86]—and the abundance of the gospel. It encourages us to seek transcendence in the transformation of a more just world.

CONCLUSION

Our theology is distinctively human. The human body fundamentally shapes the way we think about the self, the world, and God. This fact on its own tells us something about what it means to be human, bringing the body to the fore in anthropological reflection and reminding us that we are embodied wholes. Cognitive science is not a challenge that theology must respond to, it is an invitation to think carefully and empirically about the value of the body and its role in theological reflection.

In turn, this understanding of the subject calls for a theology of divine transcendence that does not depend upon false understandings of the self as divided. It also provides resources for developing one. Given our cognitive bias for thinking of God as an object like other objects, and conceiving divine transcendence as "above us" or "out there," language of divine touch may help protect against idolatrous notions of divine transcendence. In the end, such an understanding of the relationship between self, world, and God tells the truth about our existence as embodied subjects and reminds us of the mystery of God.

NOTES

1. For an introduction to this history—particularly how it is has shaped the development of robotics and artificial intelligence—see Andy Clark, *Being There: Putting Brain, Body, and World Together Again* (Cambridge, MA: MIT Press, 1997).
2. George Lakoff and Mark Johnson, *Metaphors We Live By* (Chicago: University of Chicago, 1980), 5.
3. Lakoff and Johnson, *Metaphors We Live By*, 6.
4. Ibid., 56.
5. George Lakoff and Mark Johnson, *Philosophy in the Flesh: The Embodied Mind and Its Challenge to Western Thought* (New York: Basic Books, 1999), 60.
6. Lakoff and Johnson, *Philosophy in the Flesh*, 45.
7. Ibid., 50.
8. Ibid., 46–47, 56–57.
9. Lakoff and Johnson conceptualize this in terms of atoms and molecules *Philosophy in the Flesh*, 60.
10. Lakoff and Johnson, *Metaphors We Live By*, 15–16. See also *Philosophy in the Flesh*, 54–55.
11. Lakoff and Johnson, *Metaphors We Live By*, 14.
12. Ibid., 19–24.
13. Ibid., 19, italics removed.
14. Ibid., 18.
15. Ibid., 16.
16. Mark Johnson, *The Meaning of the Body: Aesthetics of Human Understanding* (Chicago: University of Chicago Press, 2007), 136.
17. Johnson, *The Meaning of the Body*, 136–46. See also Mark Johnson, *The Body in the Mind* (Chicago: University of Chicago Press, 1987), 21–37, and Lakoff and Johnson, *Philosophy in the Flesh*, 31–37.
18. Mark Johnson, *The Meaning of the Body*, 137.
19. Lakoff and Johnson, *Metaphors We Live By*, 19.
20. Mark Johnson, *The Body in the Mind*, 73.
21. Ibid., 74.
22. Ibid., 74–76.
23. Ibid., 83–5.
24. Ibid., 85–98.
25. Lakoff and Johnson, *Metaphors We Live By*, 63–4.
26. Clark, *Being There*, 53.
27. Intelligibility in this case does not mean appropriateness. Communities may indeed structure their world in ways that are intelligible, yet harmful, to people who move in it differently.

28. For a brief discussion of this, see Michael L. Anderson, "Embodied Cognition: A Field Guide," *Artificial Intelligence* 149 (2003): 91–130, 113.

29. Johnson, *The Body in the Mind*, 102.

30. Ursula K. Le Guin, "'The Author of the Acacia Seeds' and Other Extracts from the Journal of the Association of Therolinguistics," in *The Compass Rose* (New York: Harper Perennial, 2005), the relevant section on ants can be found on 3–6.

31. Le Guin, "'The Author of the Acacia Seeds,'" 6.

32. Lakoff and Johnson, *Metaphors We Live By*, 57.

33. Mark Turner, *Reading Minds: The Study of English in the Age of Cognitive Science* (Princeton, NJ: Princeton University Press, 1991), 69–70.

34. Turner, *Reading Minds*, 70.

35. John Sanders, *Theology in the Flesh: How Embodiment and Culture Shape the Way We Think about Truth, Morality, and God* (Minneapolis: Fortress, 2016), 24.

36. I have written elsewhere about how this research can illuminate theological anthropology—see Erin Kidd, "The Subject of Conceptual Mapping: Theological Anthropology across Brain, Body, and World," *Open Theology* 4, no. 1 (2018): 117–35.

37. Lakoff and Johnson dedicate the last chapter to sketching such a philosophy in *Philosophy in the Flesh*, 551–68.

38. Noting that both transcendence and power are often spoken of in terms of the height, Brian P. Meier and his colleagues experimented whether height prompts subjects to think of godliness. They discovered that subjects were more likely to identify god(s) quickly if the pictures were higher on a screen, and more likely to rate a stranger as godly if his or her picture were higher, Brian P. Meier, et al. "What's 'Up' with God? Vertical Space as a Representation of the Divine," *Journal of Personality and Social Psychology*, 93, no. 5 (2007): 699–710.

39. Sanders, *Theology in the Flesh*, 3–4.

40. Lakoff and Johnson, *Philosophy in the Flesh*, 269.

41. Ibid.

42. There is one exception. In the Essential Self model, there are two selves, but only one is the enduring essence of a person. In this model the "I" can be aligned with either the "false" or "true" self. This structure explains phenomena such as conceptualizing an activity as "not the real me" or "trying to find oneself." While the structure of bifurcation is different in this model, it still depends on a division of the human person. Ibid., 269, 282–84.

43. Ibid., 271.

44. Ibid., 289.

45. Ibid., 269.

46. Ibid., 288.

47. Ibid., 268.

48. George Lakoff, "How to Live with an Embodied Mind: When Causation, Mathematics, Morality, the Soul, and God are Essentially Metaphorical Ideas," in *The Embodied Mind, and How to Live with One*. The Nature and Limits of Human Understanding: The 2001 Gifford Lectures at the University of Glasgow, ed. Anthony J. Sanford (New York: T&T Clark, 2003), 80.

49. Lakoff, "How to Live with an Embodied Mind," 82.

50. Lakoff and Johnson, *Philosophy in the Flesh*, 564.

51. Ibid., 565–66.
52. Ibid., 566
53. Ibid.
54. Ibid., 567.
55. Lakoff, "How to Live with an Embodied Mind," 102–3.
56. Ibid., 103–4.
57. Johnson, *The Meaning of the Body*, 14.
58. Jonathan Jong, Christopher Kavanagh, and Aku Visala, "Born Idolaters: The Limits of the Philosophical Implications of the Cognitive Science of Religion," *Neue Zeitschrift für Systematische Theologie und Religionsphilosophie* 57, no. 2 (2015): 244–66.
59. Tim Adamson, "What Is Metaphorical Cognition? Two Philosophical Models," in *The Literal and Nonliteral in Language and Thought*, ed. Seana Coulson and Barbara Lewandowska-Tomaszczyk (New York: Peter Lange, 2005), 353–79. See also Masson's discussion of Adamson's critique, *Without Metaphor*, 115–9.
60. Masson, *Without Metaphor*, 55.
61. Lakoff and Johnson, *Philosophy in the Flesh*, 124.
62. Karl Rahner, *Spirit in the World*, 2nd ed., trans. William Dych (New York: Herder and Herder, 1968), 192. Hereafter *Spirit*. For the German, see *Geist in Welt: Philosophische Schriften*, *Sämtliche Werke*, vol. 2 (Freiburg: Verlag Herder, 1996), 253. Hereafter *Geist*.
63. The phrase is Karl Rahner's. For Rahner, classical theism entails that absolute being does not exist in the world alongside other objects; neither does the subject's relationship to absolute being exist alongside her relationship to other objects. In offering a tautology—that human transcendence is directed toward a "whither"—Rahner attempts to resist any naming that might promote the reification or objectification of absolute being, see particularly *Spirit*, 117–18: *Geist*, 145.
64. Masson, *Without Metaphor*, 56.
65. Ibid., 121.
66. Ibid., 124.
67. Ibid., 122.
68. D. Stephen Long, *The Perfectly Simple Triune God: Aquinas and His Legacy* (Minneapolis: Fortress, 2016), 57–61.
69. Kathryn Tanner, *God and Creation in Christian Theology: Tyranny or Empowerment* (New York: Basil Blackwell, 1988), 47; see also her discussion of how Irenaeus makes this argument on 56–57.
70. For an example of this kind of theology in practice, where this paradox of transcendence and immanence is made clear, see Karl Rahner, "The Ignatian Mysticism of Joy in the World," *Theological Investigations*, vol. 3 (New York: Crossroad, 1967), 277–93. For the German, see "Die ignatianische Mystik der Weltfreudigkeit," in *Sämtliche Werke*, vol. 7 (Freiburg: Herder, 2013), 279–93.
71. Karl Rahner, "Current Problems in Christology," in *Theological Investigations*, vol. 1 (New York: Crossroad, 1961), 162–3. For the German, see "Probleme der Christologie von Heute," in *Sämtliche Werke*, vol. 12 (Freiburg: Herder, 2005), 271–2.
72. Jong, Kavanagh, and Visala, "Born Idolaters," 260.

73. Robert Masson, *Without Metaphor, No Saving God: Theology after Cognitive Linguistics* (Leuven: Peeters, 2014), 15.

74. Preface to Mayra Rivera, *The Touch of Transcendence: A Postcolonial Theology of God* (Louisville, KY: Westminster John Knox, 2007), ix.

75. Lakoff and Johnson list each of these among the primary metaphors in *Philosophy in the Flesh*, 50–4.

76. Preface to Rivera, *The Touch of Transcendence*, ix–x.

77. Rivera, *The Touch of Transcendence*, 10.

78. Ibid., 11.

79. Ibid., 2.

80. Ibid., 2.

81. Ibid., 88.

82. Linn Marie Tonstad, *God and Difference: The Trinity, Sexuality, and the Transformation of Finitude* (New York: Routledge, 2016), 136. See also Christopher Hadley's solution to this problem in Chapter Five in this volume.

83. Tonstad, *God and Difference*, 240–3.

84. Ibid., 242–3.

85. Ibid., 136.

86. Rivera, *The Touch of Transcendence*, 97.

BIBLIOGRAPHY

Adamson, Tim. "What Is Metaphorical Cognition? Two Philosophical Models." In *The Literal and Nonliteral in Language and Thought*, edited by Seana Coulson and Barbara Lewandowska-Tomaszczyk, 353–79. New York: Peter Lange, 2005.

Anderson, Michael L. "Embodied Cognition: A Field Guide." *Artificial Intelligence* 149 (2003): 91–130.

Clark, Andy. *Being There: Putting Brain, Body, and World Together Again*. Cambridge, MA: MIT Press, 1997.

Johnson, Mark. *The Body in the Mind*. Chicago: University of Chicago Press, 1987.

———. *The Meaning of the Body: Aesthetics of Human Understanding*. Chicago: University of Chicago Press, 2007.

Jong, Jonathan, Christopher Kavanagh, and Aku Visala. "Born Idolaters: The Limits of the Philosophical Implications of the Cognitive Science of Religion." *Neue Zeitschrift für Systematische Theologie und Religionsphilosophie* 57, no. 2 (2015): 244–66.

Kidd, Erin. "The Subject of Conceptual Mapping: Theological Anthropology across Brain, Body, and World." *Open Theology* 4, no. 1 (2018): 117–35.

Lakoff, George. "How to Live with an Embodied Mind: When Causation, Mathematics, Morality, the Soul, and God Are Essentially Metaphorical Ideas." In *The Embodied Mind, and How to Live with One*. The Nature and Limits of Human Understanding: The 2001 Gifford Lectures at the University of Glasgow, edited by Anthony J. Sanford, 75–108. New York: T&T Clark, 2003.

Lakoff, George and Mark Johnson. *Metaphors We Live By*. Chicago: University of Chicago Press, 1980.

———. *Philosophy in the Flesh: The Embodied Mind and Its Challenge to Western Thought*. New York: Basic Books, 1999.

Le Guin, Ursula K. "'The Author of the Acacia Seeds' and Other Extracts from the Journal of the Association of Therolinguistics." In *The Compass Rose*, 3–14. New York: Harper Perennial, 2005.

Long, D. Stephen. *The Perfectly Simple Triune God: Aquinas and His Legacy*. Minneapolis: Fortress, 2016).

Masson, Robert. *Without Metaphor, No Saving God: Theology after Cognitive Linguistics*. Leuven: Peeters, 2014.

Meier, Brian P., David J. Hauser, Michael D. Robinson, Chris Kelland Friesan, and Katie Schjeldahl. "What's 'Up' with God? Vertical Space as a Representation of the Divine." *Journal of Personality and Social Psychology* 93, no. 5 (2007): 699–710.

Rahner, Karl. "Current Problems in Christology." In *Theological Investigations*. Vol. 1, 149–200. New York: Crossroad, 1961. Based on "Chalkedon—Ende oder Anfang?" in *Das Konzil von Chalkedon*. Vol. 3. Edited by Alois Grillmeier and Heinrich Bacht, 3–49. Würzburg: Echter Verlag, 1954. Reprinted in "Probleme der Christologie von Heute." In *Sämtliche Werke*. Vol. 12, 261–301. Freiburg: Herder, 2005.

———. "The Ignatian Mysticism of Joy in the World." In *Theological Investigations*. Vol. 3, 277–93. New York: Crossroad, 1967. Based on a lecture Rahner gave in Vienna, originally published as "Die ignatianische Mystik der Weltfreudigkeit." In *Zeitschrift für Aszese und Mystik* 12 (1937): 121–37. Reprinted in *Sämtliche Werke*. Vol. 7, 279–93. Freiburg: Herder, 2013.

———. *Spirit in the World*. 2nd ed. Translated by William Dych. New York: Herder and Herder, 1968. Translation of *Geist in Welt*. 2nd ed. Edited by Johann B. Metz. Munich: Kösel-Verlag, 1957. Reprinted as *Geist in Welt: Philosophische Schriften, Sämtliche Werke*. Vol. 2. Freiburg: Verlag Herder, 1996.

Rivera, Mayra. *The Touch of Transcendence: A Postcolonial Theology of God*. Louisville, KY: Westminster John Knox, 2007.

Sanders, John. *Theology in the Flesh: How Embodiment and Culture Shape the Way We Think about Truth, Morality, and God*. Minneapolis: Fortress, 2016.

Tanner, Kathryn. *God and Creation in Christian Theology: Tyranny or Empowerment*. New York: Basil Blackwell, 1988.

Tonstad, Linn Marie. *God and Difference: The Trinity, Sexuality, and the Transformation of Finitude*. New York: Routledge, 2016.

Turner, Mark. *Reading Minds: The Study of English in the Age of Cognitive Science*. Princeton, NJ: Princeton University Press, 1991.

Chapter Three

Homo Symbolicus: Cognition and Communion

Julia Feder

Our bodies and our ecologies determine both the limits and opportunities for the revelation of Godself in history. In other words, material realities are not incidental to the spiritual life, but instead the divine-human relationship is structured in and through "the details of our embodiment."[1] As Robert Masson argues in *Without Metaphor, No Saving God*, "There is no 'stepping outside' our bodily, socially, and culturally constituted conceptual frameworks to gain a God's-eye view of reality independent from metaphorical and figurative conceptualizations. There is no escaping the constitutive role of embodied mind."[2] Integral to these details of our embodiment are human patterns of cognition—the "neural and cognitive mechanisms," that provide the structure for human reason[3]—both determined by and determinant of our bodies and our ecologies (our brains, the rest of our bodies, and our ecological niches).

Evolutionary anthropologists generally agree that human patterns of cognition are, in a large part, marked by the capacity for (and, indeed, the propensity toward) symbolic thought and, consequently, modes of symbolic thought organize human behavior in significant ways. Because humans are "master niche constructors," that is, they actively modify their environments in order to maximize perceived levels of quality of life, humans significantly shape their ecologies according to their symbolic worldviews and through their symbolically organized behaviors. Thus, human relationality is conditioned by human modes of symbolic thought. In this essay, I turn to literature in the field of evolutionary anthropology in order to trace the relationship between human symbolic cognition and human modes of sociality. This will help us to give weight to the claim that the saving relationship of God to humanity is mediated by distinctively human modes of symbolic or metaphorical thinking. Human modes of symbolic cognition are not simply modes of conceptual analysis, but rather they are the very condition for the possibility of human engagement with one's environment. Even further, human modes of symbolic cognition represent the conditions for the possibilities of human relationality, including relationality to God.

One of the most interesting contributions to the discussion of the shape of human cognition in contemporary evolutionary anthropology today comes from American anthropologist Terrence Deacon who argues that human beings can be distinguished from other animals by their capacity for symbolic thinking, expressed primarily through language. Language use has marked the human brain in permanent ways, such that human beings should be given a new species designation: *Homo symbolicus*. Despite his training as a scientist, he uses natively theological language to describe the effect of symbol use on the development of the human brain. Making use of Johannine imagery, symbol use has affected the development of the human brain such that "the word became flesh" and, as a result, "we are made in the image of the word." In other words, the process of niche construction employed by human beings in order to make themselves evolutionarily successful has involved symbolic communication as a primary adaptive strategy.

Deacon's turn to theological language when describing the nuances of human symbol use and its effects in the human niche may be no accident. Theological traditions have long wrestled with how to articulate the power of symbols in and for the human community. The Christian theological tradition, in particular, has customarily employed semiotic language in order to describe the significance of communal ritual practice. Since the Council of Trent in the sixteenth century, the Catholic theological tradition has commonly identified a *sacrament* as "a visible sign of an invisible grace." The use of the term *sign* is significant because, as contemporary semiotic theorists remind us, there are many different kinds of signs.

As Catholic theologian Edward Schillebeeckx describes in his early work *Christ the Sacrament of the Encounter with God* (1960), a sacrament is the kind of sign that brings about the reality which it signifies; it is a *signum efficax gratiae* [efficacious sign of grace]. In other words, a sacramental sign is an instrumental effective cause. This may push against a popular contemporary assumption that religious signs function to remind one of something that is more real or more present than the sign itself. For example, the sign of the crucifix is meant to cause the viewer to remember the crucifixion of Jesus and inspire meditation upon the Passion. However, sign-as-memorial only represents one genre of symbolic representation. For Catholics, sacramental symbols (e.g., the Eucharistic bread as a symbol of the body of Christ) make present the reality that they signify (viz., the breaking and sharing of the Eucharistic bread, in fact, an authentic encounter with Christ for the participants). In his 1960 work, Edward Schillebeeckx reformulates the traditional sixteenth century Tridentine maxim for the twentieth century with an emphasis on history: the sacramental is the supernatural expressed in history. Schillebeeckx explains, "[E]very supernatural reality which is realized historically in our lives is sacramental."[4] This symbolic expression in history of God's grace "really and actually bestows the grace it signifies."[5] The sacramental is an effective cause of grace, meaning that "grace comes visibly and is not merely a 'purely inward' matter."[6] Schillebeeckx recognizes that this unity between sign and effective cause in the sacramental is best expressed using "symbol" as a technical term.[7]

Thus, contemporary theologians like Edward Schillebeeckx use the category of *symbol* (in distinction from the broader term *sign*) to articulate the ways in which spiritual realities are communicated in and through the material world and, indeed, transform the material world. Symbols bring about that which they signify. In other words, symbols have an enduring transformative power. This resonates with Deacon's description of the way in which symbols have transformed us, as he writes, "the word became flesh," "we have been made in the image of the word" describing the coevolution of human brains and language. Language has had a transformative power, shaping us into *Homo symbolicus*: the species for whom the world is fundamentally symbolic. For Deacon, this means specifically that the world is, for us, overflowing with language(s).

In this essay I argue that human symbolic cognition and behavior are, by definition, highly cooperative and relational. The kind of conceptual blending that humans are capable of (and, indeed, predisposed toward) is a community task. Without relationality, no metaphor. First, I will turn to literature within the discipline of evolutionary anthropology in order to argue that symbolic cognition has both a social function and social consequences. In other words, symbolic human cognition implies a rich network of human relationality involving created and uncreated, biotic and abiotic elements. Next, I turn to Edward Schillebeeckx's theology of symbolic imagination, often articulated in traditional theological terms such as *sacrament*, as an example of one that takes seriously the ways in which the human symbolic imagination mediates the divine-human relationship as well as human relationships with other created realities. For Schillebeeckx, the divine is mediated in and through the material and the historical. This differs in a few critical respects from many evolutionary anthropologists' descriptions of the relationship between the material and the symbolic for humans as dualistic. Schillebeeckx's understanding of God as dialectically revealed in the material-historical order allows for a more nuanced approach to human symbolic cognition and behavior.

Before proceeding to the heart of my argument, a few clarifications need to be made. By discussing human patterns of cognition, I do not intend to suggest that *humanness* is a conceptual category that is comprised by a checklist of capacities. Instead, *humanness* functions as a category in the way that Masson describes insights about categorization from contemporary linguistics, i.e., categories are "complex," "graded and fuzzy." Categories "do not have a single precise defining characteristic or sufficient and necessary condition, but rather have a cluster of family resemblances with some features more prototypical than others."[8] Because Terrence Deacon is talking about species classifications, the relevance of categorization as a cluster of family resemblances becomes even more apparent, since human variation is a part of the very composition of the species category.[9] Relatedly, though I name symbolic cognition as a salient component of human distinctiveness and claim that the divine-human relationship is conditioned by these human particularities, I do not claim here (as some have) that the concept of creation in the *imago dei* (or any other traditional aspect of Christian theological anthropology) excludes other organisms from having a saving relationship with God.[10] It can only be a misunderstanding of the nature and purpose of theological language to make such a claim definitively. Our capacity (not as individuals, but rather as a species) for symbolic-social imagination is the condition for the possibility of human relationality with God and created others. God's saving relationality to other organisms is conditioned by their own created particularities. Theological anthropology does not and should not aim to make statements about the precise nature of the divine-ladybug relationship.[11] At the same time, however, we need to be clear about the ways in which humans relate to other organisms in and through the human symbolic-social imagination as well as the ways in which other organisms mediate the divine-human relationship to humans.[12] In other words, human relationality (to God and others) always involves other organisms. Our identity (theological or otherwise) is embedded within a network of biotic and abiotic relationships.

HUMAN COGNITION, HUMAN RELATIONALITY

Evolutionary anthropologists tend to agree that a key component of human distinctiveness as a species rests in symbolic cognition and symbolically organized behavior. This position is most clearly illustrated in Leslie White's classic essay on human thought and behavior published in 1940, "The Symbol: The Origin and Basis of Human Behavior."[13] He opens his essay with a metaphor: the symbol is to human behavior and civilization what the cell is to living organisms. Symbols are the most basic units by which we can understand what makes human life human. He writes,

> All human behavior originates in the use of symbols. It was the symbol which transformed our anthropoid ancestors into men and made them human. All civilizations have been generated, and are perpetuated, only by the use of symbols. . . . All human behavior consists of, or is dependent upon, the use of symbols. Human behavior is symbolic behavior; symbolic behavior is human behavior. The symbol is the universe of humanity.[14]

In other words, symbol use makes us who we are as a species. For White, symbols are signs that derive their meaning from their collective users. In contrast, non-symbolic signs derive their meaning from their physical form. To put it another way, one can discern the meaning of a non-symbolic sign via the senses and this, for White, implies a stability of meaning that is not present with symbolic signs. The meaning of the symbol, instead, is created and agreed upon socially. Symbols, then, are inherently "arbitrary"[15] and, therefore, illustrate the creative capacity of their generators. Human beings, as symbol-generators, create meaning while other animals merely discover meaning.[16] A consideration of the ways in which human culture is structured in and through the symbolic imagination, as White argues here, can illuminate for us some key insights into ways in which symbolic cognition influences human modes of relationality. Symbolic knowledge is a social kind of knowing; it both requires and makes possible participation in a community.

One who has some prior familiarity with White's foundational essay may have noticed that I omitted a key sentence from his above quotation—namely, "It is the symbol which transforms an infant of homo sapiens into a human being; deaf mutes who grow up without the use of symbols are not human beings."[17] This omission flags up some of the central ways in which I (along with many other contemporary thinkers) would depart from White's abelist understanding of the significance of symbol use for humanity. For White, symbol use has not only a transformative effect upon the human species as a whole but also acts upon the individual in critical ways so as to provide her access to species membership. In other words, without the active transformational work of symbol use upon the individual, one cannot be considered a member of the human species.[18] White argues that there is an immeasurable gulf between those who use symbols and those who do not[19] and that "articulate speech" is the most reliable indicator and expression of symbol use.[20] Human social organization, learning, and technological development all hinge upon articulate speech. White's analysis goes wrong in that it both (a) misunderstands humanness as a checklist of capacities rather than as a cluster of family resemblances and (b) offers a severely truncated understanding of human symbol use by limiting it to articulate speech. This joint misunderstanding of humanness and symbol use allows him to write off whole populations as not fully human. In an unfortunately common move made by those who delineate "real" humans from "subhumans," White turns to biblical language in order to condense his thesis, perhaps as a rhetorical move to provide greater authority (if not the appearance of cleverness) to his argument "'In the Word was the beginning' of culture—and its perpetuation also."[21] As we will see, John's *logos* is a frequently used shorthand for whatever anthropologists assume to be central about language for human beings. For White, the *Word* is largely "articulate speech" and human culture is identified with those behaviors that articulate speech enables. By inverting the typical expression of the opening line of John's gospel from "In the beginning was the Word," to "In the Word was the beginning," White highlights the creative agency of Word(s) in a way that Christian theologians might not protest—viz., the Word itself generates a beginning—though his identification of Word with human speech would be too narrow for most thinkers in the Christian tradition.[22] Today, most Johannine scholars agree that, in the prologue of the Gospel of John, the author is providing a midrash of the opening of Genesis 1 and claiming that the Word of God preexists creation. For John, the Word, *logos*, is the Word of God and God creates by speaking. Yet, human speech is not an analogy for the divine *logos*. Instead, the person of Jesus Christ is the divine Word made flesh. Notably, the Gospel of John is not merely a list of the sayings or speech of Jesus, but instead it is an account of his actions, teachings, healing activity, relationships, death, and resurrection. In other words, the identification of *logos* with human speech is much too narrow and betrays White's truncated vision. *Logos* is the whole human life conducted in generative love as Jesus has loved (Jn 15:12).[23]

The American biological anthropologist Terrence Deacon, writing more than fifty-five years later, takes up a similar line of argumentation as well as White's penchant for theological imagery (though somewhat more successfully) in his book, *The Symbolic Species: The Co-evolution of Language and the Brain*.[24] Building upon traditional assumptions within the field of anthropology that symbol use is salient to "humanness," as exemplified by White, Deacon argues that human distinctiveness is best understood in relationship to our capacity for symbolic thought, as expressed by language. Drawing explicitly on the work of late nineteenth-century, early twentieth-century American philosopher, Charles Sanders Peirce, Deacon enumerates three types of semiotic thought: iconic, indexical, and symbolic.[25] Iconic thought relies upon a similarity between a sign and the signified; for example, a stick figure is an iconic sign of a human person because its form resembles the human form. Indexical thought rests on a causal link in space and time between a sign and the signified; for example, smoke is an indexical sign of a fire since the smell and sight of smoke correlates historically with instances of fire. Symbolic thought turns on "social convention, tacit agreement, or explicit code" linking a sign and the signified; for example, a wedding ring is a symbolic sign of a marital covenant when the cultural context in which its wearer is embedded favors this custom.[26] Because symbolic meaning is derived from social agreement rather than causality or proximity (in contrast to indexical meaning), Deacon amplifies White's prior emphasis on the relational nature of symbolic knowing.[27] As Deacon argues, "symbolic reference is intrinsically social."[28] For Deacon, human beings are the only animals that tend toward symbolic interpretations of their environments. Thus, human-specific ways of knowing and interpreting generate and reinforce human-specific modes of relationality.

Though not impossible, Deacon argues it is difficult for other animals to cross the symbolic-learning threshold. Non-human animals are "pre-maladapted" for symbolic thought,[29] while humans are "overdesigned" for symbolic thought as evidenced by our overdeveloped prefrontal cortex.[30] Humans tend to interpret the world symbolically even when symbols are not at play. Deacon explains, "Human brain structure is an exaggerated reflection—a caricature almost—of the special demands imposed by symbol learning. We are not just adapted for symbol learning, but for *fail-safe symbol learning*."[31] He hypothesizes that symbol use in early hominids triggered a series of evolutionary developments in the brain favoring expanded symbolic behavior.[32] Thus, he makes use of the theological language of the Christian tradition, claiming that "the word became flesh"[33] and, in a later text, that humans are "made in the image of the word"[34] in order to illustrate the way in which symbol use (here represented in shorthand as "the word" and subsequently revealing his bias toward language as the paradigmatic symbolic expression) shapes the brains (i.e., flesh) of humans and has made us who we are. Distinguishing between his claims and the Christian understanding of incarnation, he explains that the process he describes is not a "divine miracle" but instead an "evolutionary miracle"[35] such that "the physical changes that make us human are the incarnations, so to speak, of the process of using words."[36] Deacon's deliberate play on "incarnation(s)" might reveal (perhaps accidentally) a deep resonance between evolutionary anthropology and the Christian tradition: namely, that the Christian sacramental worldview is a paradigmatic expression of the human symbolic imagination, revealing that for humans the symbolic is thoroughly material and the material is thoroughly symbolic.

Deacon broadens White's focus on articulate speech to a more capacious understanding of language as inclusive of any "mode of communication based upon symbolic reference (the way words refer to things) and involving combinatorial rules that comprise a system for representing synthetic logical relationships among these symbols."[37] Noting the breadth of this definition, he names "manual signing, mathematics, computer 'languages,' musical compositions, religious ceremonies, systems of etiquette, and many rule-governed games"[38] as legitimate linguistic forms. Thus, Deacon makes more space to push against White's too-easy elision of deaf and blind human beings with his theoretical category of those who "grow up without the use of symbols." Human beings participate in a wide range of forms of language and "articulate speech" is only one of those forms. There are many ways to participate in symbolic meaning-making apart from "articulate speech," including ritual, play, eating practices, and art.[39] Verbal communication, though it does not stand alone as Deacon's sole representation of language, however, remains his paradigmatic "language." This allows Deacon to focus on the ways in which language has affected the development of the human species without forcing him to make claims about the supposed relative "humanness" of specific individuals.

Symbolic cognition is never the project of an individual alone, but is always a social project. In other words, symbolic cognition is a community task. As we will note later, a description of symbolic cognition as inherently social is more helpful than a description of symbolic cognition and behavior as inherently "arbitrary" or non-functional. Symbols, Deacon argues, allow us to "offload" enormous amounts of information into the shared cultural realm. Unlike the interpretation of icons and indices, symbolic interpretation involves social dependency. Deacon explains, "If symbols ultimately derive their representational power, not from the individual, but from a particular society at a particular time, then a person's symbolic experience of consciousness is to some extent society-dependent—it is borrowed."[40] In proposing the heuristic new species designation, *Homo symbolicus* to all hominid symbol users he likens symbolic information and symbolic traditions to a closed genetic pool upon which all participants draw. He writes,

> We are all heirs of symbolic forms that were passed from one generation to the next and from one group to another, forming a single unbroken tradition. We derive all our symbolic "traits" from this common pool and contribute to its promulgation. Being a part of this symbolic information lineage is in many respects a more diagnostic trait for "humanness" than any physical trait. Evolutionary phylogenies are defined in terms of inheritance of information, but not all the information that determines a species' defining characteristics is coded in genes. So, to the extent that there are partially independent forms of information transmission that are crucial for determining a species' attributes, they too can determine potentially independent descent relationships.[41]

For example, the behavioral inheritance of stone toolmaking is not a genetic inheritance, yet it significantly affects both the fitness of subsequent generations as well as the shape of the ecologies in which these generations inhabit. As communities develop the skills of stone toolmaking and pass them on to apprentices who refine these skills, they distribute knowledge across many individuals and conserve traditions. As philosopher of biology, Kim Sterelny argues (and perhaps makes clearer than does Deacon), apprentice learning is a unique feature of human communities that enables the cultivation and preservation of symbols. Human cognition is a "collective achievement and collective legacy"[42] that rests on intensive and intentional modes of social learning, particularly apprentice learning. Apprentice learning relies not only on the high-volume transfer of information and skills to the apprentice, but also upon the organization of human environments such that they facilitate high-fidelity social learning.[43] In other words, symbolic thinking relies upon symbolically organized (social and material) environments. Consequently, some anthropologists have rejected the terminology of symbolic cognition because it can suggest a narrowly internal and individualistic set of capacities in favor of the more obviously external (behavioral) and social terms such as "symbolically organized behavior,"[44] "fully symbolic *sapiens* behavior,"[45] "human socio-cognitive niche,"[46] or even "human wisdom" as representative of a "suite of symbolic-social human interactions."[47] Whatever terminology is in play, anthropologists tend to agree that symbol use both creates and perpetuates structures of human relationality (i.e., interhuman relationality as well as extrahuman relationality[48]). White's formulation, "'In the Word was the beginning' of culture" is not then entirely poorly phrased, if we can conceive of "Word" and symbolic cognition in a broad sense and if we understand culture to be inclusive of all forms of (inter- and extra-) human relationality. As symbolic thinkers, we construct a symbolic niche—engineering our bodies, our societies, and our ecologies—such that "all the universe has become a symbol."[49] This is not simply a cognitive (re)structuring of our environment(s), but it is a constructive process that is materially significant. In other words, symbols have real creative, material agency for humans. As Deacon argues,

> Abstract symbolic objects, like the Pythagorean theorem, guide the design and construction of innumerable human artifacts every day. . . . These abstract representations have physical efficacy. They can and do change the world. They are as real and concrete as the force of gravity or the impact of a projectile.[50]

Symbolic cognition and the organization of human behavior by and through symbol use has been integral in the ongoing construction of the human niche. Deacon's approach, especially when it is supplemented with research from social learning scholars, can help us to shift away from a focus on whether individuals have achieved humanness (or not) though symbol use toward a conversation about the significance of symbol use in the human niche. This critical shift can allow anthropologists and theologians to maintain an inclusive understanding of humanity (especially inclusive of individuals with disabilities) while still saying something significant about the biological-cultural space that humans have opened up through their evolutionary development. Not all humans need to have symbolic capacities (particularly "articulate speech" as is significant for White) in order to participate in symbolically organized behavior since human relationality itself is symbolically organized. That is to say, human kinship structures are symbolically organized, human space is symbolically organized, and human care or neglect is symbolically organized. If the human symbolic imagination is foundational to the structure of human relationality, the divine-human relationship is also structured according to human modes of symbolic imagination. There is no way to "get outside" of this socially mediated kind of human symbolic cognition either through an appeal to direct experience of God or transcendence of the body.[51]

Despite the widespread recognition in evolutionary anthropology of the significance of symbol use in the human niche, it remains difficult for anthropologists to speak about the ways in which the material and the relational are symbolically structured for humans.[52] Evolutionary anthropologists tend to describe the symbolic world that humans construct as "beyond" or "beneath" the material world. For example, Terrence Deacon, in an article jointly authored with Catholic philosopher Tyrone Cashman, describes human beings as designed to view the material world as "only the surface expression of deeper hidden realities."[53] Deacon and Cashman specify the human semiotic worldview as one according to which we "conceive of the world as two-layered, so that some objects and events of mundane experience are like signs expressing meanings that concern a hidden and more fundamental level of existence."[54] Their description does not merely indicate a symbolic structure to human experience, but also implies that the symbolic and the material exist in a "dualistic" or "two-layered" relationship. If this is an accurate description, what is the precise relationship of this material world to the "second world" of symbolic meaning that is "beyond" or "invisible"? Does this other "hidden" world eclipse the natural world?[55] Or is it an extension of it? Are these worlds in competition or cooperation? To put it bluntly—is the symbolic worldview a "dualistic worldview," as Deacon and Cashman describe it,[56] or is it a "sacramental worldview"? And, what is the difference?

Anthropologists, especially Deacon, can describe well the ways in which human brains, bodies, and ecologies are thoroughly marked by the symbolic, yet when they attempt to describe the precise nature of the relationship between the material and the symbolic for humans they tend to employ dualistic language. This functions to undercut their own insights. The Christian sacramental tradition can clarify anthropologists' language about human symbol use, particularly to the degree that it prioritizes a non-competitive relationship between the material and the spiritual-symbolic. The symbolic is not behind or beneath the material, but rather it is expressed in and through the material. The symbolic is not possible without the material and the material makes the symbolic present. In other words, the symbolic and the material are not two worlds, as Deacon and Cashman suggest, rather we might talk about them, to use Edward Schillebeeckx's language, as "two dimensions" of one world. Edward Schillebeeckx's sacramental theology can help us to articulate better the relationship between the symbolic and the material for human beings.[57]

EDWARD SCHILLEBEECKX'S THEOLOGY OF SYMBOLIC IMAGINATION

Edward Schillebeeckx uses the category of symbol to articulate the ways in which spiritual realities are communicated in and through the material world and, indeed, transform the material world. Symbols bring about that which they signify. In other words, symbols have an enduring transformative power. This understanding of sacrament, for Schillebeeckx, is not limited to the seven official sacraments of the Catholic Church but instead extends to an understanding of the material world on the whole. Grounded in a rich theology of creation, all of life is symbolic of God and everything can be understood to reveal something of the supernatural to us.[58] Schillebeeckx explains,

> The world of creation then becomes an actual part of the inner yet still anonymous dialogue with God. . . . Life itself in the world then belongs to the very content of God's inner word to us. It interprets dimly at least something of that which God personally, by the attraction of his grace, is whispering in our hearts. However vaguely, life itself becomes a truly supernatural and external revelation, in which creation begins to speak to us the language of salvation, in which creation becomes a sign of higher realities. . . . All is seen to have an extraordinary, indeed a personal, purpose; a purpose which lies beyond the possibilities of nature and of earthly life.[59]

The entirety of material reality has been infused with God's grace and is capable of revealing God to us. Schillebeeckx acknowledges that many people (both Christians and non-Christians) may assume that spiritual realities are (at best) unrelated or (at worst) competitive with material realities. This is at least partly due to a misguided emphasis in Christian spirituality, beginning in the seventeenth century, on a narrowly inward form of mysticism as the complement to secular scientific advances in the West. This form of Christian spirituality strives to limit God-talk to the realm of the sheerly gratuitous or ornamental in contrast to the givenness of scientific laws of nature.[60] By foregrounding bodiliness and materiality, Schillebeeckx makes a corrective to the trajectory of Christian spirituality toward an embrace of the material world as revelatory of God. For him, God is not made present to us except in and through materiality. In contrast to a dualistic theological anthropology that divides transcendent human realities from material or biological human realities, Schillebeeckx offers a symbolic theological anthropology that insists that the spiritual reality of humanity is made visible in and through the human body. His corrective impulse is guided by a principle of Aristotelean philosophy, taken up by the Christian Thomistic tradition and carried forward into the present day by both Thomistic theologians such as Schillebeeckx, as well as non-Thomistic theologians who have a strong stake in affirming the material body, such as those committed to exploring Christian theology from feminist or ecological perspectives.[61] Schillebeeckx's impulse to affirm the material and biological as revelatory of God suggests that, though he was not aware of neurological research such as Terrence Deacon's, he would be open to its findings as contributing something to the ways that God makes Godself known in the world.

In Edward Schillebeeckx's first book, *Christ the Sacrament of the Encounter with God,* he sets the groundwork for a symbolic theological anthropology and highlights the incarnational nature of sacramental theology: human encounter with God is mediated in and through flesh and history. Schillebeeckx argues, first, that bodiliness is integral to the structure of any human encounter. Here we can substitute Deacon's *symbolic communication* for Schillebeeckx's *encounter*, since an encounter, for Schillebeeckx, is an opportunity to be open to another human person, to influence another, and to reveal oneself.[62] Secondly, the body is a sacrament of the self. That is to say, the body is a symbol of the self that actually makes the self present both to oneself and to another. As he writes, "Human bodiliness is human interiority itself in visible form."[63] Therefore, human relationality is conditioned by the symbol of the body. It is only in and through material expression that humanity comes to fulfillment. The human body reveals oneself to oneself through its activity and its experience of the world. Similarly, the body reveals oneself to others though relational and communicative acts.

Encounter between God and humanity can never be a purely inward matter, it can never fail to take material and historical form. Schillebeeckx is clear that since God is not material, the divine-human encounter need not be bodily from God's side. But, because of our material nature, we require a material mediation of God in order to experience the divine.[64] The *sacramental* is this expression of God in history, in the material.[65] Yet this is not a mere outward expression that has no effect on a "more real" inward reality; "a sacrament is a *signum efficax gratiae*, a sign which really and actually bestows the grace it signifies."[66] In other words, the sacramental is symbolic: in referring to something else, it makes the signified reality present and real. Comparing the sacramental to an intention of love, Schillebeeckx explains that a sacrament is not perfected until expressed; in other words, expression is integral to its nature.[67] Jesus is the encounter between humans and God made visible. He is the supreme realization of the relationship between God and human beings, thus Jesus is a sacrament of God and God's desire for relationship.[68] The church (i.e., the communal life and work of those who follow Jesus) is a sacrament of Jesus to the world; in other words, the church is a "sacramental extension" of Jesus after his death—it materially and historically mediates Jesus to the world after his body is no longer able to do this. In this way, then, the Church truly functions as the body of Christ, veiling and unveiling Jesus in the world.[69]

For Schillebeeckx, human relationality is conditioned by human bodiliness in at least two ways. On a personal and social level, the human body both makes visible as well as veils "human interiority," thus, either facilitating or standing in the way of human intimacy. The body functions as a symbol of the self and this body mediates the self's relationships with others.[70] Thus, the body *qua* symbol mediates the individual's and the community's relationship with God and it is only in and through this symbol that relationality with God is possible. The same can be said for any other form of human relationality (human-human relationships, human relationships with other creatures, human relationships with landscapes, etc.). According to Schillebeeckx, the symbolic nature of humanity causes humans to interpret and organize the world symbolically. That is to say, our own relationship to our bodies informs our semiotic activity. Schillebeeckx explains,

> That man's existence is *de facto* a bodily one thus provides the principle of the human tendency to create symbols. In this sense corporeality, caught up into human life, is a sign and a symbol. It is no more than a sign of the inner life of man's spirit, though belonging to it as part of his "sign-making" activity; it can be no more because it veils and alienates that life even while providing it with the means of expression. For indeed it is only in an element borrowed from the world that the human spirit can express itself.[71]

Because we are symbols, we interpret the world symbolically—always and everywhere constructing symbols. Or, to put it in anthropological language, we construct our own niche(s) as symbolic niches; we have become a "self-domesticated species."[72] The body itself is an extension of the "'sign-making' activity" of humans (as Schillebeeckx puts it) or the symbolic savant character of humans (as Deacon would phrase it). Yet, Schillebeeckx emphasizes in a unique way that the human body is the most basic human symbol. Whereas Deacon highlights "the word became flesh," Schillebeeckx could be said to argue, "flesh is word." In fact, Schillebeeckx himself does link his own theological arguments (particularly in his early work) with the early Christian insight (of Tertullian) "'*caro salutis est cardo*': corporeality is the pivot of salvation," thus foregrounding the claim that materiality is symbolic of God. That is to say, corporeality points to something else as a symbol signifies, but in doing so it does not render itself unimportant. Materiality is not a mere vehicle for something else more real. It does not leave itself behind since salvation itself is material. This becomes even more clear in Schillebeeckx's later work, especially in his last essay (notably, written on the sacraments) as he states clearly,

> From a Christian perspective human salvation is not salvation of souls, as some spiritual gurus keep insisting; it is bliss that befalls us in our full spiritual corporeality or embodied spirit. People are certainly not angels with material bodies, they are not incarnated angelic spirits, but their spirits are corporeal and their bodies are spiritual. This is not dualism but two dimensions of the one human being. In order to understand the resurrection and sacramental celebrations this sensitive, expressive corporeality is of cardinal importance: it is the *cardo* or pivot of salvation.[73]

Therefore, the theological symbols that humans generate are born in the relational, communal human space, creating and expressing shared meaning-making in and through the material.

Where Deacon's work can imply that socially agreed upon symbolic meaning and sensory material meanings (viz. indexical and iconic meanings) are positioned dualistically, Schillebeeckx's work explicitly eschews dualism and argues that a symbolic interpretation of the world is anchored in experiences of the material—that is, experiences of our own bodies as symbols and sacramental experiences of God's reliance upon materiality to express Godself in history.

THE SYMBOLIC AND THE MATERIAL

The writings of Edward Schillebeeckx can, therefore, provide an important insight into the structure of human cognition and experience and some pushback against common ways of articulating the shape of the human person in evolutionary anthropology: specifically, the symbolic is neither additive nor arbitrary. As Schillebeeckx suggests, for humans, the symbolic and the material are not "dualistic" as Deacon and Cashman argue,[74] but instead two-dimensional.[75]

Terrence Deacon is not alone in suggesting that a symbolic worldview is a dualistic worldview. Evolutionary anthropologists generally tend to describe the symbolic as additive, arbitrary, non-functional, or non-material. In distinguishing the symbolic from the indexical or the iconic (relying upon Pierce's philosophical framework), many anthropologists tend to emphasize that symbolic meaning is established by through social convention independent of any physical characteristics of either sign or object.[76]

Recall Leslie White who in 1940 argued that symbolic meaning is arbitrary, explaining that "All symbols must have a physical form otherwise they could not enter our experience. But the meaning of a symbol cannot be perceived by the senses."[77] This suggests that the only function of a symbol's physical form is as a vehicle for the communication of symbolic meaning, yet the details of this physical form are unimportant and have no influence on the kind of symbolic meaning that is socially constructed from it. Furthermore, for White and for many anthropologists who have followed him, an object *only* functions as a symbol if it has a non-sensory meaning.[78] This implies a sharp divide between on the one hand, the symbol, the social, and the (human) cultural and, on the other hand, the material, the sensory. White assumes that we can pull apart human behavior into the symbolic and the non-symbolic, the cultural and the (merely) animal as he writes,

> The behavior of man is of two distinct kinds: symbolic and nonsymbolic. Man yawns, stretches, coughs, scratches himself, cries out in pain, shrinks with fear, "bristles" with anger, and so on. Nonsymbolic behavior of this sort is not peculiar to man; he shares it not only with the other primates but with many other animal species as well. But man communicates with his fellows with articulate speech, uses amulets, confesses sins, makes laws, observes codes of etiquette, explains his dreams, classifies his relatives in designated categories, and so on. This kind of behavior is unique; only man is capable of it; it is peculiar to man because it consists of, or is dependent upon, the use of symbols. The nonsymbolic behavior of man is the behavior of man the animal; the symbolic behavior is that of man the human being. It is the symbol which has transformed man from a mere animal to a human animal.[79]

Yet, this begs the question: is it not White's larger point that humans, as a symbolic species, cannot really parse out cultural behavior from other kinds of human behaviors? Even the most basic and animal forms of human behavior—e.g., obtaining and eating food, giving birth, and excreting waste—are all shot through with cultural symbolic expression. The meaning of symbolic objects, I would argue, can be perceived by the senses because all our sensory faculties are symbolically organized from the start. In other words, our senses are conditioned by the social imaginary.[80]

For many contemporary anthropologists, a latent assumption about the dualistic nature of the symbolic and the material surfaces in definitional descriptions of the symbolic as non-functional. Modern human behavior is typically identified with the emergence of symbolic behavior and measured by the findings of artifacts with "clearly non-utilitarian purposes"[81] and symbolic "intentionality" can be measured in reverse proportion with functionality.[82] The persistent identification of the symbolic with the "arbitrary" can lead to the erroneous assumption that the cultural is the "unreal" or "less real," or even more unhelpfully, that cultural symbolic meanings can turn on mere caprice. Yet, this is a too narrow understanding of symbol that belies evolutionary anthropology's very own insights that humans are "fully cultural"[83] and "symbolic savants."[84] Human behavior is symbolically organized through and through. There is no way to pull apart the material and symbolic for humans. Similarly, there is no way to pull apart the functional from the cultural. For humans, the material is symbolic and the symbolic is material.

Anthropologists (partly by virtue of the shape of their discipline) are compelled to approach a symbolically mediated worldview by searching for material evidence of symbolic behavior. To locate symbolic cognition materially in the historical record one can only identify and analyze artifacts. Artifacts in themselves do not contain symbolic thinking—objects are always pliable, and the best symbolic objects are also vehicles of indexical and iconic thinking. Therefore, anthropologists are forced to ask of an artifact, "is this a symbol or not?" in order to infer a community who operates symbolically behind the historical object in question. When we try to classify objects as either symbolic or non-symbolic we are often forced to define symbols negatively—is there any way that what we are seeing can be understood in utilitarian terms? The consequence of this kind of interrogation, however, is an operational understanding of symbol that is not richly informed by the theory on at least two accounts: first, symbolic representation does not exist in a vacuum separate from indexical and iconic representation and, second, symbols are not non-utilitarian. While perhaps unavoidable when trying to identify a species' symbolic-learning threshold, this focus on whether an object is a symbol or not can distract from the main point: for humans, the material is interpreted symbolically and humans act in the material world from this perspective. To know in an authentic way whether something has a symbolic meaning (and to discern what that symbolic meaning is) requires participatory knowledge. This is implied in anthropologists' own description of symbols as inherently social and relational.

As Schillebeeckx's contemporary, Jesuit theologian Avery Dulles argues, symbols rely upon and generate "participatory knowledge." Dulles explains,

> An interpretative process of this kind is involved in those acts by which we know something as our own. We know our own body not by looking at it

> (though obviously we can look at some parts of our body as we look at surrounding objects) but rather by dwelling in it, by using it, by relying on it. We know it, as Polanyi says, not by attending *to* it but by attending *from* it. Because we know the body in this subjective manner, it is cognitively identified with the knowing self. Analogously, we know by indwelling when we apprehend anything at all specifically as ours—for example, our home, our country, our family, our church, our culture, our traditions [and we might add, "our species"]. None of these realities can be properly understood from without, through sheer spectator knowledge, but only from within, insofar as we appropriate and rely upon them—that is to say, by participatory knowledge.[85]

Symbols are more like landscapes or open-ended actions than objects or propositions.[86] We can't understand symbolic artifacts as mere objects, since their purpose it to draw its interpreters into communion. "By eliciting participation, symbol can convey a richer and more personal apprehension of reality in its deeper dimensions than nonsymbolic language can do. Its distinctive mark is not the absence of meaning but the surplus of meaning."[87] A symbol elicits participation in a community. Because all symbolic knowledge is participatory knowledge, investigation of symbols is always a participatory investigation. Symbols, themselves, then are technologies,[88] encoding information, providing the conditions for the possibility of traditions and innovations (i.e., social learning), and structuring human community.

Anthropologists' interrogation of the semiotic status of ancient artifacts carries the danger of limiting the symbolic to the non-functional.[89] But, this distorts the symbolic and truncates the imaginative symbolic capacity of the human. Furthermore, it feeds into the modern illusion that the religious, the transcendent, and the metaphysical is additive. As Schillebeeckx describes, in our current cultural context within which technocratic reason reigns supreme, God and a mystical relationship with the divine seems to be unnecessary in explaining the nature of humanity and the world. Comparing the divine to a gift of cut-flowers, God, in this context, is a non-essential and purely gratuitous expression of beauty to which we "honestly reply, 'You needn't have done that.'"[90] This narrowing of the symbolic and the transcendent to the non-functional and ornamental is an effect, Schillebeeckx would argue, of modern rationalism, modern political impotency, and a deliberate effort to depoliticize the spiritual by making it non-material.[91]

CONCLUSION

Conceptual blending is a community task. Without relationality, there is no metaphor. We are oriented toward relationship. Symbolic cognition isn't just conceptual analysis of the world but engagement with the world for humans. Evolutionary anthropologists argue that the symbolic cognition and behavior which is so central to our distinctiveness as a species has a social function and social consequences: symbols structure human relationality and make it possible. Symbolic thinking and behavior are community tasks. Anthropologists such as Terrence Deacon (and, in a more limited way, his intellectual predecessor Leslie White) describe this well. Yet, when pressed for images to describe the human symbolic worldview, Deacon (along with philosophical collaborator Tyrone Cashman) describes this as a dualistic worldview in which symbolic meaning is hidden behind or beneath sensory meaning. This can give the reader the impression that, for humans, the symbolic and the material are separate (and perhaps) conflicting realms of reality. This confusion is all the more amplified by many anthropologists' use of the word "arbitrary" to describe the nature of symbolic meaning. While an emphasis on the social nature of symbolic meaning is helpful for theologians, the notion that symbolic knowledge is "arbitrary" is not.

Instead, the Catholic sacramental notion that symbols bring about that which they signify can help to make clear the ways in which humans construct the world in which they live (as niche constructors) and that this construction is at once both material and symbolic. For humans, as a fully symbolic species, all the material world is suffused with symbolic meaning and, conversely, all symbols are thoroughly material. Symbolic meaning and sensory meaning function as "two dimensions,"[92] not as a dualism in which the symbolic meaning stands behind or beneath sensory meaning. Additionally, this sacramental symbolic framework can better function to open up avenues for community responsibility, especially insofar as it can help us to recognize that both sin and salvation are mediated by the thoroughly cooperative and relational human symbolic imagination. In other words, cooperation and coordination are preconditions for harm and deception as much as for human harmony and well-being. In this way then, symbols are hardly nonfunctional or arbitrary. It is in and through symbols that human community (which is so integral to our species' survival) is structured and maintained.

NOTES

1. Robert Masson, *Without Metaphor, No Saving God: Theology after Cognitive Linguistics* (Leuven: Peeters, 2014), 14.
2. Masson, *Without Metaphor*, 27–28.
3. Ibid., 14.
4. Edward Schillebeeckx, *Christ the Sacrament of the Encounter with God* (Lanham, MD: Sheed and Ward, 1963), 5, see also 6 and 15.

5. Schillebeeckx, *Christ the Sacrament*, 73.
6. Ibid., 74.
7. Ibid., 76.
8. Masson, *Without Metaphor*, 305. Theological anthropology has long suffered from a myopic view of human nature, especially to the degree that it has singled out mental capacities as a baseline for humanness. See Hans Reinders, *Receiving the Gift of Friendship: Profound Disability, Theological Anthropology, and Ethics* (Grand Rapids: Eerdmans, 2008). Biological anthropology has suffered from a similarly narrow view, as an analysis below of Leslie White will reveal. This truncated understanding of both humanity as well as the nature of human conceptual categorization has functioned as a weapon against women, the disabled, and the colonized.
9. Yet, of course, what counts as variation and what counts as worth a new species designation are political decisions and have their own history of racialized, gendered and ableist debates. See Julia Feder and Jonathan Marks, "Genetics, Race, and the Practice of Science, Part Two: On How Human Genetics Is Biopolitical," *Anthropology News* 57, no. 12 (December 2016).
10. See Christopher L. Fisher's "Animals, Humans and X-men: Human Uniqueness and the Meaning of Personhood," *Theology and Science* 3, no. 3 (2005): 291–314 as a contemporary argument that the *imago dei* cannot be applied to other animals on the basis of their lack of symbol use.
11. Karl Rahner, "Art against the Horizon of Theology and Piety," in *Theological Investigations*, vol. 23 (New York: Crossroad, 1992), 165.
12. Consider, for example, images of the divine in Scripture as a mother hen (Mt 23:37 and Lk 13:34) or the ways in which humans appeal to other animals as exemplars for moral human behavior. Adam Willows, "The Role of Non-Human Exemplars in Aquinas" *New Blackfriars* 99, no. 1081 (May 2018): 332–345.
13. Leslie A. White, "The Symbol: The Origin and Basis of Human Behavior," *Philosophy of Science* 7, no. 4 (October 1940): 451–463.
14. White, "The Symbol," 451.
15. Many anthropologists tend to write about symbols as "arbitrary" in contrast to non-symbolic signs. Yet, as I will argue below, this is not helpful, especially insofar as it can suggest that human culture is accidental or able to be modified and the "natural" world comprises the substance of material reality which is given ahead of human involvement. This obfuscates the reality that, for humans, culture and the symbolic worldview that underlies human culture shape natural landscapes (both bodies and ecologies) in concrete material ways and, conversely, that bodies and ecologies shape human culture and symbols. I favor an interpretation of the uniqueness of symbolic thought that highlights its social or relational character without describing that sociality as bestowing an "arbitrary" nature to symbols.
16. White, "The Symbol," 456f.
17. Ibid., 451.
18. Ibid., 462.
19. Ibid., 453.
20. Ibid., 460.
21. Ibid.

22. See, for example, Origen's *Commentary on John* 1.24.151 and Antonio Orbe, "Origenes y los monarquianos," *Gregorianum* 72, no. 1 (1991): 39–73.

23. Sherri Brown and Francis J. Maloney, SDB, *Interpreting the Gospel and Letters of John: An Introduction* (Grand Rapids: Eerdmans, 2017).

24. Terrence Deacon, *The Symbolic Species: The Co-evolution of Language and the Brain* (New York: Norton, 1997).

25. This tripartite understanding of semiosis is organized hierarchally such that indexical reference implies iconic semiosis and symbolic reference implies both indexical and iconic semiosis.

26. See Deacon, *Symbolic Species*, 71.

27. For Deacon, symbols (in distinction from indices) allow for stability of meaning even in the absence of a referent, e.g., unicorns. Symbolic reference can be simultaneously impossible and yet still real. In the best of circumstances, it can enable a community to, as Schillebeeckx writes, "demand a future and open it up." Edward Schillebeeckx, *Jesus: An Experiment in Christology*, trans. Hubert Hoskins (New York: Crossroad, 1979) 622. I develop this connection further in Julia Feder, "The Impossible is Made Possible: Edward Schillebeeckx, Symbolic Imagination, and Eschatological Faith," *Philosophy, Theology and the Sciences,* vol. 3, no. 2 (2016) 188–216.

28. Deacon, *Symbolic Species*, 410.

29. Ibid., 50.

30. Ibid., 413.

31. Ibid., 413.

32. In other words, early symbol use caused pre-frontalization and not the reverse, ibid., 336, 340.

33. Ibid., 321.

34. Terrence Deacon, "Beyond the Symbolic Species," in *The Symbolic Species Evolved*, ed. Theresa Schilhab, Frederik Stjernfelt, and Terrence Deacon (London: Springer, 2012), 38.

35. Deacon, *Symbolic Species*, 321.

36. Ibid., 322.

37. Ibid., 41.

38. Ibid. Note that White also acknowledges that articulate speech can be nonverbal, though his understanding is not as broad as Deacon's. He writes, "One may symbolize with the fingers, the feet, or with any part of the body that can be moved at will," White, "The Symbol," 459. Yet he also writes, "The rare cases of children who grew up without symbols because of deafness and blindness, such as those of Laura Bridgman, Helen Keller and Marie Heurtin, are instructive. Until they 'got the idea' of symbolic communication they were not human beings, but animals, they did not participate in behavior which is peculiar to human beings," 462. White likely recognizes then signing as articulate speech because it is a language that is deliberate and uses a body part, but he can't see that maybe even a deaf person who does not sign could still be participating in human symbolic meaning-making through ritualized behavior, etiquette, artistic expression, friendship, and so on.

39. Systematic exclusion from the human community threatens participation in the human symbolic imagination more than the any single ability or capacity (such as

hearing or speaking). Social isolation limits access to the shared symbolic realm and rich forms of social learning. Consequently, language perpetuating ableist conceptions of human being can isolate differently abled humans from the shared realms of meaning-making that define the human. There need to be ways that we can talk theologically and anthropologically about barriers to full relationality—especially social practices of isolation and exclusion—as fundamentally dehumanizing while still preserving a sense of the enduring humanity of the marginalized in the face of systematic measures to reduce or remove this humanity. Perhaps an emphasis on salvation and sin (both commission of sin and the interpretation of the experience of being sinned-against) as mediated by human symbolic cognition, as gestured toward in the last section of this essay, can be helpful here.

40. Deacon, *Symbolic Species*, 452.

41. Ibid., 341.

42. Kim Sterelny, *The Evolved Apprentice: How Evolution Made Humans Unique* (Cambridge, MA: MIT, 2012), xii.

43. Kim Sterelny, "Cooperation, Culture, and Conflict," *British Society for the Philosophy of Science* 67 (2016): 37.

44. See Philip Chase, "Comment on 'The Origin of Modern Human Behavior,'" *Current Anthropology* 44, no. 5 (2003): 637.

45. Christopher S. Henshilwood and Curtis Marean, "The Origin of Modern Human Behavior," *Current Anthropology* 44 (2003): 627–51.

46. Andrew Whiten and David Erdal, "The Human Socio-Cognitive Niche and Its Evolutionary Origins," *Philosophical Transactions of the Royal Society B* (2012): 2119–29.

47. Marc Kissel and Agustin Fuentes, "From Hominid to Human: The Role of Human Wisdom and Distinctiveness in the Evolution of Modern Humans," *Philosophy, Theology, and the Sciences* vol. 3, no. 2 (2016): 217–244.

48. Sterelny, *The Evolved Apprentice*, 18-19. Curtis W. Marean, "An Evolutionary Anthropological Perspective on Modern Human Origins," *Annual Review of Anthropology* 44 (2015): 545.

49. Deacon, *Symbolic Species*, 435.

50. Ibid., 453.

51. Masson, *Without Metaphor*, 27–28.

52. In many ways, my critique here has already been the subject of discussion within social scientific circles for a generation or more, yet anthropologists have yet to fully come to grips with the idea that the nature-culture divide does not reflect the reality of the human landscape as thoroughly and simultaneously "real," "narrated," and "collective." Bruno Latour, *We Have Never Been Modern*, trans. Catherine Porter (Cambridge, MA: Harvard University Press, 1993), 6.

53. Terrence Deacon and Tyrone Cashman, "The Role of Symbolic Capacity in the Origins of Religion," *Journal for the Study of Religion, Nature and Culture* 3 (2009): 16.

54. Deacon and Cashman, "The Role of Symbolic Capacity," 1.

55. Ibid., 14.

56. Ibid., 16.

57. Both Karl Rahner and Edward Schillebeeckx worked simultaneously at the forefront of thinking through symbol and sacrament in contemporary Catholic theology beginning in the mid-twentieth century. They were motivated to do this out of a concern for the reification of ritual formulas in some Catholic circles at the time. While Rahner approached this task through an appropriation of transcendental philosophy, Schillebeeckx's approach was more influenced by phenomenological philosophy and anthropological approaches to symbolic activity. Schillebeeckx explicitly names Louis-Marie Chauvet's work on symbol and sacrament as following the path that he and Rahner carved out and narrates that many others since Chauvet have taken this route such that "now this trend is fairly widely accepted." Edward Schillebeeckx, "Towards a Rediscovery of the Christian Sacraments," in *The Collected Works of Edward Schillebeeckx*, vol. 11, *Essays: Ongoing Theological Quests*, trans. Marcelle Manley, Edward Fitzgerald, and Peter Tomlinson (London: Bloomsbury, 2014), 188. Though Rahner's work is just as important as Schillebeeckx's in establishing this foundation for contemporary sacramental theology, Rahner's work has gotten significantly more attention in scholarly writings on symbol and sacramental theology. Therefore, my focus on Schillebeeckx in this essay is meant to address some of this imbalance. In addition, Schillebeeckx's approach, particularly insofar as his later writings prioritize reflection upon suffering, has the potential to pull together political and anthropological theologies in ways that complement Masson's concluding reflections on James Cone's *The Cross and the Lynching Tree* as illustrative of the ways that tectonic mapping can prompt new senses of meaning in different political contexts.

58. Schillebeeckx, *Christ the Sacrament*, 8.

59. Ibid.

60. Schillebeeckx, *Church: The Human Story of God,* trans. John Bowden (New York: Crossroad, 1990), 68.

61. See, for example, James Nelson, *Body Theology* (Louisville: Westminster/John Knox Press, 1992); Sallie McFague, *The Body of God: An Ecological Theology* (Minneapolis: Augsburg, 1993); and M. Shawn Copeland, *Enfleshing Freedom: Body, Race, and Being* (Minneapolis: Fortress, 2010).

62. Schillebeeckx, *Christ the Sacrament,* 15.

63. Ibid., 16.

64. Ibid., 43.

65. Ibid., 6.

66. Ibid., 73.

67. Ibid., 76.

68. Ibid., 18.

69. Ibid., 49. In Schillebeeckx's later work, following a lecture tour in the United States which prompted encounter with civil rights, feminist, and death-of-God movements, he began to judge this kind of approach as "too sacral" and recognized that secularization demands a reinterpretation of the Christian tradition which allows for the articulation of God as active in all human activity on behalf of humankind. See Mary Catherine Hilkert, "New Pathways in an Old Garden: Sacramental theology and Anthropology," 5–6, author's unpublished English translation of "Nieuwe Paden

in een Oude Tuin—Sacramentele Theologie en Antropologie," *Tijdschrift voor Theologie* 50, no. 1 (March 2010). He reimagines the relationship between symbolic knowledge, experience, and sacramental theology in light of the "signs of the times" such that when Christians act in the world on behalf of the human cause (which, for Schillebeeckx, is also God's cause) even the "secular . . . [can be] experienced as worship" of God. Edward Schillebeeckx, *God the Future of Man*, trans. Norman D. Smith (New York: Sheed and Ward, 1968), 102. As Mary Catherine Hilkert explains, "Schillebeeckx returns to his earlier insight that the church itself is a sacrament, but now he emphasizes that the church is not only a sacrament of encounter with Christ, but also *sacramentum mundi*, the sign of the world—'the world itself brought to epiphany'" Hilkert, "New Pathways," 11.

70. Schillebeeckx, *Christ the Sacrament*, 16.
71. Ibid., 64.
72. Deacon, "Beyond the Symbolic Species," 38.
73. Schillebeeckx, "Towards a Rediscovery," 187.
74. Deacon and Cashman, "The Role of Symbolic Capacity," 22.
75. Schillebeeckx, "Towards a Rediscovery," 187.
76. See, for example, Christopher S. Henshilwood and Curtis Marean, "The Origin of Modern Human Behavior," *Current Anthropology* 44 (2003): 635.
77. White, "The Symbol," 454, see also 457.
78. Ibid., 454.
79. White, "The Symbol," 461.
80. See, for example, Guy Deutscher, *Through the Language Glass: Why the World Looks Different in Other Languages* (New York: Metropolitan, 2010).
81. Kissel and Fuentes, "From Hominid to Human," 11. See also Henshilwood and Marean, "The Origen of Modern Human Behavior," 629.
82. Marean, "An Evolutionary Anthropological Perspective," 542. Henshilwood and Marean, "The Origen of Modern Human Behavior," 645.
83. Trenton W. Holliday, "Comment on 'The Origin of Modern Human Behavior,'" *Current Anthropology* 44 (2003): 639–40.
84. Deacon, *Symbolic Species*, 436.
85. Avery Dulles, "The Symbolic Structure of Revelation," *Theological Studies* 41, no. 1 (1980): 60–61. See Michael Polanyi, *The Tacit Dimension* (Garden City, NY: Doubleday, 1966).
86. Schillebeeckx, *Christ the Sacrament*, 100. Dulles, "The Symbolic Structure," 61. See also Nathan Mitchell, "Symbols Are Actions, Not Objects," *Living Worship* 13, no. 2 (Feb. 1977) 1–2.
87. Dulles, "The Symbolic Structure," 66.
88. See Dulles, "The Symbolic Structure," 62.
89. See example above and also Marean, "An Evolutionary Anthropological Perspective," 542.
90. Schillebeeckx, *Church*, 68.
91. Schillebeeckx, *Church*, 68.
92. Schillebeeckx, "Towards a Rediscovery," 87.

BIBLIOGRAPHY

Brown, Sherri and Francis J. Maloney. *Interpreting the Gospel and Letters of John: An Introduction.* Grand Rapids: Eerdmans, 2017.

Chase, Philip. "Comment on 'The Origin of Modern Human Behavior.'" *Current Anthropology* 44, no. 5 (2003): 637.

Copeland, M. Shawn. *Enfleshing Freedom: Body, Race, and Being*. Minneapolis: Fortress, 2010.

Deacon, Terrence. "Beyond the Symbolic Species." In *The Symbolic Species Evolved.* Edited by Theresa Schilhab, Frederik Stjernfelt, and Terrence Deacon, 9–38. London: Springer, 2012.

———. *The Symbolic Species: The Co-evolution of Language and the Brain.* New York: Norton, 1997.

Deacon, Terrence and Tyrone Cashman. "The Role of Symbolic Capacity in the Origins of Religion." *Journal for the Study of Religion, Nature and Culture* 3 (2009): 1–28.

Deutscher, Guy. *Through the Language Glass: Why the World Looks Different in Other Languages*. New York: Metropolitan, 2010.

Dulles, Avery. "The Symbolic Structure of Revelation." *Theological Studies* 41, no. 1 (1980): 51–73.

Feder, Julia. "The Impossible is Made Possible: Edward Schillebeeckx, Symbolic Imagination, and Eschatological Faith." *Philosophy, Theology and the Sciences* 3, no. 2 (2016): 188–216.

Feder, Julia and Jonathan Marks. "Genetics, Race, and the Practice of Science, Part Two: On How Human Genetics Is Biopolitical." *Anthropology News* 57, no. 12. (December 2016): e24–e28.

Fisher, Christopher L. "Animals, Humans and X-men: Human Uniqueness and the Meaning of Personhood." *Theology and Science* 3, no. 3 (2005): 291–314.

Henshilwood, Christopher S. and Curtis Marean. "The Origin of Modern Human Behavior." *Current Anthropology* 44 (2003): 627–51.

Hilkert, Mary Catherine. "New Pathways in an Old Garden: Sacramental Theology and Anthropology," 1–20. Author's unpublished English translation of "Nieuwe Paden in een Oude Tuin—Sacramentele Theologie en Antropologie," *Tijdschrift voor Theologie* 50, no. 1 (March 2010): 108–22.

Holliday, Trenton W. "Comment on 'The Origin of Modern Human Behavior." Current Anthropology 44 (2003): 639–40.

Hrdy, Sarah B. *Mothers and Others: The Evolutionary Origins of Mutual Understanding*. Cambridge, MA: Harvard University Press, 2009.

Kissel, Marc and Agustin Fuentes. "From Hominid to Human: The Role of Human Wisdom and Distinctiveness in the Evolution of Modern Humans." *Philosophy, Theology, and the Sciences* 3, no. 2 (2016): 217–244.

Latour, Bruno. *We Have Never Been Modern.* Translated by Catherine Porter. Cambridge, MA: Harvard University Press, 1993.

Marean, Curtis W. "An Evolutionary Anthropological Perspective on Modern Human Origins." *Annual Review of Anthropology* 44 (2015): 533–56.

Masson, Robert. *Without Metaphor, No Saving God: Theology after Cognitive Linguistics*. Leuven: Peeters, 2014.

McFague, Sallie. *The Body of God: An Ecological Theology*. Minneapolis: Augsburg, 1993.

Mitchell, Nathan. "Symbols Are Actions, Not Objects." *Living Worship* 13, no. 2 (February 1977): 1–2.

Nelson, James. *Body Theology*. Louisville: Westminster/John Knox Press, 1992.

Orbe, Antonio, "Origenes y los monarquianos," *Gregorianum* 72, no. 1 (1991): 39–73.

Polanyi, Michael. *The Tacit Dimension*. Garden City, NY: Doubleday, 1966.

Rahner, Karl. "Art Against the Horizon of Theology and Piety." In *Theological Investigations*. Vol. 23, 162–68. New York: Crossroad, 1992.

Reinders, Hans. *Receiving the Gift of Friendship: Profound Disability, Theological Anthropology, and Ethics*. Grand Rapids: Eerdmans, 2008.

Schillebeeckx, Edward. *Christ the Sacrament of the Encounter with God*. Lanham, Maryland: Sheed and Ward, 1963.

———. *Church: The Human Story of God*. Translated by John Bowden. New York: Crossroad, 1990.

———. *God the Future of Man*. Translated by Norman D. Smith. New York: Sheed and Ward, 1968.

———. *Jesus: An Experiment in Christology*. Translated by Hubert Hoskins. New York: Crossroad, 1979.

———. "Towards a Rediscovery of the Christian Sacraments." In *The Collected Works of Edward Schillebeeckx*. Vol. 11, *Essays: Ongoing Theological Quests*. Translated by Marcelle Manley, Edward Fitzgerald, and Peter Tomlinson, 183–210. London: Bloomsbury, 2014.

Sterelny, Kim. "Cooperation, Culture, and Conflict." *British Society for the Philosophy of Science* 67 (2016): 31–58.

———. *The Evolved Apprentice: How Evolution Made Humans Unique*. Cambridge, MA: MIT Press, 2012.

White, Leslie A. "The Symbol: The Origin and Basis of Human Behavior." *Philosophy of Science* 7, no. 4 (October 1940): 451–463.

Whiten, Andrew and David Erdal. "The Human Socio-Cognitive Niche and Its Evolutionary Origins." *Philosophical Transactions of the Royal Society B* 367, no. 1599 (August 2012): 219–29.

Willows, Adam. "The Role of Non-Human Exemplars in Aquinas" in *New Blackfriars* 99, no. 1081 (May 2018): 332–345.

Chapter Four

Conceptual Blending, Human Distinctiveness, and the Image of God

Jason P. Roberts

The question of human distinctiveness vis-à-vis other animal species is of perennial concern at the intersection of theology, ethics, and the natural sciences. A partial answer to this question may lie in the question itself. Although we are not the only communicators in the world, the creative ability to conceive, construe, and evaluate the significance of being human seems distinctive. In traditional theological anthropology, the *image of God* concept in Genesis has been a symbol of humankind's ontological, rational, axiological, relational, existential, functional, vocational, and/or eschatological distinctiveness. A cognitive linguistic perspective can help today's theologians sort through these various interpretations and generate new meanings for the concept of the image of God commensurable with contemporary, scientifically informed understandings of human distinctiveness. Not only does a cognitive linguistic perspective shed light on the meaning of the *image and likeness of God* in Genesis, it suggests that the ability to create and reformulate theological self-descriptions like this is distinctively human and a quintessential element of any contemporary interpretation of the divine image.

Cognitive linguists Gilles Fauconnier and Mark Turner have developed a plausible hypothesis that humankind's qualitatively distinct cultural-linguistic nature is a synergistic or emergent effect of neuro-cognitive evolution. Specifically, Fauconnier and Turner's conceptual integration theory (CIT) holds that among extant terrestrial species, only *Homo sapiens* readily performs the meaning-making cognitive process they call *double-scope conceptual integration*, or *double-scope blending*. Their more profound claim is that this process is also the lynchpin of the functional singularities generally associated with human distinctiveness, including "art, music, science, fashions of dress, dance, mathematics," ethics, politics, economics, religion, and so on.[1]

To the extent that CIT presents a plausible hypothesis for the origin and evolution of language and other cognitively based behavioral singularities in our species, it also bears implications for constructing a scientifically-informed Judeo-Christian anthropology and ethics. The three main sections of this chapter engage some of these interdisciplinary concerns.

The first section describes a) the central tenets of CIT and b) its merits as an explanation for why and how behaviorally modern humans became cultural-linguistic creatures through double-scope blending capacity. The second highlights recent biblical scholarship defining the concepts of the image of God and the knowledge of good and evil in Genesis in terms of humankind's ability to receive and respond to a theological vocation. Many exegetes and theologians view this vocation as a divine call to continue the process of creation with singular forms of freedom and responsibility for discerning, construing, and enacting the creator's beneficent intentions for the world and its inhabitants. In an evolutionary framework, the ability to define human being and agency against a theological backdrop may be understood as precipitating from the cognitive capacity for double-scope blending. Therefore, the final section illustrates ways to "blend" scientific and biblical understandings of human distinctiveness which highlight humankind's meaning-making abilities. Through this extended application of double-scope blending, I conclude with a series of four blends which renders a contemporized interpretation of the image of God concept. This double-scope integration of ancient and contemporary meanings yields the conclusion that bearing God's image means exercising our singularly creative capacities in ways that acknowledge the place of our species in its evolutionary community, share power, and avoid creation through violence. This conclusion also evinces the ongoing need to assess and reformulate our values-laden conceptions of human distinctiveness within and across myriad conceptual frames and academic disciplines.

CONCEPTUAL BLENDING AND HUMAN DISTINCTIVENESS

Understanding the complex realities of our physical and social environments on a daily basis comes naturally to most of us. But understanding this ability to understand has always been a much more difficult exercise. We have been at this project a long time, from Aristotle's empirical inquiry into the nature of the soul through its faculties in *De anima*, to Wittgenstein's connection of meaning to embodied action in his *Philosophical Investigations*, to Terrence Deacon's coevolutionary theory of language and the brain in *The Symbolic Species*.

This section outlines another recent attempt at this task from the perspective of cognitive linguistics. The first half of this section defines the concept of *conceptual integration* (aka *blending*), differentiates four types of conceptual integration networks, and suggests that the most complex of these—double-scope blends—enable the emergence of all the kinds of meaning which make human language and culture possible. The second half places this theory within the ongoing discourse among scientists, philosophers, and theologians concerning the precise relationship between the evolution of *Homo sapiens*' distinctive neurology and its distinctive cognitive and social functioning. Understanding these root causes of human distinctiveness in relation to the rest of the natural world must, in turn, inform the theological understanding of human distinctiveness in relation the rest of creation and its creator.

Conceptual Blending

Conceptual integration or blending projects and merges meanings from two or more packets of conceptual information, which Fauconnier and Turner call *mental spaces*, in order to frame and fill a new mental space called a *blend*.[2] This cognitive activity is creative, in that blended mental spaces often display emergent structure—conceptual relations, and thus meanings, that are not available in any of the input mental spaces, and are not predictable from them.[3] The creation of new meanings is a dynamic mental process of composing, completing, and elaborating blends. Usually with little to no conscious effort, the human brain-mind recruits and projects conceptual meanings from input mental spaces, structures conceptual relations via frames and scenarios from those same and/or other input spaces, and runs the blend "imaginatively according to the principles that have been established for the blend."[4] At the cognitive level, therefore, the emergent structure of conceptual blends constitutes the neurologically based dynamic domain of all semantic meanings, including the generative grammar which relates them. In CIT *meaning* is always a dynamic mental process, not a product or property of words, symbols, sentences, or objects themselves.

Fauconnier and Turner have identified four types of blending capacity by which we transform the material universe into our symbolic universe: "simplex," "mirror," "single-scope," and "double-scope." Simplex networks derive adequate input elements and frames from our biological and cultural history, applying those frames as values to various elements in the environment.[5] The statement "Jason is the father of Quinton" represents a simplex network of family relations which frames the two male values, "Quinton" and "Jason," according to the projected roles of father and son. The projection of framing elements and values is direct and reflects the kind of truth-conditionality often expressed in the supposedly prototypical semantic form of first-order Fregean logic.[6] However, simplex conceptual integration networks are not always so simple in their meaning. Recall, too, that completing a blend often involves recruiting framing and building materials from other mental spaces. The integration networks represented in the statements "Joseph was the father of Jesus," "The Pope is the father of all Catholics," "The Pope is the father of the Catholic Church," and "George Washington is the father of our country" all involve running more than one kind of blend simultaneously, with little or no conscious thought.[7]

In mirror networks all mental spaces involved share a single organizing frame.[8] Sharing this organizing frame is how the input spaces mirror one another in achieving a blend.[9] To illustrate this type of blending, Fauconnier and Turner recount a riddle in which a

> Buddhist Monk begins at dawn one day walking up a mountain, reaches the top at sunset, meditates at the top for several days until one dawn when he begins to walk back to the foot of the mountain, which he reaches as sunset. Make no assumptions about his starting or stopping or about his pace during the trips. Riddle: Is there a place on the path that the monk occupies at the same hour of the day on the two separate journeys?[10]

Fauconnier and Turner suggest discovering the solution by imagining the monk taking both journeys on the same day.[11] With both journeys framed by this impossible scenario, the solution emerges in the blend. One does not know exactly where it would happen, but at some point along the path, the monk would have to run into himself, as it were.

They define single-scope blending as integrating "two input spaces with different organizing frames, one of which is projected to organize the blend."[12] Many metaphors utilize single-scope blends to prompt inferences across domains of meaning that are more and/or less well-known. As Fauconnier and Turner suggest,

> The scenario of two men boxing gives us a vibrant, compact frame to use in compressing our understanding of two CEOs in business competition. We say that one CEO landed a blow but the other recovered, one of them tripped and the other took advantage, one of them knocked the other out cold.[13]

One input space is that of economic competition; the other is of a boxing match. The identities involved are projected from the CEO space, but the relations of role and causation are framed only by the boxing space. Without delving into the perhaps unfamiliar terminology of corporate transactions, the blend achieves the intended meaning via a more concrete conceptual domain.

Importantly, inferences can only be drawn in one direction: from boxing to the corporate world.

Double-scope blending involves two or more "inputs with different (and often clashing) organizing frames as well as an organizing frame for the blend that includes parts of each of those frames and has emergent structure of its own."[14] In double-scope blends, multiple—often disparate—input spaces play a role in framing the blend, giving shape and structure to new conceptual relations within the blended mental space. The new conceptual relations seeming to make sense of the reality construed by the conceptual integration are preserved in the blend. Those that do not are discarded or ignored. For Fauconnier and Turner, these conceptual relations constitute the grammar of the blend.[15]

An example of double-scope conceptual integration operates in the metaphor, "This surgeon is a butcher." As Fauconnier and Turner note, to make the inference that this is a pejorative statement, one must be able to blend automatically the neuro-cognitive structures involved in the conceptual frames of both surgery and meat-carving. The metaphor "underscores the clumsiness of the surgeon and its undesirable effects."[16] However, neither clumsiness nor undesirable effects are found in the conceptual frames of either meat-carving or surgery. Both butchers and surgeons can be quite skillful, organized, and sanitary, producing desirable results through their efforts. Both professions involve the cutting of body tissue in precise ways, making use of sharp steel instruments, and even wearing similar clothing. Yet when the blended space of the metaphor is framed by the setting, characters, and purposes of surgery along with the tools, methods, and purposes of butchery, clumsiness and its detrimental (perhaps even fatal) consequences emerge in this double-scope blend.[17] This integration of concepts creates meaning that is distinct from and not reducible to any meaning contained in or predictable from the originating conceptual frames.

The illustration in figure 4.1 is adapted from Fauconnier and Turner's "basic diagram" for visualizing the cognitive process of conceptual integration.[18] I have added explanatory notes in parentheses to label the elements of their diagram. This figure also serves as a guide for the blends I use to interpret the image of God in the final section below.

Human Distinctiveness

Why spend so much time with scientific theories, data, and figures in a piece that ultimately aims to discuss what it means to interpret and bear the divine image? The meta-analysis of language and its emergence may seem far removed from theological anthropology. However, the same hallmarks of

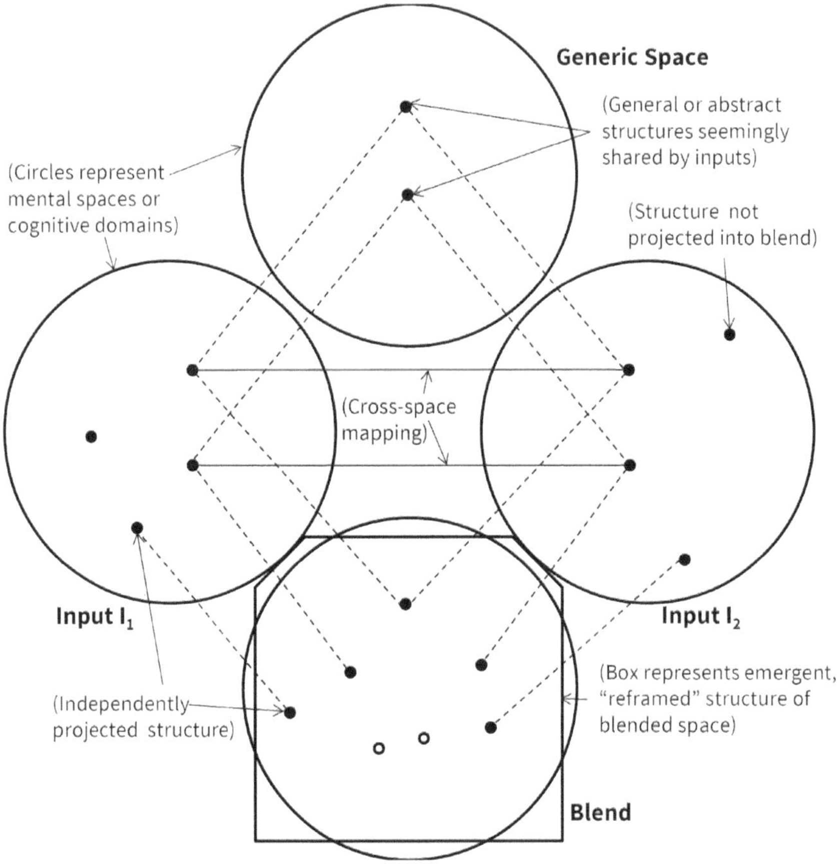

Figure 4.1. Conceptual Integration Basic Diagram

humanness highlighted by CIT also lie at the heart of what many contemporary biblical scholars and theologians interpret as the meaning of the image of God concept in Genesis. The following outline of CIT's merits in the current scientific study of human distinctiveness and its evolutionary emergence helps to establish its potential importance in contemporary theological anthropology, as well. In distinct but commensurable—blend-able—ways, CIT and Genesis depict human beings as kindred of all other creatures, while bearing a distinctively creative and conscientious relationship to themselves, their environment, and whatever conception they have of the transcendent or the divine.

According to CIT, the capacity for double-scope conceptual integration is at the epicenter of human distinctiveness, which includes the ability to define that distinctiveness. Fauconnier and Turner argue persuasively that evolutionary selection pressures are able to account for a gradual and cumulative increase in blending capacity from simplex to double-scope. They also explain how the stepwise achievement of double-scope blending capacity could correspond to a functional leap in semantic ability. But how can our species be evolutionarily ordinary and behaviorally exceptional at the same time? Put simply, CIT holds that the ability of double-scope blending to generate an expansive range of meanings from a limited vocabulary is the cognitive ratchet required for the evolutionarily rapid development of language and the associated functional singularities distinguishing behaviorally modern *Homo sapiens* from all other species, including our immediate ancestors.

Though double-scope conceptual integration is the most complex form of blending Fauconnier and Turner have identified, they propose that without this mental capacity, our species would never have developed language, not even a "simple" language utilizing only less complex forms of blending capacity. By extension, they hypothesize that the related behavior singularities epitomizing human cognition and culture—from aesthetics to zoology—would never have emerged, because these all "precipitate as products of Double-Scope conceptual integration."[19] According to Fauconnier and Turner, double-scope blending capacity accounts for why language is an all-or-nothing behavior, why it is not present in any other species, why if it is present at all it is present in abundance:

> The only way [another species] could have a simpler grammar and yet have descriptions in language for what happens would be by having separate forms and words for everything that happens in all the different domains. But the world is infinitely too rich for that to be of any use. Trying to carry around "language" of that size would be crippling. . . . If the species has not reached the stage of Double-Scope blending, it will not develop language at all, since the least aspects of grammar require it. But if it has reached the stage of Double-Scope blending, it can very rapidly develop a full language in cultural time because it has *all* the necessary prerequisites for a full set of grammatical integrations.[20]

This aspect of Fauconnier and Turner's hypothesis for the origin of language makes sense of the lacking evidence for rudimentary or grammatically simple languages in early humans, isolated tribal groups, or other animal species. This (phylogenetic) argument pertaining to our development as a species also appears to have parallels in the (ontogenetic) case of rapid language development in the majority of human toddlers. While the capacity for double-scope conceptual integration is a result of a gradual, step-wise succession of cognitive developments that were each adaptive in themselves, language appears to emerge explosively as a functional singularity made possible by this critical mass of neuro-cognitive complexity.[21]

The field of paleoanthropology gives some clues as to when double-scope conceptual blending began having a profound effect on human cognition and culture. Archeologist Steven Mithen and paleoanthropologist Ian Tattersall date the advent of behaviorally modern human beings (*Homo sapiens sapiens*) to about 50,000 BP (Before Present), in contrast to the arrival of anatomically modern human species (*Homo sapiens*) 200,000 to 100,000 BP in Africa.[22] Famous cave paintings in Europe and other artifacts from around the world have contributed to the widespread idea that the Upper Paleolithic era (ca. 45,000 to 10,000 BP) represents a "creative explosion" of and for our species.[23]

Relying on these findings, Fauconnier and Turner present their own take on how our species took this biocultural[24] evolutionary step and why it was so significant.[25] For these cognitive linguists, the suggestion of this relatively late date for the birth of our species stems largely from the choice to define behavioral modernity in terms of the capacity for double-scope conceptual integration and the paleoanthropological evidence for its inception. That is, the designation of behavioral modernity rests on the rare but reliable evidence for the rapid development of external vehicles for cultural information, including personal, social, moral, and even proto-religious concepts. In his seminal monograph on human distinctiveness, theology and science scholar J. Wentzel van Huyssteen presents the same argument in a more detailed form. With both courage and caution, he defends his reasons for calling behaviorally modern *Homo sapiens* "fully human," accepting the ethical and theological weight of this term.[26]

Although this hypothesis that human distinctiveness developed explosively has merit and many supporters, no discussion of the evolution of linguistic ability and related capacities should fail to mention competing theories which hold that both linguistic ability and use developed gradually and in step with one another. That is, these theories see our biocultural evolution as a string of creative firecrackers, rather than a single big bang or chain reaction. Examples include neuroscientist Terrence W. Deacon, archeologist Steven Mithen, and psychologist Michael Corballis, who have argued for the gradual coevolution of the human brain and language.[27]

Still, amid this ongoing conversation, there are notable points of convergence and cross-fertilization among these theorists and their respective disciplines. Fauconnier and Turner admit that they owe much to both Mithen and Deacon.[28] Now, at least with Deacon, this influence has become mutual.

More to the point, Deacon applies blending theory in a way that is immediately relevant to theological conceptions of human distinctiveness. Utilizing Fauconnier and Turner, he argues that double-scope blending capacity not only underlies humankind's symbolic abilities, but that it also involves the blending of "symbolically transformed emotions" and the synergistic emergence of "blended emotional states" that give rise to religious, aesthetic, and ethical experiences.[29] For example, Deacon suggests that the experience of religious awe emerges as a blend of elation in the face of beauty or grandeur (first input space) with feelings of terror and insignificance (second input space) at the thought of the immensity and power of the transcendent or the holy (generic space).[30] CIT may therefore hold the key to what Deacon calls the *symbolic threshold* and the functional singularities that co-emerge with it, like religion, art, and ethics.

The emergent meanings and emotions created through double-scope blending can account for a rapid development of cognitive and cultural effects that seem to outstrip the gradual evolution of their genetic and neurological causes. This portrait of human distinctiveness and its emergence depicts behaviorally modern *Homo sapiens* as bearing a number of potent functional singularities, without requiring the notion that our species is or possesses something that is ontologically disjunctive or superior. These characteristics allow us to conceptualize and affect our environments in qualitatively unique ways, but they do not separate us from the rest of the natural world and its evolutionary history.

Many recent biblical scholars find that the concept of the image of God in Genesis paints a surprisingly similar picture of human distinctiveness framed by the concept of a divine creator who shares power with creatures, names and evaluates things, does not create through violence, and calls on human creatures to exercise their singular forms of creativity in like manner.

HUMAN DISTINCTIVENESS AND THE IMAGE OF GOD

The concept of the image and likeness of God takes pride of place in the history of Christian anthropology. It has often served as a symbol of humankind's ontological, axiological, and/or existential uniqueness among animal species. Ancient and medieval interpretations of the concept traditionally placed human beings in a separate—not just distinct—category from the rest of creation. This segregation rested on the assumption that human beings are or possess something that animals do not—a rational soul or spirit capable of communion with God and eternal life.

Contemporary interdisciplinary scholarship integrating theology, biblical studies, the natural sciences, and the philosophy of science may have rendered this interpretation of the image of God and its dualistic underpinnings untenable. Deacon's work on emergence continues to be an important resource for this interdisciplinary dialogue.[31] Other monographs and anthologies featuring philosophers and theologians like Philip Clayton, Nancey Murphy, Warren S. Brown, Denis Edwards, Philip Hefner, J. Wentzel van Huyssteen, and others also argue for an emergent monist or physicalist anthropology which views human spirituality or soulfulness as an irreducible, emergent aspect of embodiment.[32]

This general perspective is presupposed here, but the biblical conception of human distinctiveness in Genesis which it helps to bring into focus pertains more directly to the topics at hand. The sections above argue that double-scope blending capacity is vital to understanding human distinctiveness in general. The current section highlights the manner in which the concept of the image of God in Genesis relates in large part to an ancient conception of human distinctiveness which comports surprisingly well with that proposed by CIT. The concluding section illustrates how this biblical concept emerged and its significance continues to develop through double-scope blending.

Many biblical scholars and theologians have all but abandoned exclusive focus on traditional conceptions of the image of God in Genesis, which I call the *rational* and *relational* interpretations. They have begun to subordinate these to the more exegetically sound *representational* or *royal* interpretation.[33] The rational conception of the image points to humanity's psycho-spiritual capacities and/or the substantive spirit possessing them as the locus of the image, as seen in Augustinian and Thomistic perspectives.[34] The relational school of thought looks primarily to interpersonal or God-human interaction to find God imaged in the "I-Thou" existential of personhood, especially as this dynamic is described by theologian Karl Barth and his followers.[35] The representational-royal conception of the image and likeness of God understands the primeval history to depict human creatures not as metaphysically or existentially unique, but as functionally and vocationally distinctive in their capacity and call to share in the creator's beneficent dominion. In Genesis human beings are wrought of the creation and embedded within it to the same extent as other creatures. At the same time, the direct address and commands of Genesis 1:26–28 suggest that in bearing the divine image, human beings possess a singular response-ability to participate in the ongoing process of creation in singularly efficacious and conscientious ways.

This functional, representational, and royal interpretation of the divine image highlights the consistent way in which the primeval history in Genesis depicts human beings and other animals as qualitatively distinguishable without being substantially different in a metaphysical sense. When reading the first several chapters as a redacted canonical whole,[36] one discovers that humankind and all other land animals are created on the sixth day from the "earth" or the "dust of the ground" (Gen 1:24–31; 2:7). The human hails from the humus. Likely an intentional play on words, *adam* (earthling; human) is created from *adamah* (earth; humus) to bear the *demut* (a likeness) to the creator. Likewise, although Gen 2:7 makes mention of a unique inbreathing of life for the first human being, the "breath of life" (*nishmat chayyim*) that is given is also borne by other creatures (7:22; cf. 6:17). Additionally, this divine in-spiration causes the human to become a "living creature/being" (*nefesh chayyah*), a designation shared by all the animal species called forth from waters and earth on the fifth and sixth days (2:7, 19; cf. 1:20, 24).

Another vital element shared by humankind and other animal species is "blood" (*dam*), which bears sacred (even cultic) significance, requiring special attention in meat preparation and retributive justice in cases of human bloodshed (Gen 9:3–6). Thus, in four interrelated terms arising in the Primeval History of Genesis, the consonants *dalet* (ד) and *mem* (מ, ם) point to a creature whose vital elements and their integration, functioning, and flourishing are consonant and contiguous with the rest of the creation. As an animated amalgam of dust, breath, and blood, the human derives every aspect of its life from the world in which it is embedded, just like the others. Even so, one of these Hebrew terms signifies a special calling and set of capacities borne for the purpose of discerning and enacting the creator's intentions for the creation with freedom and responsibility. In this way *adam* bears a *demut*, a "likeness," to God.

The visual similarity of these terms is especially apparent in the unpointed Hebrew text:

דם	*dam*	blood
אדם	*adam*	human(kind), Adam
אדמה	*adamah*	ground, earth
דמות	*demut*	likeness

The root,דם (*d-m*), is the common thread among the terms. The words אדם (*adam*) and אדמה (*adamah*) are linked by their initial guttural א (*alef*); and some may even note that the final ה (*he*) and ת (*tav*) of אדמה (*adamah*) and דמות (*demut*) are visually similar.[37]

One biblical scholar, J. Maxwell Miller, highlights evidence that the priestly editors (P), and perhaps earlier contributors to the primeval history, were well aware of this visible and audible pun, citing Genesis 9:6: "Whoever sheds the *blood* of a *human*, by a *human* shall that person's *blood* be shed; for in his own image, God made *humankind*" (NRSV; דמ terms emphasized). Conspicuously, this passage points out that that humankind deserves this special moral consideration because it is made in the "image"—*tselem*—of God, without any mention of the divine "likeness"—*demut*. These two terms are paired together in 1:26 and 5:1–3. Miller surmises that this lack of pairing and break in *d-m* consonance is to avoid any suggestion in chapter 9 that the image of God shares in the divine being. After all, human beings are made from divine blood (*dam*) in the Babylonian creation epic *Enuma Elish* and other ancient near eastern parallels.[38] The implication seems to be that even where human beings bear the divine image and likeness, there are ways in which only the creator's form of existence transcends that of creatures. In humankind, as in every other terrestrial creature, the ground breathes, not God. The breath of life may come through God's action, but it is not God's own breath.[39] Thus, in the theological anthropology of Genesis, human beings are a different kind of creature because they can act conscientiously on the creator's behalf, not because they have taken leave of the animal world and been made into or out of gods.[40]

While certainly not a scientific portrait of human nature, the anthropology of Genesis is more commensurable with an evolutionary and cognitive linguistic understanding of human distinctiveness than a dualistic conception of human uniqueness that separates spirit and matter and human beings from other creatures. In CIT evolutionary processes have afforded *Homo sapiens* a qualitatively distinct ability to generate meanings and thereby define and alter our ecological and social environments with unprecedented creativity and efficacy. Human beings are conscientious creators of meanings who fill and shape the world.

The creator God and human creatures in Genesis are depicted in much the same way—as making and naming things and evaluating them as good or not. CIT and its evolutionary portrait of humankind's functional distinctiveness helps bring this more functional interpretation of the divine image and likeness into focus, while also suggesting ways in which these seemingly disparate conceptions of human distinctiveness might blend together and generate new significance for this ancient concept.

Along this line of functional distinctiveness, many biblical scholars interpret the terms for *image* and *likeness* to overlap semantically and modify one another in both a negative and positive sense.[41] Negatively, *image* may keep *likeness* from becoming a reference to a divine substance running through human veins; *likeness* may keep *image* from becoming a reference to a mute and non-agential conduit of the divine, an object of cultic devotion, or a despotic ruler disseminating the divine will in the socio-political sphere.[42] Positively, while many exegetes point out that the definitions of "image" and "likeness" are not perspicuous, either separately or in tandem, several scholars agree that together the terms portray humanity as not merely representative of the creator, but representational as well—a likeness-bearing image.[43]

As theologian Philip Hefner suggests, "humans are, in some manner, created to be an explicit representation and presence of God's will in the creation. Humans have the created calling to articulate within the natural world what God's intentionality might be."[44] Following the ideological trajectory of Genesis in an evolutionary and emergentist view of the world, Hefner has concluded that fully embedded within creation is a created co-creator. Divinity is not the only form of self-conscious intentionality and causality. Up from the ground has come a fully creaturely form of it. The primeval history implies that one of God's intentions for creation is that one of its creatures discerns and enacts the creator's purposes with freedom and responsibility, which includes the original and ever-present possibility of getting things wrong.[45] For better or worse, Hefner infers, "what is at the core of this analogy [of the image of God] today is the character of *Homo sapiens* as a free creator of meanings, one who takes action based on those meanings and is also responsible for those meanings and actions."[46]

In parallel, complementary ways, both the biblical and natural scientific narratives of human origins indicate that this ambivalent human condition is the inevitable result of emerging as an animated amalgam of dust, breath, and blood. In cognitive linguistic terms, our distinct capacity for conceptual blending renders us free and responsible creators of meanings, who can envision the divine act of creation as the manifestation through speech of all that is real and good. CIT even suggests that this theological framing of the cosmos as a creation is a direct result of double-scope blending. Like the symbolically transformed emotions of religious experience mentioned above, theological concepts concerning a Subject or Object transcending the tangible world require the kinds of recursive conceptual mappings afforded only by double-scope blending.

Like CIT the primeval history in Genesis highlights the singularly creative power of speech. But Genesis evaluates this capacity and its outputs, intimating that humankind's distinctively linguistic nature enables them to co-create a "very good" world . . . or not. In the primeval history only human creatures are capable of naming one another and other creatures (Gen 2:19–23; 3:20), and only they gain a God-imaging, but ambivalent knowledge and freedom to pronounce and produce "good," but also "not good," "bad," or "evil" in the world (3:22).[47]According to biblical scholar Graeme Auld:

> One of the most remarkable features of the opening of Genesis (1:1–2:3) is the prominence of speech. . . . No less than 40 percent of the verbs denoting the divine actions are explicitly verbs of speaking. . . . Because the report of every "day" of creation opens with "and God said" and is followed by the divine fiat, all the making (8x), separating (2x), granting (2x), and sanctifying (1x) were also achieved by divine word. In Genesis 1, God is a God who speaks, and who acts by speaking. It stands to reason, then, that human beings created by, and made very like such a God would be preeminently speakers.[48]

The cognitive linguistic conception of human distinctiveness outlined above shares a number of features with these exegetical insights. For good and ill, much of what makes *Homo sapiens* qualitatively distinct among species is the conscientious ability to (co-)create the symbolic universe of what is and ought to be. Similarly, in Genesis, humankind may be said to bear an image and likeness of the creator God with and through their ambivalent knowledge of good and bad/evil.

Hence, cognitive linguistics not only provides hermeneutical insight as to how new meanings might emerge through integrating ancient and current concepts, but also that this distinctively human capacity did not escape the notice of the biblical writer(s). Auld's analysis suggests that the Priestly contributor(s) to the Hebrew Bible held, in a pre-scientific way, that humankind's semantic fecundity, embodied in language, made us distinct among creatures and somehow similar to the God before, behind, and beyond the creation.

After reading van Huyssteen's 2004 Gifford Lectures, which would become *Alone in the World?: Human Uniqueness in Science and Theology*, Auld urged him to make a strong connection between the place of linguistic ability in scientific portraits of human distinctiveness and his theological interpretation of the image of God in Genesis.[49] I find that the primeval history weaves another conceptual thread into its theocentric portrayal of human distinctiveness. In both CIT and the narratives of the primeval history, the human ability to create and hold ourselves accountable to concepts like "good" and "evil" is an all-pervading blessing and curse.

In Genesis 1 God's creative speech always moves toward evaluation of what is produced or what the creation is enabled to produce. "God said . . ."; "Let there be . . ."; "Let the waters bring forth . . ."; "Let the earth bring forth . . ."; "And it was so . . ."; "And God saw that it was good." In Genesis 2:18, God sees that some realities are "not good," and acts to remedy the situation. By the end of Genesis 3, God-likeness means knowing "good" and "evil" in a creaturely, imperfect, ambivalent way. Accordingly, creatures said to bear the image of God would not just be especially creative, they must evaluate what they produce and bear the divine image all the more when their actions result in what could be called "good."[50]

Thus far I have outlined the ways that conceptual blending creates new meanings. I have made a case for the hypothesis that behaviorally modern *Homo sapiens*' capacity for double-scope conceptual integration allows us to create any conceivable meaning, including anthropological, moral, and religious concepts. The concept of the image of God in Genesis blends all these types of meaning and even focuses on humankind's meaning-making abilities in ways that bear parallels to cognitive linguistic understandings of human distinctiveness.

In the final section I apply double-scope conceptual integration on a broad scale to illustrate how the biblical concept of the image of God emerged through the creative blending of ancient meanings. I then follow suit to propose ways in which these biblical meanings may construct contemporary theological understandings of human distinctiveness through the blending of concepts framed by both biblical and scientifically informed perspectives. The integration of these conceptual frames creates a blended mental space in which people of faith today can interpret and enact their capacity and call to re-present their beneficent creator with freedom and responsibility.

CONCEPTUAL BLENDING AND THE IMAGE OF GOD

The God-imaging forms of human creativity showcased in the opening chapters of Genesis may be construed in light of CIT as emerging through a capacity for double-scope blending. Proposing a neuro-cognitive indicator of what it means to be distinctively human, blending theory may shed a bright, empirically powered light on the Judeo-Christian mythic symbols of the image of God and the knowledge of good and evil. Specifically, blending biblical and biocultural understandings of humankind's functional distinctiveness recasts a portrait of the image of God and the knowledge of good and evil in which (1) these concepts and the shared human condition to which they refer are products of double-scope blending capacity; (2) the image of God, the knowledge of good and bad, and their ongoing co-creation are products of the natural world; (3) bearing the divine image is a vocation that emerges through creaturely processes—a capacity and calling to emulate God's beneficent creativity; and (4) bearing the image of God entails a morally ambivalent condition of freedom—a knowledge of good and evil.

Each of these conclusions and all of them together rely on the use of double-scope blending as a procedure for constructive interdisciplinary hermeneutics. The blending of concepts and theoretical frameworks across academic disciplines and cultural-linguistic worlds of meanings is an exercise of broad-scale double-scope conceptual integration. A fruitful way to describe the hermeneutical effects of double-scope blending across theological and scientific disciplines is through what interdisciplinary scholar Ian G. Barbour's calls a *theology of nature*. This interdisciplinary approach "starts from a religious tradition based on religious experience and historical revelation. But it holds that some traditional doctrines need to be reformulated in the light of current science," where theological and scientific concerns overlap.[51] A theology of nature perspective reframes doctrinal concepts scientifically and scientific concepts theologically in a blended mental space. Writing on the concept of the image of God in Genesis, biblical scholar J. Richard Middleton employs the phrase *hermeneutics of mutuality* to describe his own methods in very much the same way.[52] He consciously brings his subjective conceptual frameworks to his exegesis and interpretation of the biblical text, while allowing those concepts and paradigms of meaning to be transformed in turn by the world of the text. The theological conclusions of this final section employ this procedure and diagram the hermeneutical process in a series of double-scope blends.

Conclusion 1: Blending in the Image of God

Concerning the first conclusion about the concepts and shared human condition that are the image of God and knowledge of good and evil, many historical and biblical scholars argue convincingly that the opening chapters of Genesis were likely edited together during and/or shortly after the Babylonian captivity of the sixth century BCE. This school of thought has recently been distilled and extended in Middleton's monograph *The Liberating Image*. He argues that in a post-exilic context, the cosmogony and themes of Genesis 1–11 bear the marks of blending ancient Israelite and Neo-Babylonian ideologies as a means of critiquing the latter. Utilizing common mythic and narrative elements found in the Babylonian epic *Enuma Elish* and other ancient Near Eastern parallels, the Priestly editor(s) of Genesis 1 appear to have framed the ancient Mesopotamian understandings of creation via Israelite conceptions of God as the one and only redeeming deity of the exodus experience, and vice versa.

What appears to take place in Genesis 1 is the co-framing, or double-scope blending, of the polytheistic cosmogony of Babylonia and a monotheistic cosmogony of ancient Judaea-Israel. The concept that all people bear royal dignity and the potential to re-present the beneficent intentions of the creator as shapers of history emerges through this blend. In the face of the Babylonian captivity, this elevated status and function of human creatures vis-à-vis their creator is not the exclusive prerogative of the militarily mighty and their rulers. The concept of the image of God in Genesis emerges from the double-scope blend of a monotheistic cosmogony with a polytheistic cosmogony. In the latter conceptual frame, the power structures among the gods are intended to be recapitulated among their human representatives and slaves.

Surprisingly, this blending of monotheism and Neo-Babylonian royal ideology yields a universalized royal divine image. Where only one deity is preserved in the blend, there are no superior and inferior gods for various castes or tribes of people to represent. In this divine image, all are called to have dominion over the earth, not over one another, and no one can shed another's blood with impunity.[53] The double-scope blending of these competing ideologies is summarized by the following three points and figure 4.2.

First, as stated above, the cosmogony of Genesis 1, along with its mention of the image of God, is very likely a polemical ideological critique of the Babylonian cosmology depicted in *Enuma Elish*, in which the god Marduk ascends to power through military and political conquest.[54] After becoming chief among the gods, Marduk creates the heavens and earth by killing and mutilating the body of Tiamat, the goddess representing the chaos of the deep salt seas. He and his ally Ea create human beings from the blood of Tiamat's consort, Qingu, as a means of punishing this rival and for the purpose of conscripting creatures who toil in order to provide the gods with sustenance and occasion to rest. This creation-by-combat theme is conspicuously absent from the conceptual inputs contributing to the primeval history, and it is not projected into the blended concept of the image and likeness of God.[55]

Second, the order and means of creation and the purposes of created entities are similar in Genesis and *Enuma Elish*. Both Marduk and Elohim create through fiat[56] and separating—light from dark, waters from waters, heavens from earth, and water from land. Heavenly luminaries also bear similar functions in each account. Both cosmologies define the role of the sun, moon, and stars in marking the passage of days and seasons. However, since the ancient Israelites do not involve heavenly bodies in worship, the luminaries are given a lower status—they "serve" not as divine sources of light but as carriers of light to govern the day and night.[57] Further, Elohim does not create by separating the body parts of dead deities. The forces of chaos Marduk must overcome in order to create are utterly de-personified in the Genesis cosmology. The goddess Tiamat is almost unrecognizable as the *tehom*—the deep sea—over which the breath (*ruach*) of God so effortlessly hovers. In Genesis 1:21 great sea monsters issue forth from earthly waters, not vice versa. By contrast, Marduk must breathe or otherwise conjure a great wind to disturb the insides of Tiamat, affording him the opportunity to kill her before he can create. The Lord God is not a mere replacement of Marduk. The Israelites' God has no personal rivals, and whatever semblance of primordial chaos can be found in Genesis 1, it is brushed aside by the constitutive utterance, "Let there be . . ."[58] In Genesis, created reality and its purposes come about through acts of divine freedom and generosity, rather than retribution and necessity. God empowers the creation to "bring forth" what it will and sees "that it was good." Creation in the Hebrew Bible is an act of liberation rather than subjugation.

Third, both cosmogonies call for political and ethical mimesis.[59] With *Enuma Elish* the move from myth to ritual and politics is more straightforward than with the Genesis cosmology. Imperial conquest, such as that of the Southern Kingdom of Judah ca. 587–538 BCE, is a reenactment of Marduk's rise to power over the forces of chaos. Captive peoples then provide the labor force on which Babylonian society and its elite depended. In the drama surrounding the annual New Year's festival (*Akitu*), the Babylonian king stood in as Marduk, a representation or *image* of this god on earth, set there to implement divine purposes.[60]

Blended with a Neo-Babylonian conceptual framework, the cosmogony and anthropology of Genesis 1 democratizes this royal *image* concept. It still bears a functional purpose, but in very different ways. In the midst of being "subdued" and "ruled over" in captivity, the Israelites are called in hope against hope to bear the image and likeness of God, as they "fill the earth, and subdue it; and have dominion over" its creatures, while deriving sustenance from its plant life (Gen 1:26–30; NRSV). God is able to rest after creating humankind, but not due to the fruits of human labor (Gen 2:3). Rather, this creator calls humankind to take part in this Sabbath rest, as Exodus 20:8–11 records. More than a despotic ruler, royal statue, or a mute idol, all humankind bears an "image" of God that is a "likeness" unto divine agency. This co-framing of concepts yields a creation account in which the primordial forces of chaos with which the creator must battle have been de-personified. Without having to slay other gods in order to create, the Lord God is depicted as creating through fiat. Those who bear an agential image and likeness to *this* creator are called to emulate this non-violent, power-sharing mode of creativity. They are not to bring order to the cultural world through the violent assertion of dominion over other human beings. In fact, Genesis 3:16 implies that the tendency for humans to "rule over" one another belongs to the shadow side of imaging a God who knows good from bad/evil.

Figure 4.2 illustrates the double-scope blend that yields one foundational aspect in the first conclusion listed in this section. That is, the notion that the image of God refers to a shared human vocation emerges in the clash of ancient Near Eastern ideologies, perhaps exacerbated by the context of the Babylonian Exile.

But can people of faith today simply repeat and apply this ancient conception of the image of God? In some ways, yes; emerging from this exegesis are theological, anthropological, and moral principles that are fruitful in themselves. At the same time, those questing for these ancient meanings are laden with twenty-first-century methods, concerns, and values. The conceptual, social, and ecological environments surrounding the image of God concept are radically different today. Some have sought to reduce the notions of divine and human creativity to epiphenomena of quantum particles and forces. Additionally, the human capacity to "fill the earth and subdue it" has so far outstripped the hopes of ancient exiles that our species is causing global climate change and mass extinctions, making the creation less habitable and fecund.[61] For these reasons and more, the theologian is obliged to integrate

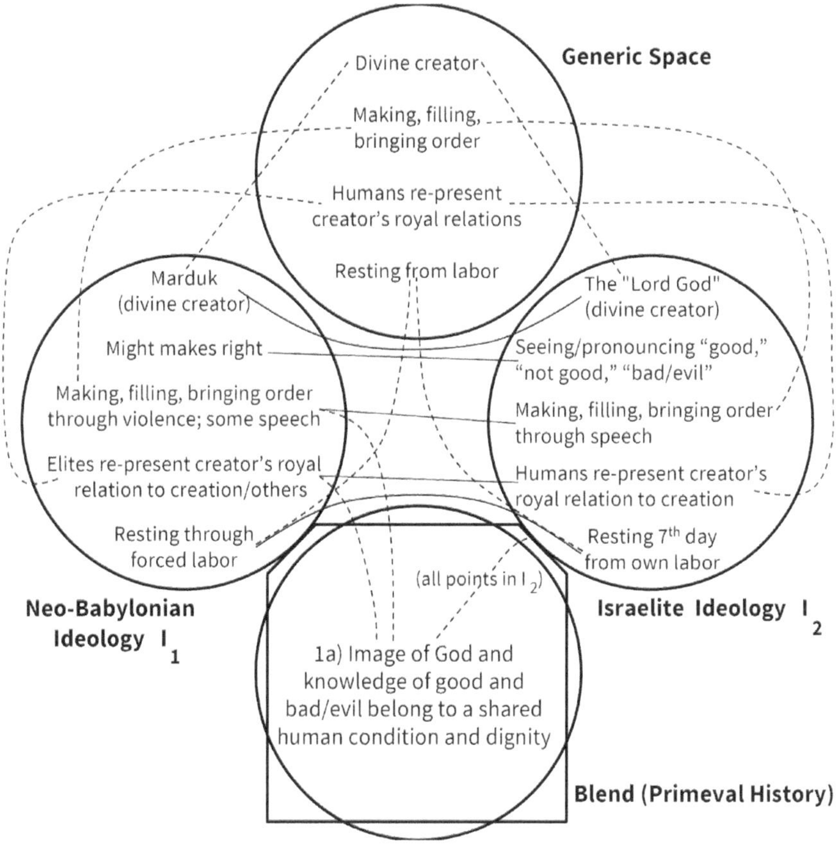

Figure 4.2. Image and Knowledge in Primeval History

biblical and contemporary concepts and paradigms, lest the great symbols of the faith lose their intellectual credibility and moral fruitfulness. CIT helps to show *how* the concept of the image of God originally emerged by blending disparate meanings in desperate times. These contemporary concerns are just a few reasons *why* readers today ought to follow suit.

The blend illustrated in figure 4.3 makes room for a biocultural evolutionary perspective to shape the way we think about human distinctiveness in the image of God. Blending these ancient and current anthropologies generates the interpretive inference that the human condition described in the primeval history is largely a result of double-scope blending capacity. The biocultural and cognitive linguistic view that *Homo sapiens* have emerged through natural processes helps to specify those naturally occurring human capacities and creations which re-present the God of creation.

Waxing theoretical for a moment, figure 4.3 also illustrates one of the reasons that conceptual integration is as complex a process as it is creative. The various solid and dotted lines represent connections and projections among meanings in the input, generic, and blended mental spaces. The solid lines between the input spaces connect meanings that are projected in some way into both the generic and blended spaces. These projections are pictured by dotted lines connecting elements of those same concepts to the generic and blended spaces. At the same time, figures 4.1 through 4.4 show disparate meanings, not connected to the generic space, being projected into the blend from one or both of the input spaces.[62] These independently projected meanings, as well as concepts not projected from one or more input spaces can have a profound effect on the emerging conceptual structures. For example, the concept of a divine creator is projected into the blend in figure 4.3, which frames and is framed by the evolutionary concepts in the other input space. What is more blended meanings like these can contribute to the input spaces of other

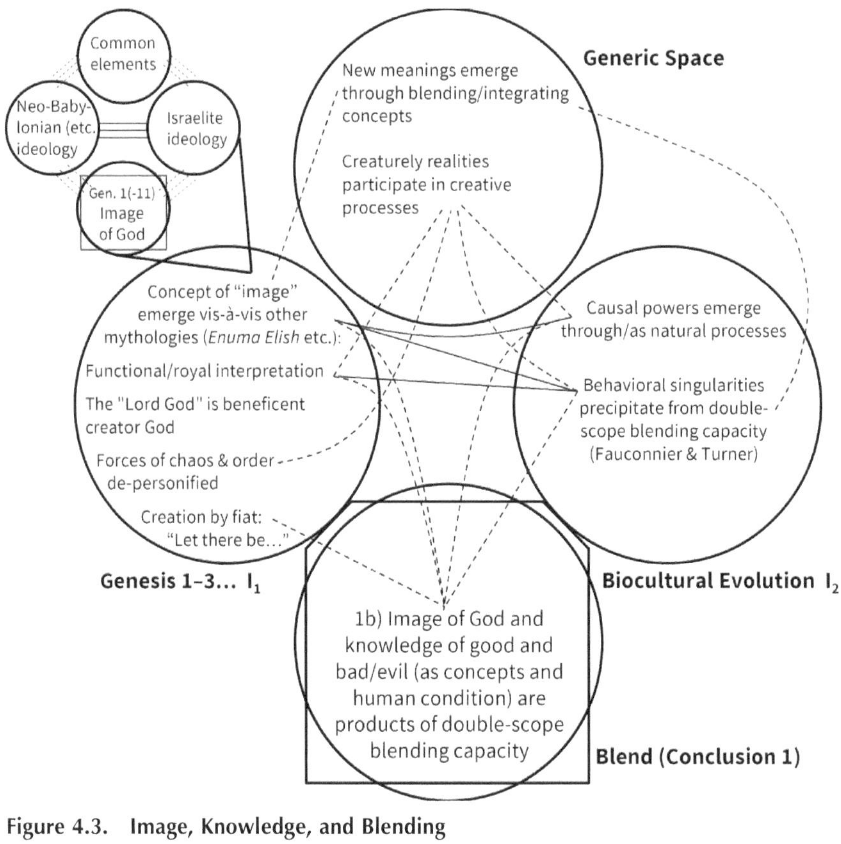

Figure 4.3. Image, Knowledge, and Blending

blends, as in the "theological presupposition" that "God creates through evolutionary processes" found in figures 4.4 through 4.6. This compound use of blended meanings is illustrated even more explicitly through the projection of the blend pictured at the top left of figures 4.3 and 4.5.

Conclusion 2: Evolving in the Image of God

My second interpretive conclusion is that the image of God, the knowledge of good and bad/evil, and their ongoing co-creation are products of the natural world. An evolutionary conception of humankind's biocultural distinctiveness brings into focus and blends with elements in the early chapters of Genesis where human creatures and their God-imaging creative abilities emerge from the creation itself. Recall that in the primeval history, humankind is brought forth from the earth along with other creatures as an animated amalgam of dust, breath, and blood. Ontologically ordinary in every respect, *adam* (humankind) does bear a distinguishing capacity to think and act in ways that show a *demut*—a likeness—to the creator who can see and say that created realities are "good" or not. Gaining this ambivalent form of freedom and responsibility is also facilitated by creaturely entities in Genesis 2–3—the serpent and the tree of knowledge. Blending biblical and scientific conceptions of human distinctiveness allows one to interpret the image of God and the knowledge of good and evil as products and processes of *Homo sapiens'* biocultural evolutionary nature. Blended meanings like these appear in contemporary theological anthropologies like Hefner's, where human beings are characterized as "created co-creators" and "defined self-definers."[63] Contemporizing these biblical concepts through blending allows them to remain intellectually honest and morally fruitful conceptions of the human condition in new contexts.

In sum figure 4.4 shows the results of blending biblical and scientifically-informed conceptions of creativity (divine, cosmic, human) and humankind's kinship with other creatures. From this integration of concepts emerges the inference that the image of God and knowledge of good and bad/evil (as human concepts and condition) are evolved and evolving products and processes of our biocultural nature.

Conclusion 3: Re-Presenting the Image of (a Good) God

Blending the first two interpretive inferences supports the theological conclusion that bearing the image of God with a knowledge of good and evil is humankind's evolved and evolving response-ability. Our species emerges with a capacity and call to re-present the intentions of the creator who shares

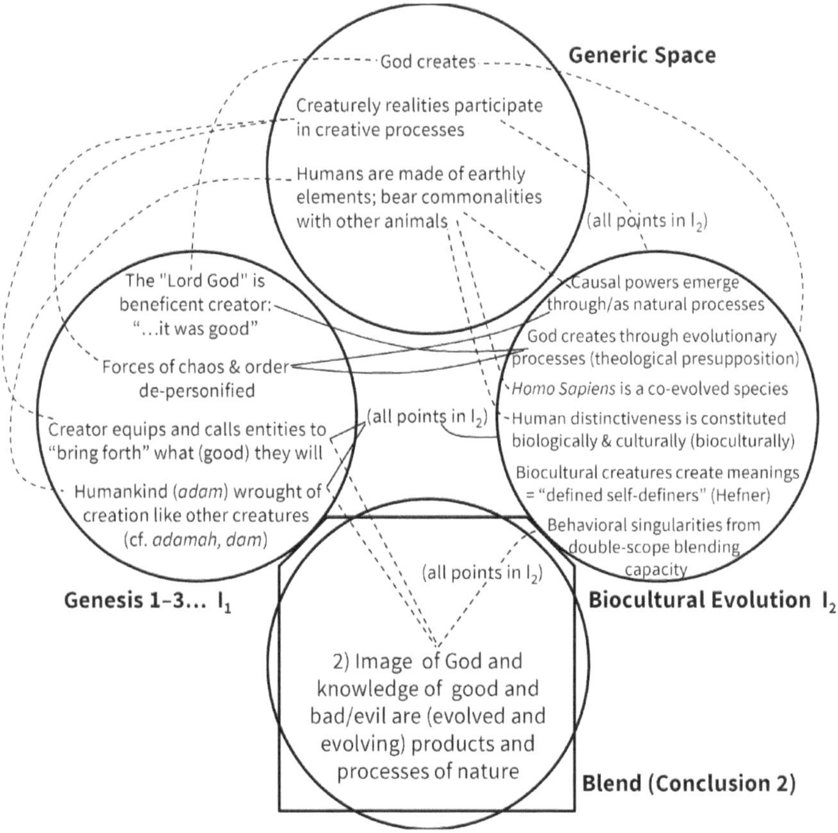

Figure 4.4. Image, Knowledge, and Nature

power and does not create through violence. According to this perspective visualized in figure 4.5, being the creator's beneficent representatives in/to the creation is *Homo sapiens'* theological vocation.

Note also that the biocultural evolution input space in figure 4.5 does not really change from that of figure 4.4. However, the combination of the Genesis input spaces (left side) from figures 4.3 and 4.4 generate a new blend in figure 4.5. This new conclusion builds upon concepts of the royal-representational nature of the image of God in Genesis, as well as the anti-violent ethical inferences generated by the monotheistic cosmogony of the primeval history. A God without rivals has no need to create through violence, because the raw materials for the creation are not the dead bodies of those rivals. Further, there is no mention of the creator's own body in Genesis 1, even in the creative acts of speaking, seeing, blessing, and so on. With no mention of a physical form to maintain, the created purpose or vocation of human beings

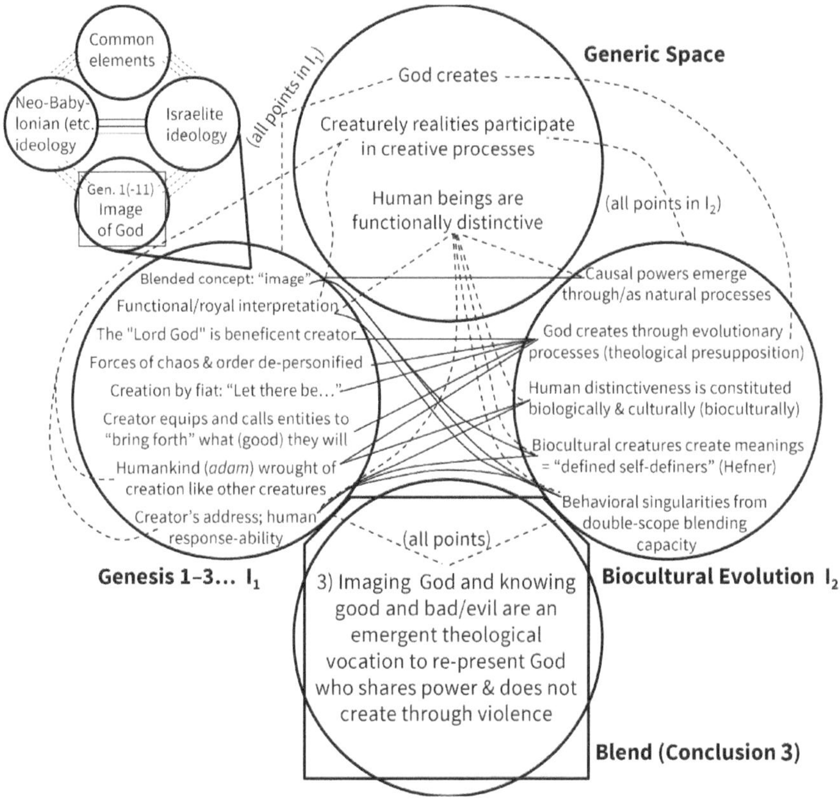

Figure 4.5. Image, Knowledge, and Emergent Vocation

is not tied to providing sustenance and leisure for the gods and their human representatives.

With these distinctions from *Enuma Elish* and other ancient mythology in mind, the direct address to human beings created in the image and likeness of God in Genesis 1:28–30 is conspicuously lacking in a call for some of them to subdue and have dominion over others. Because everyone is blessed to bear the creator's image and likeness, no one is intended by God to be subjugated by another. Rather, all are called to "fill the earth and subdue it; and have dominion over" other kinds of creatures.

Yet even this cannot be an invitation for exploitation, because bearing the image of *this* creator would naturally entail "filling" and having "dominion" in analogous ways to those God exercises in the previous verses. That is, God and those who would bear this creator's image enable and invite others to "let there be . . ." to "be gathered," to "put forth," to "bring forth," "to be fruitful," and so on. Bearing the image of this creator, human beings also come to bear a distinctive capacity to evaluate that which they and the world around them produce. They can see and say whether or not "it is good." The implication throughout the primeval history is that the attempt to create cosmic or social order through exploitation and subjugation is never good and denies the divine image in oneself and others.[64]

Conclusion 4: Choosing in the Image of God

This last point about humankind's evaluative capabilities leads into a final conclusion. Understanding distinctive forms of human agency as catalyzed by natural and cultural selection pressures paints an ambiguous and ambivalent portrait of human freedom and creativity. Blending this insight with depictions of human nature in Genesis 1–3 relativizes traditional "paradise lost" interpretations of the Garden narrative. That is, "Eden" was never a historical context of human bliss and juridical righteousness before God from which a pair or group of humans "fell" in an act of disobedience. An evolutionary worldview brings into focus narrative elements implying that a God-imaging creaturely existence in life as we know it must entail a morally ambivalent condition of freedom. The harsh verbs of dominion in Genesis 1:28, the presence of the crafty serpent and the tree of knowledge in the garden, and the ambiguous form of wisdom that makes the human creatures more like their creator in Genesis 3:22 are just a few hints that humankind is ultimately meant to make its home outside the mythical garden. Humanity's home is actually the wild places where the challenges and opportunities to bear the image of their beneficent creator are greater, and from which humankind originated.[65]

Further, if Genesis 1 is to be read canonically alongside the Garden Narrative of chapters 2–3, then being barred from Eden cannot only be a punishment for a creature called to fill the whole earth, of which Eden is but a small cultivated corner. Biblical scholar Phyllis Bird also points out that the command to fill the earth is directly connected with the command to have dominion over it. While the harsh verbs of 1:28 certainly imply the cursed drudgery emphasized by the Yahwist in 3:17–19, the Priestly creation account holds that the capacity, call, and opportunity to master land and beast is also part and parcel of the blessing pronounced to the bearers of the divine image. Even in their ambivalence, all of these elements contribute to the "very good-ness" of the creation as a whole (Gen 1:31).[66]

Thus, there is good reason to believe that the divine first person plural "us" in 1:26 and 3:22 frames a narrative about coming to a mature knowledge of the good *and* bad/evil (*tov va-ra*) that goes along with bearing the image and likeness of God as finite, fallible creatures in a good but dangerous world. These two verses are the only ones in all of scripture in which God speaks in the first person plural to confer or describe similarity of humanity to divinity. While

Genesis 2–3 cannot be characterized as a benign coming-of-age story, it also does not narrate a unilateral fall from righteousness so much as an ambivalent stumble out of innocence. The so called "curses" of Genesis 3 list the looming trials of one kind of creature who has come to a conscientious awareness, somehow similar to God's, that maintaining and producing life can be fraught with all sorts of hardship, that conflict and power disparities can arise in the most intimate of relationships. There are dangerous animals lurking in the Garden, crafty creatures of God's own making (Gen 3:1), sources of wisdom able to open human eyes to all these dangers and more. Overall, the primeval history suggests that relating to the creation, one another, and God in distinctively human ways means being aware of the original and ever-present possibility of fulfillment and frustration, cooperation and conflict, good and evil.

This view of human distinctiveness in Genesis comports with a biocultural anthropology informed by CIT. Figure 4.6 illustrates how the blending

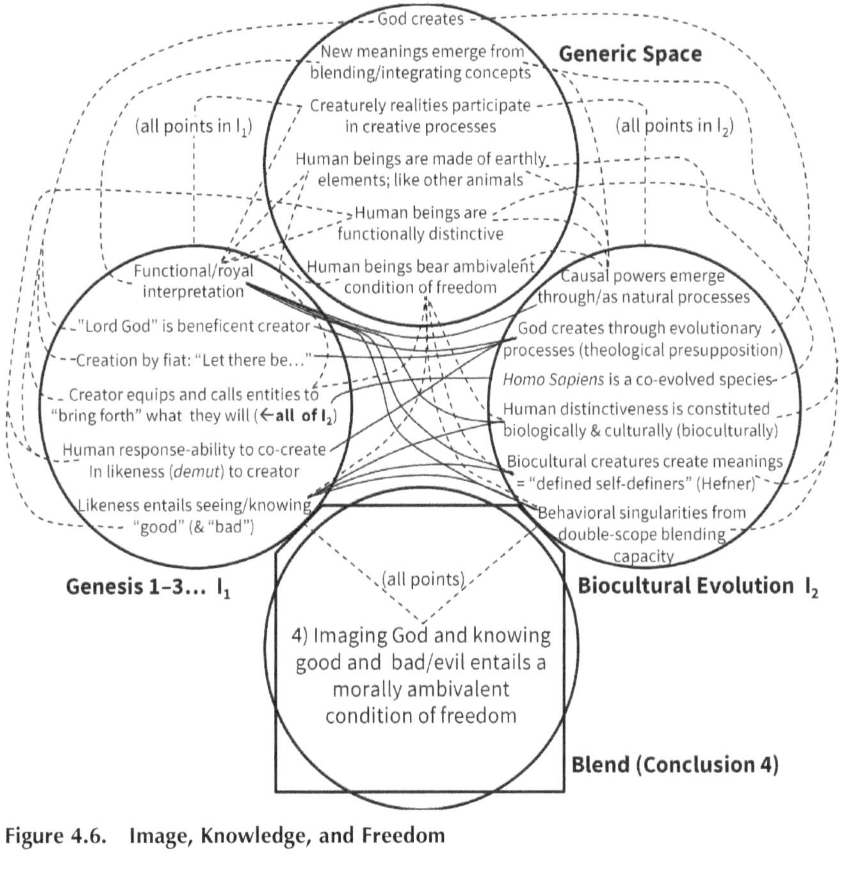

Figure 4.6. Image, Knowledge, and Freedom

of these two conceptual frames yields the inference that the evolutionary emergence of creatures who can define themselves as bearers of the image and likeness of God necessarily entails a morally ambivalent condition of freedom.

Philip Hefner's definition of *freedom* is a helpful one to adopt in this case. It emerges from a similar integration of biblical and biocultural concepts and encapsulates both the ambivalence and inescapability of this human condition. For him freedom is "the condition of existence in which humans unavoidably face the necessity both of making choices that govern their behavior and of constructing the stories that contextualize and hence justify those choices."[67] I have attempted here to propose that this capability and necessity emerge in no small part from humankind's distinctive capacity for double-scope blending. In this view the inescapable blessing and curse of creating and filling our worlds of meanings with everything that is conceivably real, true, and good is part and parcel of bearing the image and likeness of God.

The illustrations and considerations of this chapter are intended to showcase the distinctive human capacity they define—the meaning-making process of double-scope blending. According to this interpretation, conceptual blending, human distinctiveness, and the image of God are an indissociable constellation of concepts. Conceptual integration theory provides a plausible explanation of how *Homo sapiens* evolved to become a species capable of self-definition, including theological self-definition. The ways in which CIT illuminates the emergence of our species and its ever-evolving symbolic worlds equips scholars at the interdisciplinary crossroads of the sciences, theology, and ethics with powerful hermeneutical tools for reformulating what it means to bear the image of God as a creature with a knowledge of good and evil.

NOTES

1. Gilles Fauconnier and Mark Turner, "The Origin of Language as a Product of the Evolution of Modern Cognition," in *Origin and Evolution of Languages: Approaches, Models, Paradigms*, ed. Bernard Laks et al. (London: Equinox, 2008), 133.

2. Gilles Fauconnier and Mark Turner, *The Way We Think: Conceptual Blending and the Mind's Hidden Complexities* (New York: Basic Books, 2002), 40, 47.

3. Ibid., 42–49; cf. "The Origin of Language," 133–35; "Principles of Conceptual Integration," in *Discourse and Cognition: Bridging the Gap*, ed. Jean-Pierre Koenig (Stanford, CA: CSLI Publications: 1998), 269–73, 278–82; "Rethinking Metaphor," in *The Cambridge Handbook of Metaphor and Thought*, ed. Raymond W. Gibbs (New York: Cambridge University Press, 2008), 53–55.

4. Fauconnier and Turner, *The Way We Think*, 48.

5. Ibid., 120
6. Ibid.
7. Ibid., 140–41.
8. Ibid., 47
9. Ibid., 123.
10. Ibid., 39.
11. Ibid., 122–26.
12. Ibid., 126.
13. Ibid.
14. Ibid., 131.
15. Fauconnier and Turner, "The Origin of Language," 134, 144, 146–47, 150.
16. Fauconnier and Turner, "Principles of Conceptual Integration," 279.
17. Ibid.
18. Fauconnier and Turner, *The Way We Think*, 46.
19. Fauconnier and Turner, "The Origin of Language," 133.
20. Ibid., 144, 146; emphasis in original.
21. Ibid., 142, 146.
22. Steven Mithen, *The Prehistory of the Mind: The Cognitive Origins of Art, Religion, and Science* (London: Thames and Hudson, 1996); Ian Tattersall, *Becoming Human: Evolution and Human Uniqueness* (New York: Harcourt Brace, 1998); *The World from Beginnings to 4000 BCE* (Oxford: Oxford University Press, 2008), 100–108.
23. See Tattersall, *Becoming Human*, 5–29, 68, 225–33.
24. Defined by theologian Philip Hefner, the term *biocultural evolution* refers to (1) the emergence, within the physical realm, of biological processes of evolution that themselves generate the phenomenon of culture; and (2) to the distinctive, non-Darwinian, dynamic processes by which culture proceeds, while at the same time existing in a relationship of symbiosis with the physical-biological processes in which it emerged and in which it continues to operate." Philip Hefner, "Biocultural Evolution and the Created Co-Creator," *Dialog* 36, no. 3 (1997): 197.
25. Fauconnier and Turner, "The Origin of Language," 139, 148, 151–53; cf. Ian Tattersall, *Becoming Human*, 5–29, 225–35; J. Wentzel van Huyssteen, *Alone in the World? Human Uniqueness in Science and Theology* (Grand Rapids: William B. Eerdmans, 2006), 47–48, 60–67, 169, 176–79.
26. Van Huyssteen, *Alone in the World?*, 47; cf. 66–67, 176–79, 187–93, 246–51, 318; cf. "Human Origins and Religious Awareness: In Search of Human Uniqueness," *Studia Theologica* 59 (2005): 105–106. To issue a word of caution on normative terms like "fully human," there have been several recent studies involving gene flow between Neanderthals and anatomically modern humans in Eurasian regions. At the same time, the general model for the emergence of behaviorally modern *Homo sapiens'* cognitive and cultural distinctiveness in the Upper Paleolithic remains plausible. *Homo neanderthalensis* may have borne enough genetic and behavioral similarity to *Homo sapiens* to interbreed with some of our ancestors as recently as around 45,000 BP. However, studies of the Neandertal genome, as well cranial and vocal morphology suggest that they likely could not conceptualize or communicate with the same

kinds of complexity that were emerging among *Homo sapiens*. For a summary of this line of thought, see Eric Trinkaus, "Late Neandertals and Early Modern Humans in Europe, Population Dynamics and Paleobiology," in *Continuity and Discontinuity in the Peopling of Europe: One Hundred Fifty Years of Neanderthal Study*, ed. Silvana Condemi and Gerd-Christian Weniger (Dordrecht: Springer, 2011), 315–29.

This set of hypotheses has several implications for defining and evaluating human distinctiveness. For one thing, we behaviorally modern humans may not be all that different from our extinct hominin cousin. Like the conceptual frameworks through which we construct and navigate our worlds of meanings, the boundary of human distinctiveness is porous. Under different circumstances or on other planets where life has evolved, we might not currently be "alone in the world," as van Huyssteen phrases it. Our functional distinctiveness is not only a human possibility, even if, as far as we know, it is only a human actuality. If nothing else, the contingent and evolutionary nature of human distinctiveness ought to garner humility when attempting to define its cosmic, axiological, or theological significance in relation to other species and their environments.

27. See Terrence W. Deacon, *The Symbolic Species: The Co-Evolution of Language and the Brain* (New York: W.W. Norton & Company, 1997); Steven Mithen, *The Prehistory of the Mind*; *The Singing Neanderthals: The Origins of Music, Language, Mind, and Body* (London: Weidenfeld & Nicholson, 2005); Michael Corballis, *The Truth about Language: What It Is and Where It Came From* (Chicago: University of Chicago Press, 2017).

28. Mithen, for example, uses the term *cognitive fluidity* in *The Prehistory of Mind* to describe humankind's adaptive ability to combine various behavioral and cognitive domains conceptually through symbolization, 70, 136; cf. *The Signing Neanderthals*, 263–66. Cognitive fluidity allows our species to create meanings and artifacts of a potentially limitless variety. Mithen hypothesizes that the advent of language predates and feeds into the cognitive fluidity that resulted in the rapid development of culture. By contrast, Fauconnier and Turner argue more coherently that both language and the so called creative explosion of the Upper Paleolithic period "came about once the continuous improvement of blending capacity reached the critical level of Double-Scope blending," "The Origin of Language," 147; cf. 139. Cognitively fluid minds are, to revise Mithen's hypothesis, the result of the capacity for double-scope conceptual integration.

Fauconnier and Turner's hypothesis also addresses lingering questions left by other theorists, such as Deacon. They argue that Deacon's theory of the co-evolution of language and the brain provides fuel for a false dichotomy that sometimes arises when interpreting paleoanthropological data. This false dichotomy resides in the seeming impasse between "gradualist" and "punctuated equilibrium" models of evolution, surfacing in the face of peculiar or puzzling data. To summarize, the advent of language and other singularly human forms of cognitive fluidity and creativity seems punctuated, while the genetically based encephalization process which led to the sudden emergence of the human mind and culture was almost definitely gradual. The main difficulty left by Deacon's original theory is that it includes a gradual accumulation of both vocabulary and grammar. For Fauconnier and Turner this type of development would demand the "crippling" kind of language mentioned above, because a simple grammar can only support a language bearing "separate forms and words for everything that happens in all the different domains," "The Origin of Language," 144; cf. 138.

CIT explains how a biological step can facilitate a functional leap. As it stood two decades ago, Deacon's co-evolution theory is unable to surmount the theoretical difficulty of explaining how everything human language is and does could evolve in a gradual, step-wise manner. Fauconnier and Turner conclude that when provided with the tools to explain behavioral leaps through biological steps, Deacon's theoretical framework for the co-evolution of language and the brain is basically right. They note simply that "his theory is missing an explanation of the mental operations underlying [the] relational ability" behind the biocultural emergence of behaviorally modern *Homo sapiens*, "The Origin of Language," 150. For Fauconnier and Turner, "conceptual blending is a good candidate for a continually evolving mental ability that could produce the singularity of language. This opens up new possibilities that Deacon could not have considered" when he developed his theory in *The Symbolic Species*, ibid.

29. Terrence W. Deacon and Tyrone Cashman, "The role of Symbolic Capacity in the Origins of Religion," *JSRNC* 3, no. 4 (2009): 21, 22–23; cf. Terrence W. Deacon, "The Aesthetic Faculty," in *The Artful Mind: Cognitive Science and the Riddle of Human Creativity*, ed. Mark Turner (New York: Oxford University Press, 2006): 40–52.

30. Deacon and Cashman, "The Role of Symbolic Capacity," 21. In a word, Deacon and Cashman appear to be hypothesizing about the neuro-cognitive causes of what Rudolf Otto calls an experience of the numinous as *mysterium tremendum et fascinans* in *The Idea of the Holy*, 2nd ed., trans. John W. Harvey (Oxford: Oxford University Press, 1950).

31. See Terrence W. Deacon, *Incomplete Nature: How the Mind Emerged from Matter* (New York: W. W. Norton and Company, 2012.

32. See Philip Clayton, *Mind and Emergence: From Quantum to Consciousness* (Oxford: Oxford University Press, 2004); Warren S. Brown and Nancey Murphy, eds., *Whatever Happened to the Soul: Scientific and Theological Portraits of Human Nature* (Minneapolis: Fortress Press, 1998); Denis Edwards, *Partaking of God: Trinity, Evolution, and Ecology* (Collegeville, MN: Liturgical Press, 2014), 116–29; Philip Hefner, *The Human Factor: Evolution, Culture, and Religion* (Minneapolis: Fortress, 1993); van Huyssteen, *Alone in the World*, 111–62; cf. contributions by some of these authors in Philip Clayton and Paul Davies, eds., *The Re-Emergence of Emergence: The Emergentist Hypothesis from Science to Religion* (Oxford: Oxford University Press, 2006); Nancey Murphy and William R. Stoeger SJ, eds. *Evolution and Emergence: Systems, Organisms, Persons* (Oxford: Oxford University Press, 2007).

33. See van Huyssteen, *Alone in the World*, 126–62; J. Richard Middleton, *The Liberating Image: The Imago Dei in Genesis 1* (Grand Rapids: Brazos Press, 2005); cf. Jason P. Roberts, "'Fill and Subdue'? Imaging God in New Social and Ecological Contexts," *Zygon: Journal of Religion and Science* 50, no. 1 (2015): 49.

34. As this characterization implies, these "rational" anthropologies have typically assumed a form of ontological dualism, whether of a more radical neo-Platonic

variety or a more holistic Aristotelian-Thomistic hylomorphism. In this spectrum of perspectives, one can legitimately ask whether the image of God is something that pertains to the whole person as a living body, the soul alone, or the body only with respect to the soul.

Van Huyssteen calls these traditional and highly influential characterizations of the image of God "substantive interpretations," in that they have to do with understanding the human being as a certain kind of substance bearing a nature created independently of other living species, *Alone in the World*, 126–32. Emphasized in the Protestant traditions, early Reformers like Luther emphasized Augustine's psychological analogy of Trinity in the soul's faculties of memory, understanding, and will as bearing God's image, ibid., 129. In book XIV, chapter 4 of *De Trinitate*, however, Augustine himself asserts that the image of God does not lie in these mutable powers of the soul, but in its immortal and rational nature. Admittedly, Thomas Aquinas, whose anthropology remains influential in the Catholic magisterial understanding of human distinctiveness, moves away from this neo-Platonic dualism. He concludes in questions 75–76 of the *Prima Pars* of his *Summa Theologica* that the human person who bears the image of God is an indivisible substance composed of both the matter (*hyle*) of the body and the form (*morphe*) of the rational soul. This hylomorphic conception of human nature is nonetheless at odds with the much more tenable understanding in the contemporary philosophy of science that human soulfulness, mindfulness, or spirituality emerges as a dynamic function of the living body-brain in its environment. Hylomorphism essentially reverses this causal relationship in holding that the life and development of the body-brain is animated by the already existing soul.

35. Karl Barth, *Church Dogmatics*, vol III/1, *The Doctrine of Creation*, ed. G. W. Bromiley and T. F. Torrance (Edinburgh: T & T Clark, 1958), 182 ff.

36. There are a large number of reasons to view the first eleven chapters of Genesis as a coherent textual unit, despite the diversity of source material contributing to it. Biblical scholar Andreas Schüle, for example, notes the many parallels between the creation of humankind in the Garden Narrative of Genesis 2–3 and the ancient Near Eastern "mouth opening" ceremony through which cultic images of gods were crafted. At the end of Genesis 1 (typically associated with Priestly source material) and the end of Genesis 3 (typically associated with much older Yahwist source material), the creator speaks in the first person plural to note the similarity of human creatures to the divine. This parallel is likely intentional, as it is unique to the primeval history. What is more, Shüle argues convincingly that in light of 1:26–28 and 3:22, Genesis 2–3 reads like a mythic tale narrating the creation and completion of living, autonomous images of God which outstrip the significance and capabilities of mute idols. See "Made in the 'Image of God': The Concepts of Divine Images in Gen. 1–3," *Zeitschrift für die Alttestamentliche Wissenschaft* 117, no. 1 (2005): 11–20. With respect to the concept of the divine image, another, more general reason to view the primeval history as a single textual unit is that its three direct references to the image and/or likeness of God are dispersed throughout these passages (i.e., 1:26–27; 5:1–3; 9:6) and found nowhere else in the Hebrew Bible.

37. Note that these noun forms are simplified from those found in Genesis. In the Massoritic Hebrew text, many of these terms are prefixed and suffixed with inseparable prepositions, the article, and/or pronominal forms. At the same time, the root

forms would have been both audibly and visually recognizable, especially in the original unpointed text, which did not contain spaces between words, making the prefix-suffix distinction moot.

38. J. Maxwell Miller, "In the 'Image' and 'Likeness' of God," *Journal of Biblical Literature* 91 (1972): 299–302, 304.

39. One of the strongest clues to this exegetical conclusion can be found by interpreting the use of the verb "breathed" in Genesis 2:7 in light of the way God issues life-giving breath more indirectly in Ezekiel 37:9. The latter passage is the only verse in the Hebrew Bible outside Genesis 2:7 in which the primitive Hebrew verb *naphach* means "breathe." In this famous resurrection prophesy of Ezekiel, however, it is clear that the breath or spirit that gives life comes from early winds, even if God's agency is needed to instill their life-giving quality. Given the lack of any literal reference to divine embodiment in the primeval history, in conjunction with the ubiquity of the breath of life among creatures in Genesis 6:17 and 7:22, God's seemingly direct manner of breathing in 2:7 may be closer to the more indirect divine action of Ezekiel 37 than is suggested by verb form found in the Garden Narrative.

40. Cf. Psalm 8. This Psalm contains the nearest direct reference the image of God and its royal/representational significance outside Genesis. It states that in bearing dominion with and over other creatures on God's behalf, human creatures are always "lower than *elohim*," v.5. This plural Hebrew term, often translated as *heavenly beings* or *gods*, is also the word used for the single creator "God" in Genesis 1.

41. See Gordon J. Wenham, *Word Biblical Commentary, Volume 1: Genesis 1–15* (Waco: Word Books, 1987), 29; David J. A. Clines, "The Image of God in Man," *Tyndale Bulletin* 19, no. 1 (1968): 90–92; Miller, "In the 'Image' and 'Likeness' of God," 293–94, 299–304; Graeme Auld, "*imago dei* in Genesis: Speaking in the Image of God," *Expository Times* 116, no. 8 (2005): 161.

42. See Walter Brueggemann, *Genesis: A Commentary for Teaching and Preaching* (Atlanta: John Knox Press, 1982), 31–32; Middleton, *The Liberating Image*, 88–90, 176–84; J. F. A. Sawyer, "The Meaning of 'מיהלא מלצב' in Genesis I–XI," *Journal of Theological Studies* 25 (1974): 420–21; Schüle, "Made in the 'Image of God,'" 11–20.

43. See Clines, "The Image of God in Man," 90–92; Middleton, *The Liberating Image*, 88; Sawyer, "The Meaning of 'מיהלא מלצב' in Genesis I–XI," 424–26; Van Huyssteen, *Alone in the World?*, 156–57.

44. Hefner, "Biocultural Evolution and the Created Co-Creator," 197.

45. See Jason P. Roberts, "Emerging In the Image of God to Know Good and Evil," *Zygon: Journal of Religion and Science* 46, no. 2 (2011): 471–81.

46. Hefner, *The Human Factor*, 239; cf. Roberts, "Emerging In the Image of God," 471–81; "'Fill and Subdue'?," 50.

47. Cf. Genesis 1:4, 10, 12, 18, 21, 25, 31; 2:18. Human beings are the only kind of creature in Genesis 1–3 depicted as a direct addressee of a divine pronouncement or command, 1:28; 2:16–17; 3:9 ff. The cursing of the serpent in 3:14–15 is the only exception to this pattern. However, the Garden Narrative never depicts the serpent as addressing God or becoming like God in knowing "good" and "bad" or "evil."

48. Auld, "*imago dei* in Genesis," 259–61.

49. Ibid., 162.

50. See Roberts, "'Fill and Subdue'?," 54; cf. 58–60.

51. Ian G. Barbour, *Religion and Science: Historical and Contemporary Issues* (San Francisco: Harper Collins, 1997), 100.

52. Middleton, *The Liberating Image*, 40–42.

53. See Genesis 1:28; 9:6.

54. Middleton, *The Liberating Image*, 160–67; cf. Alexander Heidel, *The Babylonian Genesis: The Story of the Creation* (Chicago: University of Chicago Press, 1963), 3–10, 13–14.

55. Middleton, *The Liberating Image*, 235–54.

56. Ibid., 66. After accepting the challenge to defeat Tiamat on the condition he is declared chief among the rebel gods, Marduk's allies test his potency by placing a constellation before him, which he destroys then recreates by speaking to it.

57. Gerhard F. Hasel, "The Significance of the Cosmology in Genesis 1 in Relation to ancient Near Eastern Parallels," *Andrews University Seminary Studies* 10, no. 1 (1972): 14.

58. See Middleton, *The Liberating Image*, 261, 264–65.

59. Ibid., 177.

60. Ibid., 161; 181–84.

61. See Roberts, "'Fill and Subdue'?," 42–63.

62. See Fauconnier and Turner, *The Way We Think*, 48.

63. Hefner, *The Human Factor*, 27, 118, 119; cf. 45, 47, 120–21, 265, 277.

64. See Middleton, *The Liberating Image*, 204–31, 244–69, 287–97; cf. Roberts, "'Fill and Subdue'?," 48–50, 55–56, 60.

65. See Genesis 3:23; John Baker, "The Myth of Man's 'Fall': A Reappraisal," *Expository Times* 92 (1981): 235–37; Phyllis A. Bird, "'Male and Female He Created Them': Genesis 1:27b in the Context of the Priestly Account of Creation," *Harvard Theological Review* 74 (1981): 129–159; Warren Malcolm Clark, "The Legal Background to the Yahwist's Use of 'Good and Evil' in Genesis 2–3," *Journal of Biblical Literature* 88 (1969): 266–78; John F. A. Sawyer, "The Image of God, The Wisdom of Serpents, and the Knowledge of Good and Evil," in *A Walk in the Garden: Biblical, Iconographical and Literary Images of Eden*, ed. Paul Morris and Deborah Sawyer (Sheffield: JSOT Press, 1992), 64–73; Schüle, "Made in the 'Image of God,'" 1–20; William N. Wilder, "Illumination and Investiture: The Royal Significance of the Tree of Wisdom in Genesis 3," *Westminster Theological Journal* 68 (2006): 51–69.

66. Bird, "'Male and Female He Created Them,'" 153.

67. Hefner, "Biocultural Evolution and the Created Co-Creator," 197.

BIBLIOGRAPHY

Auld, Graeme. "*Imago dei* in Genesis: Speaking in the Image of God." *Expository Times* 116 (2005): 259–62.

Baker, John. "The Myth of Man's 'Fall': A Reappraisal." *Expository Times* 92 (1981): 235–37.

Barbour, Ian G. *Religion and Science: Historical and Contemporary Issues*. San Francisco: Harper Collins, 1997.

Barth, Karl. *Church Dogmatics*. Vol. III/1, *The Doctrine of Creation*. Edited by G. W. Bromiley and T. F. Torrance. Edinburgh: T & T Clark, 1958.

Bird, Phyllis A. "'Male and Female He Created Them': Genesis 1:27b in the Context of the Priestly Account of Creation." *Harvard Theological Review* 74 (1981): 129–159.

Brown, Warren S. and Nancey Murphy, eds., *Whatever Happened to the Soul: Scientific and Theological Portraits of Human Nature*. Minneapolis: Fortress Press, 1998.

Clark, Warren Malcolm. "The Legal Background to the Yahwist's Use of 'Good and Evil' in Genesis 2–3." *Journal of Biblical Literature* 88 (1969): 266–78.

Clayton, Philip. *Mind and Emergence: From Quantum to Consciousness*. Oxford: Oxford University Press, 2004.

Clayton, Philip and Paul Davies, eds. *The Re-Emergence of Emergence: The Emergentist Hypothesis from Science to Religion*. Oxford: Oxford University Press, 2006.

Clines, David J.A. "The Image of God in Man." *Tyndale Bulletin* 19, no. 1 (1968): 53–103.

Corballis, Michael. *The Truth about Language: What It Is and Where It Came From*. Chicago: University of Chicago Press, 2017.

Deacon, Terrence W. "The Aesthetic Faculty." In *The Artful Mind: Cognitive Science and the Riddle of Human Creativity*. Edited by Mark Turner, 40–52. New York: Oxford University Press, 2006.

———. *Incomplete Nature: How the Mind Emerged From Matter*. New York: W. W. Norton and Company, 2012.

———. *The Symbolic Species: The Co-Evolution of Language and the Brain*. New York: W. W. Norton & Company, 1997.

Deacon, Terrence W. and Tyrone Cashman, "The Role of Symbolic Capacity in the Origins of Religion," *Journal for the Study of Religion, Nature and Culture* 3, no. 4 (2009): 1–28.

Edwards, Denis. *Partaking of God: Trinity, Evolution, and Ecology*. Collegeville, MN: Liturgical Press, 2014.

Fauconnier, Gilles, and Mark Turner. "The Origin of Language as a Product of the Evolution of Modern Cognition." In *Origin and Evolution of Languages: Approaches, Models, Paradigms*. Edited by Bernard Laks with Serge Cleuziou, Jean-Paul Demoule, and Pierre Encrevé, 133–56. London: Equinox, 2008.

———. "Principles of Conceptual Integration." In *Discourse and Cognition: Bridging the Gap*. Edited by Jean-Pierre Koenig, 269–83. Stanford, CA: CSLI Publications, 1998.

———. "Rethinking Metaphor." In *The Cambridge Handbook of Metaphor and Thought.* Edited by Raymond W. Gibbs, 53–66. New York: Cambridge University Press, 2008.

———. *The Way We Think: Conceptual Blending and the Mind's Hidden Complexities*. New York: Basic Books, 2002.

Hasel, Gerhard F. "The Significance of the Cosmology in Genesis 1 in Relation to Ancient Near Eastern Parallels." *Andrews University Seminary Studies* 10 (1972): 1–20.

Hefner, Philip. “Biocultural Evolution and the Created Co-Creator.” *Dialog* 36, no. 3 (1997): 197–205.

———. *The Human Factor: Evolution, Culture, and Religion*. Minneapolis: Fortress Press, 1993.

Heidel, Alexander. *The Babylonian Genesis: The Story of the Creation*. Chicago: University of Chicago Press, 1963.

Middleton, J. Richard. *The Liberating Image: The* Imago Dei *in Genesis 1*. Grand Rapids: Brazos Press, 2005.

Miller, J. Maxwell. “In the ‘Image’ and ‘Likeness’ of God.” *Journal of Biblical Literature* 91 (1972): 289–304.

Mithen, Steven. *The Prehistory of the Mind: The Cognitive Origins of Art, Religion, and Science*. London: Thames and Hudson: 1996.

———. *The Singing Neanderthals: The Origins of Music, Language, Mind, and Body*. London: Weidenfeld & Nicholson, 2005.

Murphy, Nancey, and William R. Stoeger SJ, eds. *Evolution and Emergence: Systems, Organisms, Persons*. Oxford: Oxford University Press, 2007.

Otto, Rudolph. *The Idea of the Holy*. 2nd ed. Translated by John W. Harvey. Oxford: Oxford University Press, 1950.

Roberts, Jason P. “Emerging in the Image of God to Know Good and Evil.” *Zygon: Journal of Religion and Science* 46, no. 2 (2011): 471–81.

———. “‘Fill and Subdue’? Imaging God in New Social and Ecological Contexts.” *Zygon: Journal of Religion and Science* 50, no. 1 (2015): 42–63.

Sawyer, John F. A. “The Image of God, The Wisdom of Serpents, and the Knowledge of Good and Evil.” In *A Walk in the Garden: Biblical, Iconographical and Literary Images of Eden*. Edited by Paul Morris and Deborah Sawyer, 64–73. Sheffield: JSOT Press, 1992.

———. “The Meaning of ‘מיהלא מלצב’ in Genesis I–XI.” *Journal of Theological Studies* 25 (1974): 418–26.

Schüle, Andreas. “Made in the ‘Image of God’: The Concepts of Divine Images in Gen 1–3.” *Zeitschrift für die Alttestamentliche Wissenschaft* 117 (2005): 1–20.

Tattersall, Ian. *Becoming Human: Evolution and Human Uniqueness*. New York: Harcourt Brace & Company, 1998.

———. *The World from Beginnings to 4000 BCE*. Oxford: Oxford University Press, 2008.

Trinkaus, Eric. “Late Neandertals and Early Modern Humans in Europe, Population Dynamics and Paleobiology,” in *Continuity and Discontinuity in the Peopling of Europe: One Hundred Fifty Years of Neanderthal Study*. Edited by Silvana Condemi and Gerd–Christian Weniger, 315–29. Dordrecht: Springer, 2011.

Van Huyssteen, J. Wentzel. *Alone in the World? Human Uniqueness in Science and Theology*. Grand Rapids: William B. Eerdmans, 2006.

———. “Human Origins and Religious Awareness: In search of Human Uniqueness.” *Studia Theologica* 59 (2005): 104–28.

Wenham, Gordon J. *Word Biblical Commentary, Volume 1: Genesis 1–15*. Waco: Word Books, Publisher, 1987.

Wilder, William N. “Illumination and Investiture: The Royal Significance of the Tree of Wisdom in Genesis 3.” *Westminster Theological Journal* 68 (2006): 51–69.

Chapter Five

Kenosis as a Pauline Metaphor within a Double-Scope Blend

Christopher M. Hadley, SJ

The word *kenosis* has had a complex history in recent theological discourse. For some people it denotes self-giving love poured out for the sake of others. For others it is a baptizing of masochism, a kind of sacralized self-annihilation in accordance with imbalanced religious norms. The noun *kénōsis* is biblically rooted in a passage from Paul's letter to the Philippians (2:7), a complex and nuanced text in itself. My thesis in this chapter is that *kénōsis* is most fruitfully interpreted in its original New Testament context of the letter to the Philippians and other Pauline letters, and that this reading is enhanced in light of recent cognitive linguistic studies.

More particularly, my claim is that *kénōsis* is best interpreted as the product of a complex metaphoric process called a double-scope blend that operates in Paul's thinking in Philippians. There is more than one layer of blending in Paul's use of *kénōsis*, the most fundamental of which is found in the inspired New Testament proclamation that "Jesus is Lord" in Philippians 2:11. The blend JESUS IS LORD places the human and the divine together by identifying Jesus's name with a title for God. The more localized double-scope blend of which *kénōsis* is a part involves a word from chapter 3 of Philippians (3:13), *epéktasis* in Greek,[1] often rendered "straining forward" in English. The thesis is that the self-emptying to which Paul refers in Philippians 2:7 must always be held in creative tension with both the exaltation of 2:11 and the straining for the "prize" of eternal life in 3:13–14. The proposed blend is therefore given as KÉNŌSIS IS EPÉKTASIS.[2] I further suggest that this complex network of double-scope blending is also operative in the work of a modern kenotic theologian, the twentieth-century Swiss writer Hans Urs von Balthasar. He is a controversial but ultimately fruitful modern thinker whose trinitarian theology and Christology can, and should, be retrieved by virtue of the blend KÉNŌSIS IS EPÉKTASIS. The rationale for the study is inspired by the pastoral urgency of a New Testament theology that speaks to those who suffer oppression in any form.

In the first section of the essay I provide some background on double-scope blends in the work of Robert Masson. Masson provides the paradigmatic double-scope blend (JESUS IS THE MESSIAH) from which all those I propose take their form. I then proceed to exegeses of Philippians 2:5–11 and 3:7–16 to bring out the meanings of key terms such as JESUS, LORD, KÉNŌSIS, and EPÉKTASIS. The last part consists of an analysis of key areas in Balthasar's Christology and trinitarian theology together with commentary on some of his significant critics in light of double-scope blend theory.

ON DOUBLE-SCOPE BLENDS IN THEOLOGICAL RESEARCH

In his book *Without Metaphor, No Saving God*, Robert Masson proposes JESUS IS THE MESSIAH as a theological example of a metaphoric process called a *double-scope blend*. A double-scope blend occurs when input from two different and formerly incompatible fields of meaning are mapped together to create a new field of meaning allowing for new metaphors, new conceptualizations, new questions, and new knowledge. The religious claim that JESUS IS THE MESSIAH forces a new equivalence between a carpenter who was crucified as a criminal and Israel's hopes for redemption and the restoration of their kingdom. Robert Masson's diagramming of this equivalence is figure 5.1.[3]

Masson describes the context and process of the new equivalence's emergence:

> Rather the first Christians' claim tectonically reconfigures the meaning of "Messiah," the identity of Jesus, and the field of meanings associated with messianic hope and God's relation to Israel. Affirming that Jesus is the Messiah makes possible logical moves otherwise unavailable and lays the groundwork for later moves otherwise unthinkable. It inaugurates a new worldview—ultimately a new religion. This tectonic reconfiguration of the fields of meanings is the fundamental characteristic of the process Mary Gerhart and Allan Russell call "metaphoric."[4]

The operative sense of *metaphoric* here is that of "a conceptual process underlying a wide range of expressions such as metaphor, metonymy, and analogy that are typically described as figurative."[5] Masson defines the double-scope blend JESUS IS THE MESSIAH as *tectonic* because it signifies something deeper than a relevant likeness or analogy between two things. In this blend, the one field of input, JESUS, is not simply applied to another field, MESSIAH,

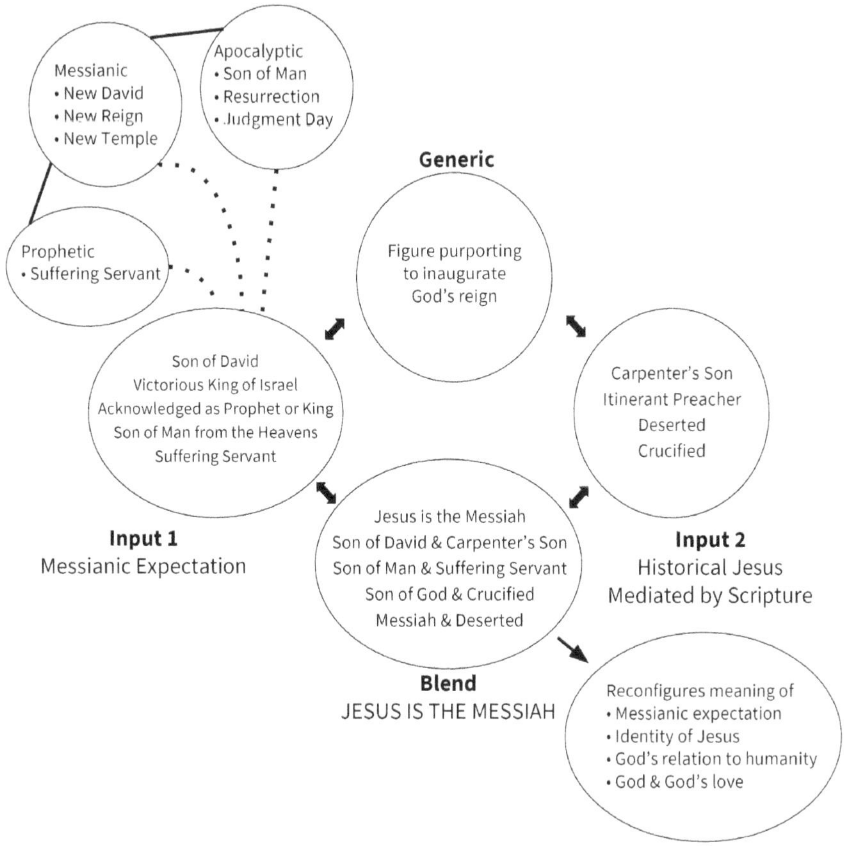

Figure 5.1. JESUS IS THE MESSIAH **from Robert Masson "Are Aquinas and Whitehead Metaphorical and Analogical All the Way Down?"** ***Open Theology*** **1 (2015), 531.**

in a way that facilitates a new understanding of the latter or vice versa as in a single-scope blend. Rather, the tectonic overlapping of the two fields creates an entirely new field of meaning—a new continent as it were—that radically changes the meanings of the original two terms, JESUS and MESSIAH.[6] This blend reconfigures meanings of messianic expectation, the identity of Jesus, God's relation to humanity, the very person of God, and the nature of God's love for the world. In particular, the figure of Jesus of Nazareth is reconfigured as salvific, that is, able to effect a new wholeness in sinful and broken persons and communities in a way that has eschatological or everlasting significance. The concept of *messiah* is reconfigured as someone who must go through the process of being rejected by the world in order to enter definitively into his domain, which is inclusive of a broader reality than previously expected.

Sometimes these combined inputs are already fairly rich metaphoric fields of meaning that result in even richer ones, which Gilles Fauconnier and Mark Turner have called integration networks.[7] In Masson's double-scope blend, JESUS IS THE MESSIAH, the resulting field of meaning forms the structure for the entire Christian revelatory and theological linguistic system; the former fields of meaning are realigned so that all doctrine, spirituality, and morality are rooted in an integration network made possible by the blend. The cognitive processes involved in the blend now function from a higher viewpoint. Masson's hypothesis is that "*there is no saving God without conceptual mappings that are metaphorical (cross-domain) and that entail tectonic equivalence (or double-scope integration)*."[8] What is salvific about this "saving God" is now seen in terms of the reconfiguration of JESUS and MESSIAH in the double-scope blend: the experience of divine forgiveness is now possible because the life of the man Jesus is now seen to have eternal and universal significance by its mapping with *messiah*, and the domain of this Messiah is now seen to include everyone everywhere, including those rejected and condemned by society for whatever reason and even those who do the rejecting.

With this background in place, the following exegeses of the two passages in Paul will highlight the terms to be included in the blends that I am proposing.

EXEGESIS OF PHILIPPIANS 2:5–11 AND 3:7–16

Chapters 2 and 3 of the canonical NT book of Philippians are probably separated at the abrupt shift in tone that occurs at 3:2 as parts of two different original letters to the same audience.[9] In this view the first letter would be an exhortation to continue in spiritual growth as a community and the second a stark warning against false prophets who try to impose Mosaic law on the community. Any kind of blend of terms drawn from these two contexts of separate letters would have to be a theological construction based on the canonical unity of Philippians, but this is not necessarily at odds with the senses of the two words in their contexts of Paul's two exhortations to the Philippian community to be of the same mind with each other and with Christ. The first of the two passages to be exegeted introduces the notion of *kénōsis* and the proclamation "Jesus Christ is Lord." The second introduces the notion of *epéktasis*.

Philippians 2:5–11: KÉNŌSIS and the Divine Name

5Let the same mind be in you [*phroneite*] that was in Christ Jesus,

6who, though he was in the form of God,
did not regard equality with God as something to be grasped* [*harpagmòn*],[10]

7but emptied himself [*eautòn ekénōsen*],
taking the form of a slave, being born in human likeness.
And being found in human form,
8he humbled himself and became obedient to the point of death—
even death on a cross.

9Therefore God also highly exalted him
and gave him the name that is above every name,
10so that at the name of Jesus every knee should bend,
in heaven and on earth and under the earth,
11and every tongue should confess
that Jesus Christ is Lord,
to the glory of God the Father.

The NRSV translation given above closely follows the Greek text decided upon in both Nestle-Aland (NA27) and Bruce Metzger's *Textual Commentary*.[11] The wider context of the passage is Paul's reflection that it would be more conducive to the Philippians'' joy and progress in the faith for him to "remain in the flesh" (1:24–25) even though his "desire is to depart and be with Christ, for that is far better" (1:23). And yet, if he remains "in the flesh" and visits them, he will be able to "share abundantly in [their] boasting in Christ Jesus" (1:26). In the chapter following the pericope above to be analyzed in the next section, Paul exhorts the community to persevere in progress out of hope for the "goods" they will receive (3:13–14). The form of the pericope is most likely a hymn, excepting the first verse (5), which I have set off as an introduction. Paul may not have composed this hymn but he clearly had rhetorical intentions for it as an enhancement of his exhortation to the community to a union of hearts and minds, which is the purpose of the whole letter. The imperative verb in v.5, *phroneite* or "have the same mind," which is the same verb used at the beginning of the present chapter (2:2) as well as in the next (3:15), implies more than just rational deliberation but rather a determining mindset.[12]

The verb *ekénōsen*, the aorist form of the verb *kenóō*, occurs in v.7 combined with the reflexive pronoun *eautòn*: "he emptied himself." Within the context of Philippians 2:5–11, this verb and reflexive pronoun has yielded the traditional theological concept of *kénōsis* or self-emptying. The verb could also mean "negate" or "make vain,"[13] and in the context of the hymn it could also carry a sense of vulnerability and a lack of power vis-à-vis being "in the form of God" (*en morphē theou*) and having "equality with God" (*tò einai* ísa *theo*). The sense of vulnerability or lack of power would suggest either "something to be grasped" or "something to be exploited" for *harpagmòn* in v.7, the latter of which the NRSV uses. I have changed it to "something to be grasped," a more literal sense that accords more directly with the opposite sense of *eautòn ekénōsen* as "he emptied himself." A similar opposition occurs between the verbs *etapeínōsen*, "he humbled himself," in v.8 and *huperúpsōsen*, "God highly exalted him," in v.9.[14] In the resulting parallel structure, Jesus's and God's actions form a complement of humility and exaltation, of renunciation and possession. These analogous counter-movements also correspond to the emptying of a visible divine form in vv.6–7 and the bestowal of equality with the divine name *Lord* upon Jesus's own name in v.9 and v.11.

The word *Lord* in the text is, of course, ambiguous. It translates *kúrios*, which means "sir" or "master" in addressing a man, and is found in many instances in the Septuagint (LXX), in the NT, and throughout Greek literature of all ages. It could also be an epithet for a god, corresponding to many other ancient Semitic titles that bear the same ambiguity. *Kúrios* was often the substitute for the divine name "I Am" or *eigō eimi* in the LXX.[15] It would have been unthinkable for Paul as a first-century Jew committed to monotheism to state directly and unambiguously that "Jesus is God," but the ambiguity suggested by the word *Lord* served a positive function in conveying meaning in the ancient world.[16] Paul's extensive use of "Lord" is therefore not a simple ascription of a title to Jesus but rather the proclamation of Jesus's true identity as the proper recipient of divine worship,[17] of which Phil 2:10–11 is the most prominent example.

There is a parallel with the title *Lord* in Johannine literature in Jesus's investiture with the divine name in the so-called "High-Priestly Prayer." Here the divine name has to do with Jesus's "frequent use of the divine self-referential formula *egō eimi* (I Am)."[18] The text of John 17:11–12 saturates the rest of the Gospel text with an explanatory power that guides the interpretation of many of that texts key narrative features: "Holy Father, protect them in your name that you have given me, so that they may be one, as we are one. While I was with them, I protected them in your name that you have given me." Given the theological parallel with Philippians 2, as far as Jesus is "in the form of God" and "equal with God," his exaltation involves the manifestation of his name as *Lord*. Larry Hurtado writes in his study of first-century Christologies, *Lord Jesus Christ: Devotion to Jesus in Earliest Christianity*:

> To speak of Jesus as invested with the divine name, as coming with and in the name of God, as given the name, and as manifesting God's name in his own words and actions, was to portray Jesus as bearing and exhibiting God in the most direct way possible in the conceptual categories available in the biblical tradition, and within the limits of the monotheistic commitment of that tradition.[19]

Considering JESUS IS LORD as a double-scope blend of a tectonic nature reveals how John's investiture of Jesus with the divine name must now be seen in terms of Paul's hymn in Philippians, that is, in light of *kénōsis*, obedience, and the cross, in figure 5.2.

The emptied, humiliated, and publically executed man JESUS (the first field) is mapped together with the very One in the form of God Who is endowed with the divine name itself, LORD (the second field). These two terms, JESUS and LORD, now reconstitute each other in the Christian experience of revelation and enable the emergence of the symbolic worlds of divine-incarnational Christology, of a soteriology characterized by Christ's own humble service and self-giving love, and of (what is now seen as) trinitarian orthodoxy in the early church. JESUS and LORD are now conceptually linked by way of Jesus's exaltation, which is the Father's glorification of him for the Father's own

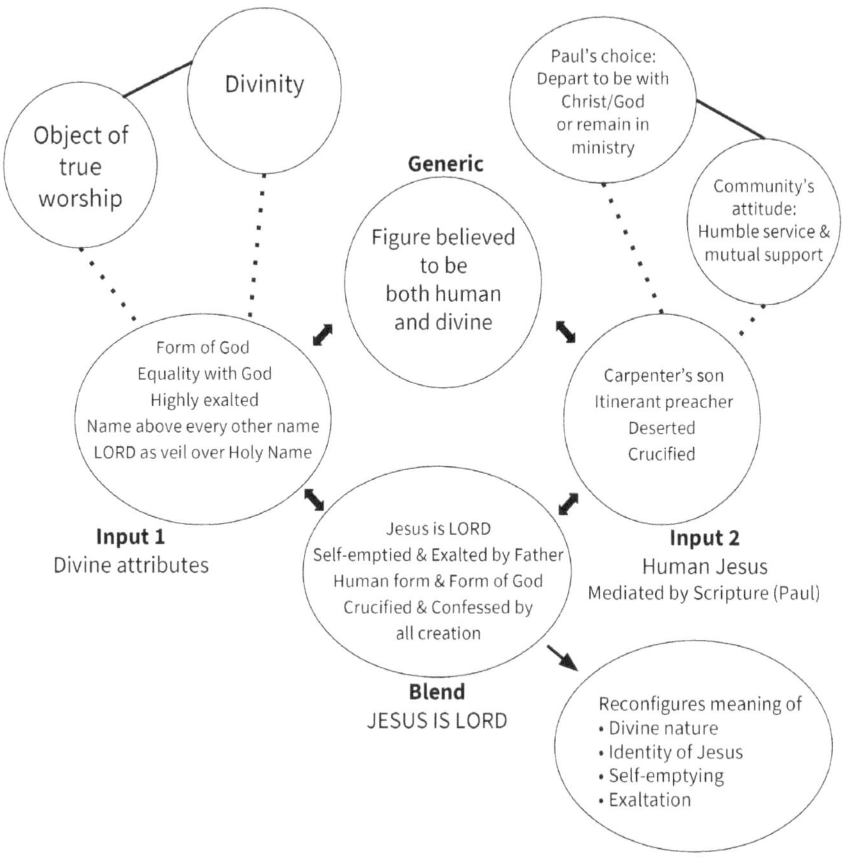

Figure 5.2. JESUS IS LORD **in Phil 2**

glory. God's (the Father's) spiritual exaltation of the incarnate Son corresponds to what Paul calls the "prize" and "heavenly calling" of the Christian in Philippians 3, to which I now turn.

Philippians 3:7–16: EPÉKTASIS and Receiving a "Prize"

Both chapter 2 and chapter 3 of Philippians contain exhortations, the latter being Paul's warning to the community against Judaizers that have evidently come among them. The second pericope in chapter 3 contrasts with the heavily theological focus of the first pericope from Philippians 2 in its emphasis on the attitude that Paul seeks to inculcate in the community:

> 7Yet whatever gains I had, these I have come to regard as loss because of Christ.
> 8More than that, I regard everything as loss because of the surpassing value of
> knowing [*gnōseōs*] Christ Jesus my Lord. For his sake I have suffered the loss
> of all things, and I regard them as rubbish, in order that I may gain Christ 9and
> be found in him, not having a righteousness of my own that comes from the law,
> but one that comes through faith in Christ, the righteousness from God based on
> faith. 10I want to know Christ and the power of his resurrection and the sharing
> of his sufferings by becoming like him in his death, 11if somehow I may attain
> the resurrection from the dead.
>
> 12Not that I have already obtained this or have already been perfected*
> [*teteleíōmai*]; but I press on to make it my own, because Christ Jesus has made
> me his own. 13Beloved, I do not consider that I have made it my own; but this
> one thing I do: forgetting what lies behind and straining forward [*epekteinómenos*] to what lies ahead, 14I press on towards the goal for the prize of the heav-
> enly call of God in Christ Jesus. 15Let those of us then who are mature be of the
> same mind [*phronōmen*]; and if you think differently about anything, this too
> God will reveal to you. 16Only let us hold fast to what we have attained.

The only significant textual issue in this pericope arises in 3:12 where some copyists have put "have declared myself righteous" in place of *teteleíōmai*, "have been perfected," perhaps to tone down any possible implication of actively attaining some kind of perfection.[20] The NRSV renders *teteleíōmai* as "reached the goal," which is also possible and accords with the ascetical tone and athletic imagery of the rest of the passage.

What Paul has "lost" in v.7 is any confidence in his observance of Torah as a means of salvation. The "knowing" of "Christ Jesus my Lord" in v.8 suggests a deep intimacy and not a mere acquaintance, much less the possession of information about someone.[21] This kind of knowing is the basis for the faith that he speaks of in v.9, a deep existential orientation toward and dependence on the person of Christ. The knowing includes "sharing in his sufferings by becoming like him in his death" in v.10, which bears strong resonances with

Christ's own *kénōsis* in the previous chapter (2:8). In 3:16 Paul does not want the community to lose what they have gained, which is this intimate knowledge of Jesus as Lord (v.8) and the "righteousness from God based on faith" (v.9) that obviates all self-righteousness based on Torah observance.

And yet there is something worth striving for toward which Paul exhorts his readers. The key word comes in v.13, *epekteinómenos*, which I have kept as "straining forward" along with the RSV, NRSV, and NAB. The verb *ekteínō* can have the sense of a tensed resoluteness and eagerness, suggesting athletic effort and eventually occurring as the designation of certain prayer litanies in Byzantine liturgy (as in "ekteny").[22] This is consistent with the athletic imagery of v.14, according to which I have translated *tēs anō klēseōs* as an "upward calling" as toward a stage in an award ceremony to receive one's prize (*brabeion*) after a competition (the NRSV has "heavenly calling"). Paul exhorts the people in 3:15 as he does in 2:5 to think the same way and have the same mind (the verb is *phronéo* in both verses) regarding this *epéktasis*. The self-emptying of Christ out of love for God and others is to govern their communal mindset; but because of God's promise and love for them, striving *together* for the goal of eternal life is also to govern their thinking.

The Blend KÉNŌSIS IS EPÉKTASIS

If JESUS IS LORD is truly a double-scope blend, then *kénōsis* and *epéktasis* mutually interpret each other in Paul's letter to the Philippians by implication of the new field established. The resulting double-scope blend would be KÉNŌSIS IS EPÉKTASIS, figure 5.3.

The opposing dynamics of *kénōsis* vs. *epéktasis*, self-emptying vs. attaining a prize, generosity to others vs. desire for one's own goal in their respective input fields can be held together in a creative tension in the blend. But without the blend, each metaphor risks suggesting an isolated movement that is distorted without the other: *kénōsis* would be spiritualized masochism and *epéktasis* would be spiritualized ambition or greed. Paul's exhortation of his readers to "be of the same mind" thus allows the community to exist in response to Christ's *kénōsis* through an act of *epéktasis* "toward the fullness of his form."[23] KÉNŌSIS IS EPÉKTASIS makes possible the language for a path of growth for both the individual believer and for the community.

The larger goal of this essay is to show how the fuller theological meaning of the new blend I have proposed, KÉNŌSIS IS EPÉKTASIS, emerges in what could be a double-scope blend of the two double-scope blends, JESUS IS LORD and KÉNŌSIS IS EPÉKTASIS, figure 5.4.

The first blend is interpreted by the second, and vice versa. *Kénōsis* first characterizes Jesus's attitude and then the individual Christian's and the

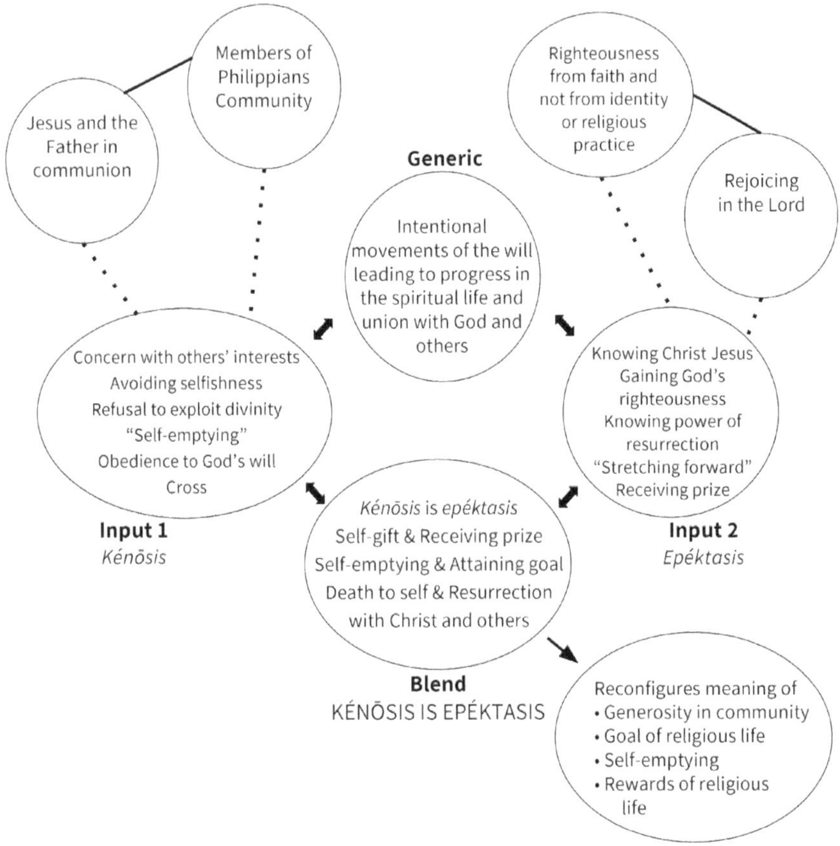

Figure 5.3. KÉNŌSIS IS EPÉKTASIS

Church's attitudes. *Epéktasis* is more directly applicable to the Christian and the Church (as creaturely entities), but in Hans Urs von Balthasar's thinking it also characterizes God in an analogical sense. His short book *Heart of the World* is characteristic of what I consider to be a fundamental movement in his thought, in which the symbol of the cross functions together with the image of *epéktasis* as a mode of divine self-expression:

> The very form of the Cross, extending out into the four winds, always told the ancient Church that the Cross means solidarity: its outstretched arms would gladly embrace the universe. According to the *Didache*, the Cross is *sēmeion epektaseōs*, a "sign of expansion," and only God himself can have such a wide reach: "On the Cross God stretched out his hands to encompass the bounds of the universe" (Cyril of Jerusalem). "In his suffering God stretched out his arms

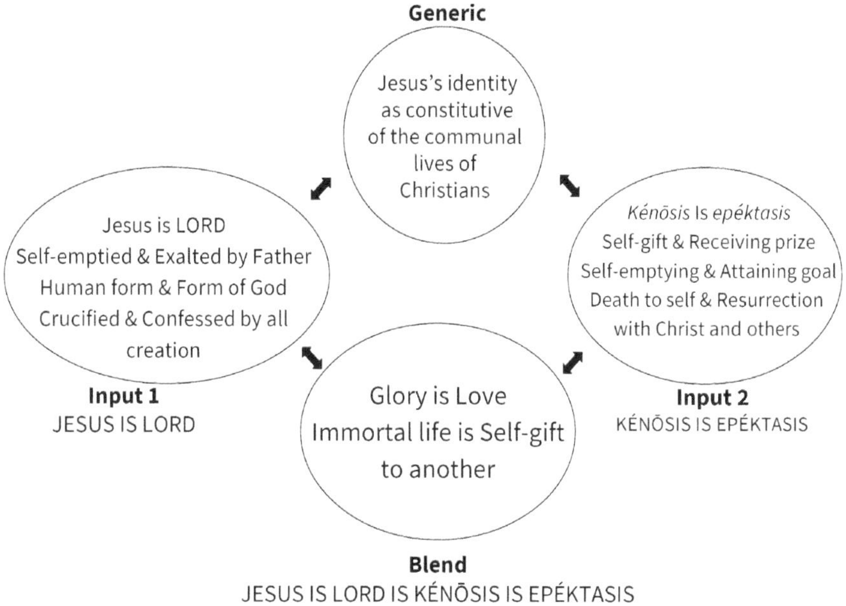

Figure 5.4. Blending JESUS IS LORD and KÉNŌSIS IS EPÉKTASIS

> and embraced the world, thus prefiguring the coming of a people which would, from East to West, gather under his wings" (Lactantius).[24]

This brief series of patristic aphorisms sets the tone and establishes the theme of the entire book. Here the triune God performs an *epéktasis* toward the world out of love via the Son's own act of *kénōsis*, the language for which movement is made possible by the historical and/or spiritual *event* of Jesus's manifestation as LORD to the individual Christian and to the Church. The blend JESUS IS LORD is essential to understanding how *kénōsis* and *epéktasis* condition one another, but now *kénōsis* and *epéktasis* are also theologically essential to understanding the way *Lord* and *Jesus* mutually interpret each other. The claim is that the emergent character of the human language here reflects how the blend of blends makes higher levels of theological thought possible.

JESUS IS LORD is a theological statement, and so its causal priority as a blend vis-à-vis the more anthropologically and psychologically based blend of KÉNŌSIS IS EPÉKTASIS might best be understood in terms of Christology and pneumatology. First, regarding Christology, the blend of the blend appears to be governed by yet another blend, JESUS'S LIFE IS OUR LIFE. In this single-scope blend, the new meaning of the second input field (OUR LIFE) is now determined by the first (JESUS'S LIFE) but not the other way around.

Jesus's life now determines the fullest meaning of our life, but he conforms to the limitations of our life ultimately and only as an expression of God's generosity (Philippians 2:6–8). That is to say, the origin of meaning for his own life—and ours by extension—lies in God and not in our humanity. This could be seen as a Johannine Christology rooted in the Last Supper Discourse (John 13–16) and the High Priestly Prayer (John 17), where Jesus speaks of the disciples as extensions of him as branches are of a vine, who live now by the very life that he has imparted to them from the Father.

The unity of vine and branches in John's Gospel relates directly to the second aspect of the theological explanation of the single-scope blend JESUS'S LIFE IS OUR LIFE, which can be seen in Paul's theology of the Holy Spirit in the first letter to the Corinthians. Paul begins the section of 1 Corinthians 11:17–13:13 with a rebuke of the Corinthians for their lack of discernment regarding their unity as Christ's Body and the resulting segregation of rich from poor at the Lord's Supper (11:17–22). The reference to Jesus's eucharistic "institution narrative" ("this is my body that is for you… this cup is the new covenant in my blood"; 11:23–26) is set squarely in the context of Paul's advocacy for the poor in their community. He proceeds by insisting on the need to examine one's own participation in the Supper according to Jesus's command and according to the dictates of one's own conscience regarding one's participation in building community (11:28–29). His claim that one can proclaim JESUS IS LORD only under the influence of the Holy Spirit (12:3) goes hand in hand with his list of the Spirit's gifts for building up the body and with his relativization of the value of those gifts under the absolute condition of how they express love (12:4–13:13). The practice of the Lord's Supper according to the Risen Jesus's intention and the Spirit's influence takes place in a context of mutual self-giving between members of a community, or communion (*koinonia*) as Paul would call it. Paul's exhortation takes its context and gains its force from this intersubjective, liturgical, and eucharistic mentality. One only overcomes one's natural compulsions to indulge and exclude by means of God's self-offering in the person of Christ and the gifts of the Holy Spirit. The proclamation of JESUS IS LORD is therefore an expression of the person's "ultimate concern," as Lutheran theologian Paul Tillich puts it, but it is also a statement of one's new relation to the God of Jesus Christ and through that relation to all others in the community.

Paul's Christology and pneumatology in 1 Corinthians are therefore consistent with his teaching on self-emptying or *kénōsis* in Philippians: Jesus the divine Son is revealed in the form of a servant, the Divine One who emptied himself out of obedience to the Father but also out of love for others, producing in the believer the paradoxical conviction that JESUS IS LORD. The implication of the presence of the Spirit in the proclamation that JESUS IS LORD also suggests that it is the Spirit who offers the goods of the Kingdom. The individual Christian and the corporate body of the community are called to extend all care, intentionality, and even passionate desire toward these goods—that is, toward eternal life with the risen Christ and each other—even as they offer their lives in love for each other and for God in *kénōsis*. In Gregory of Nyssa's terms, the mind of Christ is one of the "goods" to be desired by the soul in its *epéktasis* toward the risen life with Christ, only to be had when one empties oneself in humbleness of heart and in imitation of Christ who emptied himself for the benefit of others.[25] This was the very "mind that was in Christ" (Philippians 2:5), albeit a very human Christ at the point of death as he joined himself in suffering and longing for the Kingdom with the Good Thief on the cross in Luke's passion narrative: "Truly I tell you, today you will be with me in Paradise" (Luke 23:42).

What follows is a consideration of how the biblical-metaphoric blend KÉNŌSIS IS EPÉKTASIS operates, somewhat imperfectly, as a backdrop to the thought of one prominent modern theologian who is heavily influenced by the Christology of Philippians.

HANS URS VON BALTHASAR, *KÉNŌSIS*, AND CURRENT THEOLOGICAL DISCOURSE

In my exegeses of the two Philippians passages and analyses of the conceptual blends JESUS IS LORD and KÉNŌSIS IS EPÉKTASIS, I have sought to show how the triune relations are characterized by Christ's *kénōsis*, seen not only as an event in God but also between God and the cosmos. The God-world relation, which both Paul and Balthasar see as grounded in the triune relations, is characterized by both *kénōsis* and *epéktasis* and can thus serve as the attitude or "mind" that Paul wants to inculcate in the Christian community. But positive readings of *kénōsis* in scripture and the Christian tradition have been far from universal in the history of Christian theology and pastoral practice.

Balthasar's theology offers possibilities for a retrieval of his own work and of *kénōsis* based on the blend KÉNŌSIS IS EPÉKTASIS. His sometimes wildly imaginative thought has also provided material for critics who are suspicious of *kénōsis*. If the sense of *kénōsis* as qualified by *epéktasis* in a double-scope blend that I have proposed here were the only operational feature of Balthasar's theology, it would perhaps be more plainly evident to more people and might have precluded many of the controversies and criticisms that we now have. Balthasar's kenoticism becomes controversial when what is expected in the Christian community is increasingly, and unintentionally, construed in earthly and culture-bound terms and then projected back onto

God, thus disturbing the logic of the blend. A look at the main contours of Balthasar's kenoticism and its critics will provide a fuller context for considering the possibilities of my proposed blends.

Critiques of Balthasar

It must be admitted that the "minds" that have been historically transmitted in churches have not always been governed by the conceptual blends that I have seen at work in Paul, and thus might not qualify as "the mind that was in Christ Jesus" (Phil 2:5). Some of these negative attitudes have been cryptically operational in Balthasar's own kenotic theology, undermining its more positive aspects. Some feminist critics point to understandings and appropriations of *kénōsis* that threaten women's sense of self and agency within patriarchal systems.[26] Tina Beattie's argument in *New Catholic Feminism* is that Balthasar's kenotic trinitarian theology is based on an irredeemably patriarchal theological anthropology that places the masculine in a violent and dominant position vis-à-vis the feminine.[27] It is true that in *Theo-Drama, Vol. III: Person in Christ* Balthasar reads an ontological, and not just temporal, "priority" of men over women into the creation account of Genesis 2:4–25.[28] He then maps this gender binary on to Christ's masculine relationship to a feminine church and a feminine soul based on Ephesians 3:25–33, and from this he extrapolates wildly in *Theo-Drama, Vol. V: The Last Act* with regard to the trinitarian relations among the ultimately "hyper-masculine" and "active" Father and the primarily "hyper-feminine" and "passive" Son and Spirit.[29] In such a divine ontology the idea of *kénōsis* is particularly risky to women and to any subjugated persons when read back into Christ's humiliation on the cross in Philippians as a model of discipleship. Daphne Hampson, writing from a post-Christian perspective in response to prevalent notions of *kénōsis* in the tradition, wishes to abolish it altogether from theological discourse as a hopelessly masochistic concept.[30] It is as if the dominant person's *kénōsis* or pseudo-self-emptying were hiding, at best, a patriarchal condescension to the other and a cryptic instrumentalism with regard to the dominant's own self-cultivation, while the submissive is called upon in his or her *kénōsis* in response to empty out even the little that he or she has for the dominant. Hampson's point regarding *kénōsis* as an expression of the moral demands of love incumbent upon those who are oppressed is that self-emptying makes no sense if their very selves are unjustly embattled from the start.[31] The possibilities for mutual love and growth in relationship are precluded by the existence of any kind of hierarchy, which is inextricably linked both to gender difference and to an understanding of *kénōsis* that imports suffering and violence into God. Greek Orthodox theologian Aristotle Papanikolaou agrees that, under these conditions, critics of *kénōsis* and of Balthasar are right to be suspicious of "an ethic of *kenosis*."[32] The more loving and truly moral imperative for the victim of abuse would be, in such a case, to maintain oneself in the face of unjust opposition and to take on one's rightful role in co-determining reality with others.

Linn Marie Tonstad, a constructive theologian at Yale Divinity School, provides a contemporary interpretation of Karl Rahner's axiom, "the economic Trinity is the immanent Trinity" in her critique of Balthasar's *Theo-Drama*:

> God's being is in God's action, which means that what is said about God's modes of self-relation cannot contradict the kinds of relationships that are established by God's action in the world. Jesus preaches the kingdom of God, but it is a kingdom without masters and servants, which manifests the logic of friendship without flattening the difference beyond difference. The logic of that kingdom is a logic of superabundance, or better, an economy of plenitude.[33]

Tonstad pursues this logic of superabundance at greater length in her book, *God and Difference*,[34] via a focus on Christ's resurrection and the coming resurrection of all, seen in light of Christ's transformation of sinful human relations mired in the economy of lack and competition. Although she is open to some renewed and carefully qualified understandings of *kénōsis*, the concept generally does not play a positive role in her vision of trinitarian theology. Too often, she says, *kénōsis* has been responsible for the destructive and masochistic currents of interpersonal economies of lack.

Balthasar can and must be challenged on his consistency in how he appropriates this Pauline kenoticism. Adrienne von Speyr speaks of "the weakness of the Son in *shéol*" as an expression of the Son's kenotic relation to the Father even in the immanent Trinity,[35] a position that Balthasar adopts as his own in *Mysterium Paschale*, *Theo-Drama IV: The Action*,[36] and *Theo-Drama V*. Both Speyr and Balthasar interpret this image from Holy Saturday to mean that the kenotic, self-emptying passivity of Christ in death as he waits to be raised up by the Father expresses something positive in his relation to the Father from eternity, but Beattie and Tonstad suspect that such imagery valorizes masochism as a response to oppression. In a masochistic or crypto-nihilist appropriation of *kénōsis*, one's Christology and soteriology become accordingly dubious and dangerously unorthodox: Jesus would be said to annihilate himself, almost in suicide, in order for the Father's will—and thus the Father's very person—to be somehow fulfilled. That this would constitute human salvation or a foundation for spiritual and moral life would be incoherent and abhorrent.

My argument in this essay has been that *kénōsis* is in fact a part of Paul's own theology of God's "superabundance." Paul calls the Philippian and Corinthian communities to nurture relationships that respond more adequately to God's generous action in the world and do not merely perpetuate the byproducts of worldly hierarchicalism. The Christ-centered *kénōsis* that he imagines for his communities is also an *epéktasis* toward the fullness of life as a member of Christ's body in communion with others, not in competition with them.

A Pauline Retrieval of Balthasar's Kenoticism

Although it is certainly an attitude and a "mind" to be adopted and imitated that is held by the human being, Jesus of Nazareth, *kénōsis* is also an act that originates in the eternal Son's sharing fully in the divine will to reconcile the world to God. As Tonstad also says (in the quotation above), "God's being is in God's action." Such is Ignatius of Loyola's interpretation of the incarnation in his *Spiritual Exercises*,[37] which has had its influence on the former Jesuit Balthasar. Just as Karl Barth argues that Jesus makes known the "whole God" across the "all-encompassing" (*umgreifenden*) distance between the eternal Son's procession from the Father and the incarnate Son's death on the cross, Balthasar argues that this "all-encompassing distance" is "sufficient" to make known the Father's "whole name."[38] *Kénōsis* is an aesthetic manifestation of God's being, of God's way of being, and thus it is neither a change in God's being nor, at bottom, an alienation of the Son from the Father.[39] Balthasar's sense of "theological aesthetics," which I use here, indicates the structuring of a person's spiritual and intellectual perception that originates from within God. Since *kénōsis* is a divine *Self*-manifestation, this aesthetic structuring of the believer's perception is grounded not in any preconceived objectivity but in God's own subjectivity. The most surprising thing about Christianity, theologically speaking, is not that Jesus is God. It is rather that God, the Lord, has expressed God's Self as Jesus.

For Balthasar, the eternal Son does not lose the divine nature either in whole or in part in his self-emptying and human incarnation. Lucy Gardner and David Moss name *kénōsis*, and more particularly "the *kenosis* of the Son prefigured in the *Urkenosis* of the Father" as the central theme in Balthasar's thought around which all other themes revolve in an increasingly deepening symbolism.[40] His borrowing of Russian Orthodox theologian Sergei Bulgakov's idea of the "primal kenosis" or *Ur-Kenosis* (Balthasar's term) of the Father out to the Persons of the Son and Spirit in generation and spiration serves the purpose of illustrating the core feature of God's Self-expression as God: the triune act of being of the eternally generating Father, the eternally "being-generated" Son, the eternally spirating Father and Son, and the eternally "being-spirated" Spirit. Balthasar conceives of these four sets of relations, expressed in their Latin-Western formulation, as sets of mutual kenoses between and among divine persons that constitute one act of being in the Godhead.

The Son's incarnation is a *kénōsis* of one of the Trinity so that God might enter the non-divine realm with other human beings. Jesus's cross is both a self-expression of God and an event in history, revealing in an earthly mode what Balthasar calls a trinitarian "process." Jesus's sensible, incarnate, aesthetic relation to the Father is a symbolic representation of God's freedom in the salvific-economic decision to reconcile the world on the cross: "In this whole process lies that which Jesus calls his glorification through the Spirit [John 16:14], which is nothing other than the bringing to light of the love that lies in obedience, of the identity with the loving Father that lies in the distance," as he says in his New Testament theology, *Glory of the Lord VII: The New Covenant*.[41] Balthasar further defends his theological use of "process" in *Theo-Drama V: The Last Act*, where he investigates "the dynamic relationship between creature and Creator, or the way in which *becoming* is rooted in absolute *Being*."[42] Saying what "process" is in reference to God requires, first of all, a stipulation that it is not a univocal term applied to both God and human beings. God does not need the world to trigger some cruciform mechanism by which God can truly become God. The meta-symbol of *Ur-Kenosis*, the "super-kenosis" of the Father's Self-emptying to the Son in the Godhead, does not constitute a loss of the Godhead by God but rather the will and "mode" of the Father's being: the Father will be God *only* as the Father of the Son and the Spirator of the Spirit. Likewise, the Son will only be God as the Son of the Father, and so on. But the blend KÉNŌSIS IS EPÉKTASIS suggests that the element of "process" in the analogy for the dynamism of God's triune life is also *epéktasis*, in that the divine persons move toward each other in what the Greek theologians called *perichoresis* and the Latins *circumincessio*, just as much as they "give space" to each other in *kénōsis*.

CONCLUSION

Supporters of Balthasar and those who maintain the theological legitimacy of *kénōsis* would agree that trinitarian difference, creation, incarnation, the sending of the Spirit, and even differences within the created world must in no way be characterized by lack, involuntary emanation, or the degradation of pure being. My point has been that the blend KÉNŌSIS IS EPÉKTASIS operates implicitly in their thinking. Aristotle Papanikolaou rethinks *kénōsis* and the element of risk in relationship by pointing to Balthasar:

> *Kenosis* for Balthasar is not self-sacrifice, but the movements of self-giving toward the other in order to receive the other that are constitutive of divine and

> human personhood. Personhood, for Balthasar, is not a quality possessed, but a unique and irreducible identity received in relations of love and freedom that can only be labeled as *kenotic*.[43]

The Pauline blend KÉNŌSIS IS EPÉKTASIS explains the mutuality between this giving and receiving of oneself in communion with others. Jennifer Martin observes that for Balthasar, *kénōsis* both allows for and presumes (in a dynamic back-and-forth) a fundamental "distance between Father and Son," which allows not only for the very possibility for the embodiedness of the Son in his incarnation but also for human embodiedness in creation itself.[44] KÉNŌSIS IS EPÉKTASIS implies a bond of togetherness, even if this implication is proleptic and includes a distance across which the community must strive.

In Balthasar's Trinity, infinite distance is eternally being opened up in the Father's *Ur-Kenosis* to the Only Begotten, a true self-emptying so that the Son may truly be and the Spirit may proceed from them both. The Son and Spirit then open themselves to receive the fullness of Godhead from the Father, and this constitutes the persons in their relations. The desire for the "goods" of the resurrection in *epéktasis* and in the human experience of *kénōsis*, as we read it in its authentic NT sense in Philippians 2:5–11 and 3:7–16, refers to its own foundation in the proclamation that JESUS IS LORD. This retrieval of *kénōsis* in a genuinely Pauline and theologically valid sense points to an inner-divine reality that obviates any fundamentally unhealthy dynamics of strife and competition at the heart of Balthasar's understanding of the hypostatic relations.

NOTES

1. I have given the noun forms of these two lexemes in their Greek transliterations for the sake of parallel structure, neither of which occur as nouns in Paul's texts but both of which have become common expressions in patristic and theological scholarship. I will not refer to the English word "kenosis" as it would normally be given without diacritical marks and italics unless it so occurs within a quotation.

2. The inspiration for this study comes from Jakob Rinderknecht, who in the question period of my public dissertation defense on Balthasar's trinitarian theology suggested that just such a blend as KÉNŌSIS IS EPÉKTASIS might be active in the thought of Paul, Gregory of Nyssa, and Balthasar.

3. Masson, *Without Metaphor, No Saving God: Theology After Cognitive Linguistics* (Leuven: Peeters, 2014), 107. At the author's request, we are reproducing a slightly simplified version of the figure, originally published in Robert Masson, "Are Aquinas and Whitehead Metaphorical and Analogical All the Way Down?," *Open Theology* 1 (2015), 531.

4. Robert Masson, *Without Metaphor*, 59.

5. Masson, *Without Metaphor*, 4.

6. Masson, *Without Metaphor*, 63–65.
7. Gilles Fauconnier and Mark Turner, "Rethinking Metaphor," in *The Cambridge Handbook of Metaphor and Thought*, ed. Raymond W. Gibbs (New York: Cambridge University Press, 2008), 53.
8. Masson, *Without Metaphor*, 111.
9. See Brendan Byrne, "Letter to the Philippians," *The New Jerome Biblical Commentary* (*NJBC*), ed. Raymond E. Brown, Joseph A. Fitzmeyer, and Roland E. Murphy (Englewood Cliffs, NJ: Prentice Hall, 1990): 48:4, p. 791. There could be parts of a third letter in the canonical book as well.
10. All of the biblical translations are from the New Revised Standard Version (NRSV). The asterisks (*) mark places where I have preferred a different possible word choice.
11. Erwin Nestle and Kurt and Barbara Aland, *Nestle-Aland Novum Testamentum Graece et Latine* (Stuttgart: Deutsche Biblegesellschaft, 1983, 1994); Bruce M. Metzger, *A Textual Commentary on the Greek New Testament* (Stuttgart: Deutsche Biblegesellschaft, 1994). There are some slight grammatical and lexical variations among authoritative ancient manuscripts. The one major textual issue is the lack of an article "the" in front of "name" in v.9 in some major textual traditions, but NA27 and Metzger are convinced that it should be included.
12. Byrne, "Letter to Philippians," *NJBC*, 48:17, p. 794.
13. Albrecht Oepke, "*kenóō*," *Theological Dictionary of the New Testament [TDNT]: Abridged in One Volume*, ed. Gerhard Kittel and Gerhard Friedrich, trans. Geoffrey W. Bromiley (Grand Rapids, MI: Eerdmans, 1985), 427. The sense of *kenóō* as making vain and useless or a more general negation can be seen in 1 Cor. 9:15, 2 Cor. 9:3 regarding Paul's "boasting." The cross being "emptied of its power" in 1 Cor. 1:17 is another place where the verb strongly carries this meaning.
14. *NJBC*, 48:20–21, p. 795.
15. Larry Hurtado, *Lord Jesus Christ: Devotion to Jesus in Earliest Christianity* (Grand Rapids, MI: Eerdmans, 2003), 108–9.
16. See Donald N. Levine, *The Flight from Ambiguity: Essays in Social and Cultural Theory* (Chicago: University of Chicago Press, 1988) for a full account.
17. Hurtado, *Lord Jesus Christ*, 112.
18. Hurtado, *Lord Jesus Christ*, 385.
19. Hurtado, *Lord Jesus Christ*, 385.
20. Metzger, *Textual Commentary*, 547.
21. *NJBC*, 48:26, 796.
22. Ernst Fuchs, "*ekeíno*," *TDNT*, 219–20.
23. David Bentley Hart, *The Beauty of the Infinite: The Aesthetics of Christian Truth* (Grand Rapids, MI: Eerdmans, 2003), 339. Hart, an Orthodox systematic theologian, builds upon Gregory of Nyssa for his theological anthropology: "To be human is to be an 'act,' thoroughly dynamic (in either one's sensible or intelligible aspect), in transit, without center in oneself, borne away or driven toward what lies beyond," ibid., 189–90. According to Gregory's *Life of Moses*, his allegorical reading of Exodus, human nature's perfection consists of the "endless desire for beauty and more beauty, this hunger for God (*De vita Moysis* 1.10; *GNO* 8.1:4–5)."

24. Hans Urs von Balthasar, *Heart of the World* (San Francisco: Ignatius Press, 1979), 13.

25. Gregory of Nyssa, *In Cant.* 4; Richard A. Norris, trans., *Homilies on the Song of Songs*, Homily 4 (Atlanta: Society of Biblical Literature, 2012), 138–39.

26. A recent Syndicate symposium on Anna Mercedes' book, *Power For: Feminism and Christ's Self-Giving* (London: T&T Clark International, 2011) explores the possibilities of positive feminist reclamations of kenosis. Mercedes' proposal (in a nutshell) is that the selfless and "agapic" element in kenosis is counterbalanced by an inherent erotic and desiring element, something not so far from what I have proposed here. The Syndicate participants' responses voice many remaining concerns regarding the risks of pastorally and morally misappropriating kenosis in Christian life. See the exchange here: https://syndicate.network/symposia/theology/power-for/. Accessed June 3, 2017.

27. Tina Beattie, *New Catholic Feminism: Theology and Theory* (London: Routledge, 2006), 160.

28. Balthasar, *Theo-Drama: Theological Dramatic Theory*, vol. III, *Dramatis Personae: Person in Christ*, trans. Graham Harrison (San Francisco: Ignatius Press, 1992), 285–87.

29. Balthasar, *Theo-Drama: Theological Dramatic Theory*, vol. V, *The Last Act*, trans. Graham Harrison (San Francisco: Ignatius Press, 1998), 91.

30. In fact, Hampson makes no investment whatsoever in retrieving the integral whole of the Christian tradition, particularly regarding the Trinity.

31. Daphne Hampson, "On Power and Gender," *Modern Theology* 4, no. 3 (1988): 240. Carolyn Chau engages Hampson's and Sarah Coakley's debate on kenosis, cautiously proposing a positive retrieval of it based on Coakley's arguments in Hampson's edited volume, *Swallowing a Fishbone?: Feminist Theologians Debate Christiantity*, ed. Daphne Hampson (London: SPCK, 1996) and on Aristotle Papanikolaou's arguments, in Carolyn Chau, "'What Could Possibly Be Given?': Towards an Exploration of *Kenosis* as Forgiveness—Continuing the Conversation between Coakley, Hampson, and Papanikolaou," *Modern Theology* 28, no. 1 (January 2012): 1–24.

32. Aristotle Papanikolaou, "Person, Kenosis and Abuse: Hans Urs von Balthasar and Feminist Theologies in Conversation," *Modern Theology* 19, no. 1 (2003): 42.

33. Linn Marie Tonstad, "Sexual Difference and Trinitarian Death: Cross, Kenosis, and Hierarchy in the Theo-Drama," *Modern Theology* 26, no. 4 (2010): 625.

34. Tonstad, *God and Difference: The Trinity, Sexuality, and the Transformation of Finitude* (New York: Routledge, 2016).

35. See Georges De Schrijver, *Le merveilleux accord de l'homme et de Dieu : l'analogie de l'*être *chez Balthasar* (Leuven: Leuven University Press, 1983), 313.

36. Balthasar, *Mysterium Paschale*, trans. Aidan Nichols (Edinburgh: T&T Clark, 1990); *Theo-Drama: Theological Dramatic Theory*, vol. IV, *The Action*, trans. Graham Harrison (San Francisco: Ignatius Press, 1994).

37. The "Contemplation on the Incarnation" [101-09], a perennial influence on Balthasar's trinitarian thought; *The Spiritual Exercises of Saint Ignatius,* trans. and commentary George E. Ganss, S.J. (St. Louis: Institute of Jesuit Sources, 1992), 56–58.

38. For the "whole God" reference, see Balthasar, *The Theology of Karl Barth: Exposition and Interpretation*, trans. Edward T. Oakes (San Francisco: Ignatius Press, 1992), 87; for "the Father's whole name," *The Glory of the Lord: A Theological Aesthetics*, Vol. VII, *The New Covenant*, trans. Brian McNeil (San Francisco: Ignatius Press, 1989), 248. The passage in *Glory of the Lord VII* is one of Balthasar's rare mentions of the Divine Name in the *Glory of the Lord* series. The historical-critical and philological examination of how it functions in the OT does not enter much into his discussion of God's being, but the Name of God as revealed to Moses in Exodus 3:13–16 is perhaps the most fundamental echo of the OT in Jesus's High Priestly prayer in John 17:6, 11–12; Hurtado, *Lord Jesus Christ*, 382.

39. See especially Hart, *Beauty of the Infinite*, 356–57.

40. Lucy Gardner and David Moss, "Something Like Time," in *Balthasar at the End of Modernity*, ed. Gardner, Moss, et al., (Edinburgh: T&T Clark, 1999), 71–72.

41. Balthasar, *Glory of the Lord* VII, 252.

42. Balthasar, *Theo-Drama* V, 77.

43. Papanikolaou, "Person, Kenosis and Abuse," 42. In this line of argument Papanikolaou makes common cause with Sarah Coakley (who is not directly in dialogue with Balthasar's work). Coakley finds a locus for the understanding of *kénōsis* in a kind of "power-in-vulnerability" in silent prayer. This willing act of vulnerability that lets God be God actually undermines the damaging gender essentialism that favors patriarchy and male dominance; "Kenosis and Subversion: On the Repression of 'Vulnerability' in Christian Feminist Thinking," in *Swallowing a Fishbone?: Feminist Theologies Debate Christianity,* ed. Daphne Hampson (London: SPCK, 1996), 110–11. The kind of vulnerability to God, and to God *alone* in prayer, that Coakley advocates for is not essentially subject to exploitation but rather to an abundant reception of love from the Other. In her Gregory of Nyssa-influenced theology of the dynamics of kenotic prayer, God is the solicitous guarantor of the Christian's well-being when "the circle of divine desire [is] perfectly enacted, under the aegis of the Spirit's own longing love," *God, Sexuality and the Self: An Essay 'On the Trinity'* (Cambridge: Cambridge University Press, 2013), 255–56. She maintains that to repress this kind of vulnerability before God and to refuse God's access to the soul in prayer would be harmful in the spiritual life.

44. Jennifer Newsome Martin, "The 'Whence' and the 'Whither' of Balthasar's Gendered Theology: Rehabilitating Kenosis for Feminist Theology," *Modern Theology* 32, no. 2 (April 2015): 214.

BIBLIOGRAPHY

Balthasar, Hans Urs von. *The Glory of the Lord: A Theological Aesthetics: Volume VII: Theology: The New Covenant*. Translated by Brian McNeil, C.R.V. San Francisco: Ignatius Press, 1989.

———. *Heart of the World*. Translated by Erasmo S. Leiva. San Francisco: Ignatius Press, 1979.

———. *Mysterium Paschale: The Mystery of Easter*. Translated by Adrian Nichols. Edinburgh, UK: T & T Clark, 1990.

———. *Theo-Drama: Theological Dramatic Theory*. Vol. III, *The Dramatis Personae: The Person in Christ*. Translated by Graham Harrison. San Francisco: Ignatius Press, 1992.

———. *Theo-Drama: Theological Dramatic Theory*. Vol. IV, *The Action*. Translated by Graham Harrison. San Francisco: Ignatius Press, 1994.

———. *Theo-Drama: Theological Dramatic Theory*. Vol. V, *The Last Act*. Translated by Graham Harrison. San Francisco: Ignatius Press, 1998.

———. *The Theology of Karl Barth: Exposition and Interpretation*. Translated by Edward T. Oakes. San Francisco: Ignatius Press, 1992.

Beattie, Tina. *The New Catholic Feminism: Theology, Gender Theory and Dialogue*. London; New York: Routledge, 2005.

Brown, Raymond E., Joseph A. Fitzmyer, and Roland E. Murphy, eds. *The New Jerome Biblical Commentary*. Englewood Cliffs, NJ: Prentice Hall, 1990.

Chau, Carolyn A. "'What Could Possibly Be Given?': Towards an Exploration of Kenosis as Forgiveness—Continuing the Conversation Between Coakley, Hampson, and Papanikolaou1." *Modern Theology* 28, no. 1 (January 2012): 1–24.

Coakley, Sarah. *God, Sexuality, and the Self: An Essay "On the Trinity."* Cambridge, UK: Cambridge University Press, 2013.

Fauconnier, Gilles, and Mark B. Turner. "Rethinking Metaphor." In *The Cambridge Handbook of Metaphor and Thought*. Edited by Raymond W. Gibbs, 53–66. New York: Cambridge University Press, 2008.

Gardner, Lucy, David Moss, Ben Quash, and Graham Ward, eds. *Balthasar at End of Modernity*. Edinburgh, UK: T&T Clark, 1999.

Gregory of Nyssa. *Homilies on the Song of Songs*. Edited by Richard A. Norris, Jr. Atlanta: Society of Biblical Literature, 2013.

Hampson, Daphne. "On Power and Gender." *Modern Theology* 4, no. 3 (April 1988): 234–250.

———, ed. *Swallowing a Fishbone?: Feminist Theologians Debate Christianity*. London: SPCK Publishing, 1996.

Hart, David Bentley. *The Beauty of the Infinite: The Aesthetics of Christian Truth*. Grand Rapids, MI: Eerdmans, 2004.

Hurtado, Larry W. *Lord Jesus Christ: Devotion to Jesus in Earliest Christianity*. Grand Rapids, MI: Eerdmans, 2005.

Ignatius of Loyola. *Spiritual Exercises of Saint Ignatius: A Translation and Commentary*. Translated and edited by George E. Ganss. Chicago: Loyola Press, 1992.

Kittel, Gerhard, Gerhard Friedrich, and Geoffrey W. Bromiley, eds. *Theological Dictionary of the New Testament: Abridged in One Volume*. Grand Rapids, MI: Eerdmans, 1985.

Levine, Donald N. *The Flight from Ambiguity: Essays in Social and Cultural Theory*. Chicago: University of Chicago Press, 1988.

Martin, Jennifer Newsome. "The 'Whence' and the 'Whither' of Balthasar's Gendered Theology: Rehabilitating Kenosis for Feminist Theology." *Modern Theology* 31, no. 2 (April 2015): 211–34.

Masson, Robert. *Without Metaphor, No Saving God: Theology after Cognitive Linguistics*. Leuven: Peeters, 2014.

———. "Are Aquinas and Whitehead Metaphorical and Analogical All the Way Down?" *Open Theology* (January 1, 2015): 524–27.

Mercedes, Anna. *Power For: Feminism and Christ's Self-Giving*. London: T&T Clark, 2011.

Metzger, Bruce M., ed. *A Textual Commentary on the Greek New Testament*. Revised edition. Hendrickson Publishers, 2005.

Papanikolaou, Aristotle. "Person, Kenosis and Abuse: Hans Urs von Balthasar and Feminist Theologies in Conversation." *Modern Theology* 19, no. 1 (January 2003): 41–65.

Schrijver, G. De. *Le Merveilleux Accord de L'homme et de Dieu. Etude de l'analogie de l'etre chez Hans Urs von Balthasar*. Leuven: Peeters, 1983.

Tonstad, Linn Marie. *God and Difference: The Trinity, Sexuality, and the Transformation of Finitude*. New York: Routledge, 2015.

———. "Sexual Difference and Trinitarian Death: Cross, Kenosis, and Hierarchy in the Theo-Drama." *Modern Theology* 26, no. 4 (October 2010): 603–631.

Chapter Six

Eucharistic Spirituality and Metaphoric Asymmetry

Stephen R. Shaver

Broadly speaking, it is possible to distinguish between two basic approaches to Christian eucharistic spirituality. The first—identified most closely with Roman Catholic and Eastern Orthodox traditions, but also found among many Anglicans and Lutherans—places a strong emphasis on the sacred character of the consecrated elements of bread and wine, identified as the body and blood of Christ. These elements are treated with reverence and carefully consumed or reserved; they may become the focus of adoration within or even outside the liturgy. In churches following this approach, the celebration of the eucharist is typically considered the central act of Christian worship and the normative liturgical action for Sundays and feast days.[1]

In the second approach—characteristic of many Reformed and free-church traditions—believers feed on Jesus not with their mouths but, in the words of Thomas Cranmer, in their hearts by faith.[2] Eucharistic piety centers less on the consecrated bread and wine and more on the act of prayer and worship, with the elements themselves seen primarily as tokens or reminders of an invisible and spiritual reality. Reservation and adoration are not practiced, and in many cases the elements may be treated as ordinary food and drink once the liturgy is over. While early reformers such as Cranmer and John Calvin sought to foster weekly celebration, many Protestant churches have moved over time toward a less frequent practice in which the eucharist may still be highly valued but is not seen as a *sine qua non* of Sunday worship. Some evangelical and Pentecostal churches tend to find the primary emotional and spiritual focus of worship instead in practices like reading scripture, singing praise music, or praying in tongues.[3] Yet, as Sarah Koenig has noted, such practices can be spoken of in strikingly sacramental-sounding terms, raising the possibility of a kind of eucharistic piety without the eucharist itself.[4] As one popular praise song puts it:

This is my daily bread
This is my daily bread
Your very word spoken to me.[5]

The liturgical and ecumenical movements of the twentieth century have seen remarkable convergences, and neither of these two strands of piety exists in isolation. Still, the difference in ethos between them remains noticeable, especially at the level of local practice and popular devotion.[6] The concept of metaphoric asymmetry, a core principle in the cognitive understanding of metaphor, can help account for the emergence and the stability of both.

These two strands of eucharistic spirituality are in fact grounded in two distinct core metaphors. The first is THIS BREAD AND WINE ARE JESUS'S BODY AND BLOOD. The second is JESUS'S FLESH AND BLOOD ARE HEAVENLY LIFE-GIVING BREAD AND DRINK. Both these metaphors are scriptural, and at first glance they may appear almost identical. From a cognitive standpoint, however, they are two different metaphors with opposite directionality. The first maps the attributes of Jesus's body and blood onto (earthly) elements of food and drink. The second maps the attributes of heavenly food and drink onto Jesus's (crucified and risen) flesh and blood. The differences between the entailments of these two metaphors tend to give rise to very different experiences of eucharistic practice and spirituality. Yet metaphors do not exist in a vacuum, and these two pieties can also interact to create complex blends. A truly ecumenical theology of the eucharist will need to do justice to both metaphors, separately and together, without treating them as contradictory or relying exclusively on either at the expense of the other.

METAPHORIC ASYMMETRY

Asymmetry in conceptual metaphor theory refers to the fact that metaphorical thinking is invariably directional. In conceptual metaphor, one area of human experience (the target frame) is conceptualized in terms of another that is more immediately cognitively accessible (the source frame).[7] Often this is because the target frame is more abstract and the source frame more amenable to direct sensory experience. An example is the metaphor AFFECTION IS WARMTH, which has been shown to exist in a variety of cross-cultural settings. This metaphor underlies a variety of ordinary expressions:

I'm really *warming up* to her.
He behaved quite *coldly* to me.
She gave me an *icy* stare.

There was a *thaw* in bilateral relations.
Their chance encounter *kindled* his affections.

As can be seen from these examples, conceptual metaphor is a matter of mapping between *concepts*, not of the particular *words* used in any given expression. Metaphor is not simply a surface-level rhetorical flourish, but a matter of the underlying thought process at work. The phrase "affection is warmth" need not appear as such: in fact, it rarely does appear explicitly, since the underlying conceptual mapping in this particular metaphor is so well entrenched as to go without saying. In AFFECTION IS WARMTH, which likely arises from early childhood experiences of being held close in which these two experiences occur simultaneously, the more concrete frame of warmth is used to understand the more abstract one of affection.

Importantly, however, the reverse is not true. We do not typically use our experience of affection to structure and organize our experience of warmth. In other words, expressions like these are not familiar like those above but seem odd and difficult to understand:

* Is the oven *friendly* enough yet?
* It's twelve below zero out—Brr, I'm *standoffish!*[8]

This asymmetry is true in general of primary metaphors—those metaphors grounded in direct bodily experience which form the building blocks of much of our capacity for abstract thought. A few of these, as identified by Joseph Grady, include AFFECTION IS WARMTH, IMPORTANT IS BIG, HAPPY IS UP, INTIMACY IS CLOSENESS, and UNDERSTANDING IS GRASPING.[9] A handful of additional examples illustrating the asymmetric character of these metaphors are given below (the reader is invited to come up with others):

IMPORTANT IS BIG:
This acquisition is *huge* for the corporation.
* Four foot two! Honey, you're so much *more important* than you were last year!

HAPPY IS UP:
You're really *flying high* today!
* After takeoff, the plane *felt better and better* until it reached cruising altitude.

INTIMACY IS CLOSENESS:
My college roommate and I used to be *tight*, but eventually we *drifted apart.*
* I'm glad you moved back home—it's so good having you *dearer* to me.

UNDERSTANDING IS GRASPING:
I just can't quite *get a handle on* integral calculus.
* Okay, *understand* the handlebars and pedal!

It is not only primary or deeply entrenched metaphors that exhibit this type of directionality: novel and creative metaphors show the same asymmetry. Consider the pair of sentences below:

This surgeon is a butcher.
This butcher is a surgeon.[10]

Each of these sentences is perfectly understandable, but the implications are very different. The difference lies in which of the two frames (SURGERY, BUTCHERY) is having its attributes mapped onto the other. In the first, the characteristics of a butcher—who must hack forcefully through meat and bone to carve up a dead animal into its parts—are mapped onto the surgeon. In the second, the characteristics of a surgeon—who, prototypically at least, makes careful and precise incisions—are mapped onto the butcher.

DIAGRAMMING METAPHORS

In contemporary cognitive linguistics metaphor is generally understood as a subcase of the wider set of thought processes known as conceptual blending.[11] As Gilles Fauconnier and Mark Turner have shown, much imaginative thought is the result of what appears to be a uniquely powerful human ability to integrate multiple mental spaces, or "small conceptual packets constructed as we think and talk."[12] This integration happens continually, and usually subconsciously, as we "compress complex ideas to a scale at which they can be easily manipulated by human minds."[13] A blend can be depicted as a network of four mental spaces: two input spaces; a generic space, which includes whatever cognitive structure the two input spaces have in common; and a blended space in which elements from the input spaces combine to generate emergent structure.[14] The basic diagram for illustrating a blend is shown in figure 6.1. Each space is represented by a circle; solid lines indicate mappings between elements in the two input spaces, and dotted lines indicate connections between the input spaces and the generic space or the blended space.

From the standpoint of conceptual blending theory, metaphor is what is known as a *single-scope* blend: one in which the blend is asymmetrically structured by one of the two input spaces (i.e., the source frame). The generic space contains whatever schematic structure the two input frames have in common. The blended space combines content from both input spaces,

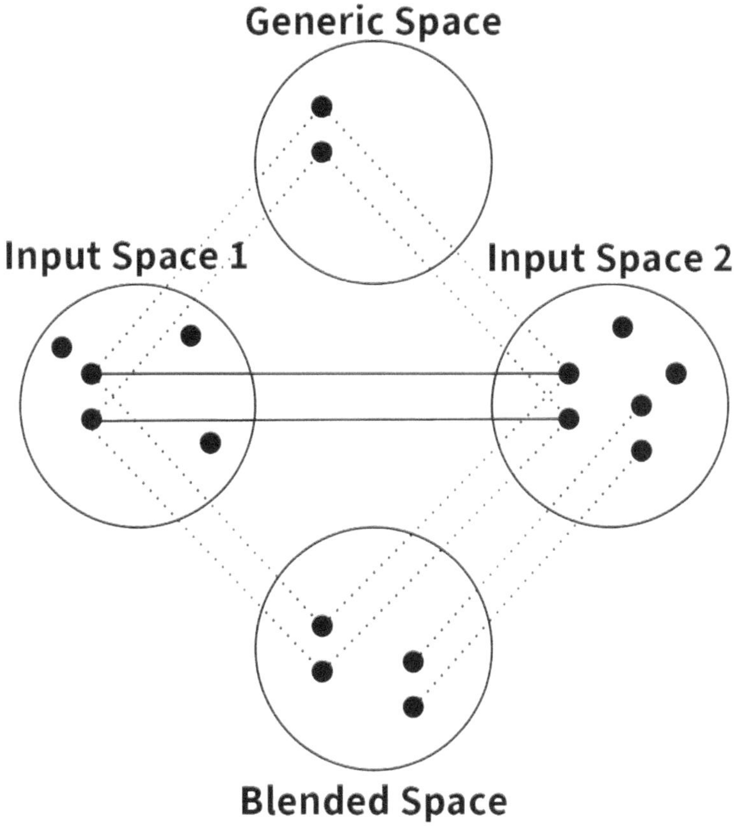

Figure 6.1. Basic Blend Diagram

inheriting some structure from the target frame but allowing some elements of the source frame to override their target-frame counterparts. Importantly, in a single-scope blend, while the source frame remains unaltered, inferences from the blended space can be "floated" up to the target frame.[15] This means that reasoning done in the blend can result in new conclusions being drawn about the target frame.

The example from above, "This surgeon is a butcher," can be diagrammed as seen in figure 6.2.

The generic space contains what the two input spaces have in common: several basic roles shared by both the BUTCHERY and SURGERY frames as well as a basic shared image structure. Although the detailed visual scene of a surgeon's operating room is different from that of a butcher's workroom, there is considerable similarity between the two at a more abstract level.[16] In

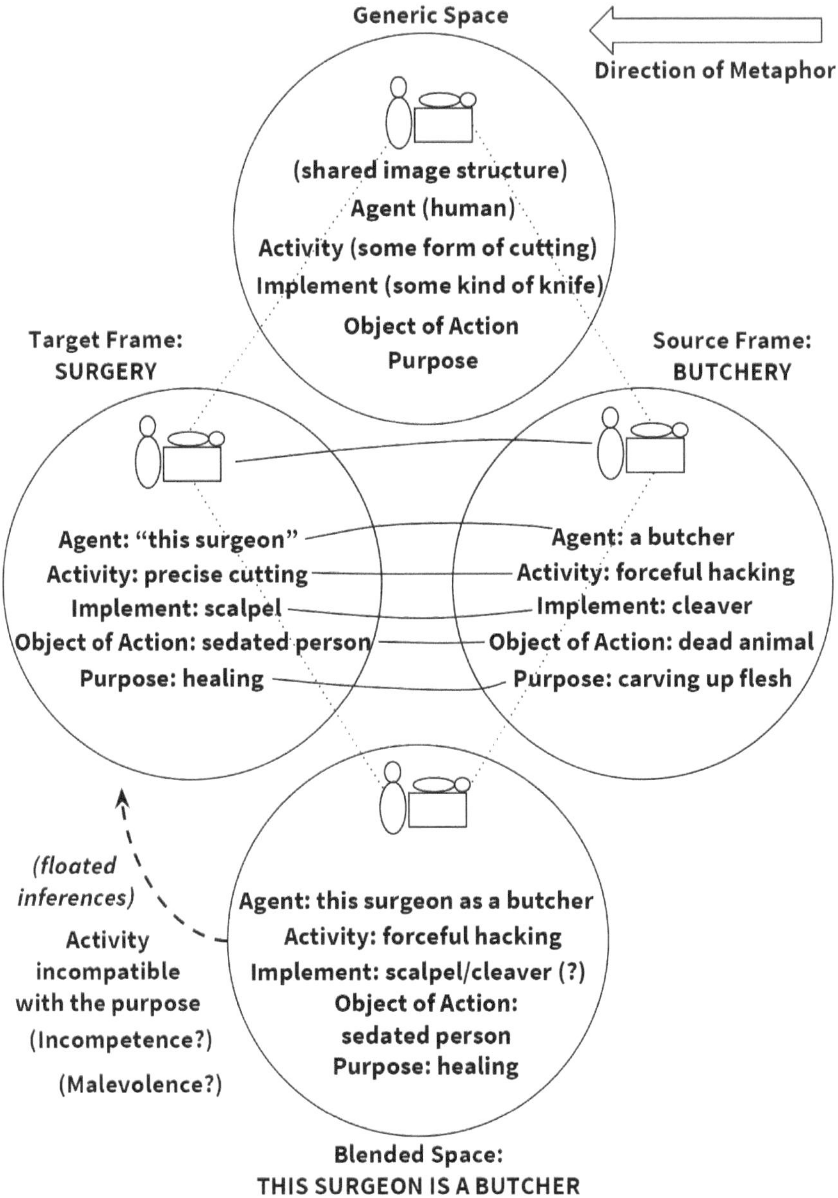

Figure 6.2. THIS SURGEON IS A BUTCHER

each, a standing human agent wields a sharp instrument on a person or animal stretched out on a table. This shared image structure is a major factor enabling the mappings in this metaphor.

The target space includes "this surgeon" acting in a SURGERY frame, while the source frame draws from a prototypical scene of butchery. In the blend, this particular surgeon is envisioned *as* a butcher, mapping content from the source frame onto the target and overriding some of it. Precisely how much content is overridden will be individual to each hearer: for example, some may conjure up an image of the surgeon-as-butcher still dressed in surgical scrubs, while others may import some material from the source frame and imagine him or her in a butcher's apron. The imagined surgeon-as-butcher may continue to hold a scalpel or may wield a butcher's cleaver. Blending is not deterministic: rather, clashes between source- and target-frame structure are resolved creatively, drawing upon the individual's encyclopedic knowledge about both input spaces as well as the pragmatic situation at hand. However, the more salient and prototypical a feature is to the source frame, the more likely it is to be mapped over. In this case, almost all hearers are likely to map the butcher's prototypical manner of activity—forceful hacking—into the blend, overriding the surgeon's ordinary careful precision.

This leads to an inference not available in the source frame. A butcher practicing butchery is just doing his or her job. But a surgeon who acts this way is doing surgery in a way that cannot possibly achieve the goal of healing. In other words, this surgeon is either incompetent or perhaps even actively malevolent. This inference is *emergent* in the blend—it does not arise from either target or source frame alone but only from the combination of the two. However, having emerged, it is now available to be floated back to the target frame. The real-world surgeon does not wear a butcher's apron or wield a cleaver, but the speaker does indeed believe she is a very poor surgeon.

The reverse sentence, "This butcher is a surgeon," can be diagrammed in a similar way, as in figure 6.3.

Here it is the prototypical manner of activity from SURGERY that is mapped into the blend, overriding that of BUTCHERY. Again there are emergent inferences—although this time they are perhaps more ambiguous: is this butcher-surgeon's precise cutting a sign of great skill or of overcaution? Depending on the situation, the speaker's tone of voice, and so on, "This butcher is a surgeon" might be understood in either way.[17] In either case, however, the inferences become real-world assertions about the behavior of this particular butcher.

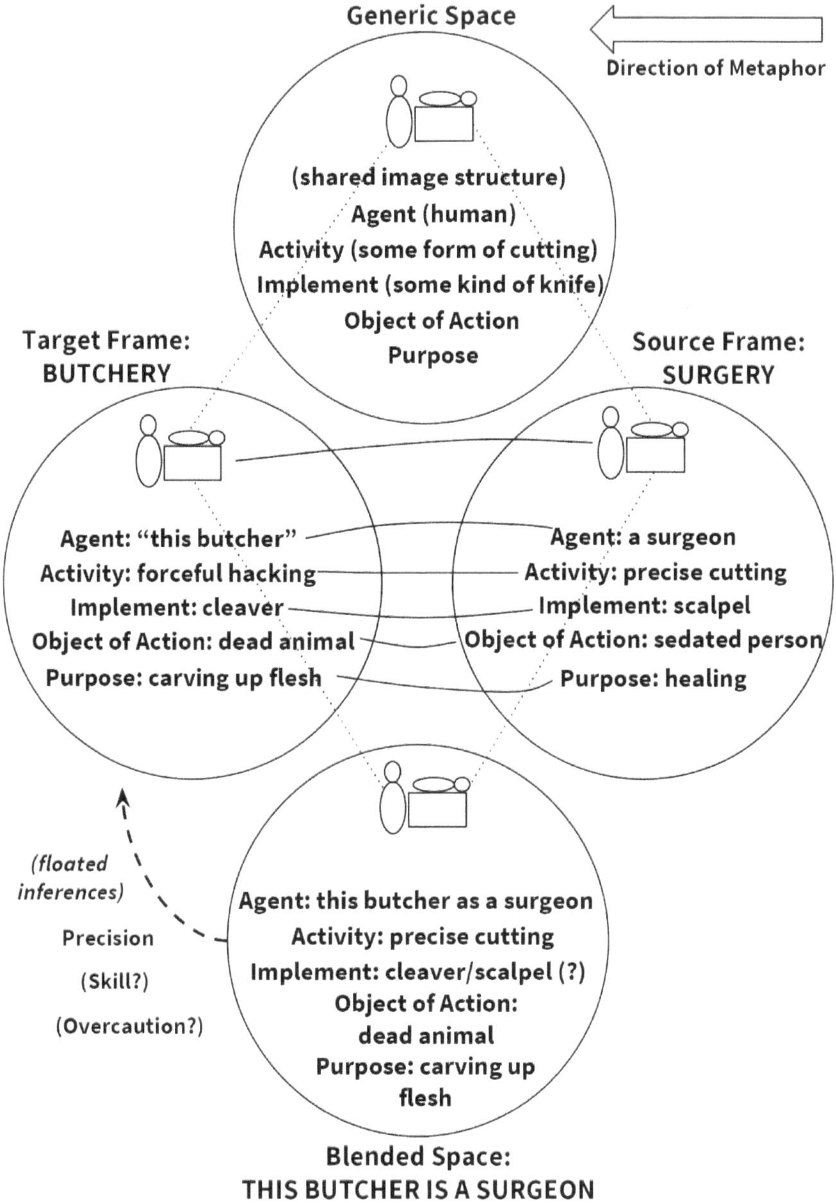

Figure 6.3. THIS BUTCHER IS A SURGEON

BREAD IS JESUS/JESUS IS BREAD

It is the same type of asymmetry that accounts for the significant difference between the two strands of eucharistic piety described above. They are grounded in metaphors that operate on similar frames but create very different mappings between them. Consider this portion of a sixth-century communion instruction by the Syrian bishop Philoxenus of Mabbug:

> When you have extended your hands and taken the body, bow, and put your hands before your face, and worship the living Body whom you hold. Then speak with him in a low voice, and with your gaze resting upon him say to him: "I carry you, living God, who is incarnate in the bread, and I embrace you in my palms, Lord of the worlds whom no world has contained. You have circumscribed yourself in a fiery coal within a fleshly palm—you, Lord, who with your palm measured out the dust of the earth. You are holy, God incarnate in my hands in a fiery coal which is a body. See, I hold you, although there is nothing that contains you; a bodily hand embraces you, Lord of natures whom a fleshly womb embraced. Within a womb you became a circumscribed body, and now within a hand you appear to me as a small morsel.
>
> "As you have made me worthy to approach you and receive you—and see, my hands embrace you confidently—make me worthy, Lord, to eat you in a holy manner and to taste the food of your body as a taste of your life."[18]

The governing metaphor in this passage is striking. The presence of Jesus is so strongly identified with the morsel of consecrated bread that the faithful recipient can "worship the living Body whom you hold." To hold the bread ("God incarnate in my hands") is to hold Jesus. To look at the bread ("your gaze resting upon him") is to look at Jesus. To eat the bread is to eat Jesus and thus to partake of his immortality ("to taste the food of your body as a taste of your life"). Philoxenus' prayer rests on a metaphoric blend in which the attributes of Jesus are mapped unidirectionally onto the eucharistic bread: BREAD IS JESUS.

A profoundly different type of spirituality is at work in this modern evangelical hymn:

> 1. Some, these days, would tell us that our Jesus is not food,
> That we only need to know about Him and do good,
> But we're glad to tell you, brothers, it's just not that way—
> Jesus is the bread of life; we eat Him every day.
>
> *Refrain:* We love the church life, eating, drinking, breathing Jesus.
> We love the church life, taking in God's Word.
> We love to hear those "O Lord, Amen, Hallelujahs!"
> We love the church life, feasting with the Lord.

2. When He fills our inward parts, we're never quite the same,
So much richness we can taste by calling on His name.
"Services" but once a week for us will never do.
Every day we need the fellowship to take us through. (*Refrain*)[19]

Like Philoxenus' prayer, this hymn is about Jesus, bread, and eating: the frames involved here are very similar. But the direction of the metaphoric mapping is completely the reverse. No particular eucharistic meal is mentioned; no consecrated morsel of bread is being addressed. Instead, feeding on Jesus is a matter of the whole "church life": hearing scripture proclaimed ("taking in God's Word"); shouts of praise ("O Lord, Amen, Hallelujah!"); acts of prayer and "calling on His name." Formal worship "services," while not ruled out, are clearly treated as secondary. Eating Jesus every day is not a matter of attending a daily eucharistic celebration but of having an intimate relationship with Jesus in the texture of one's daily life. The metaphoric mapping in this song is as clear as in Philoxenus' prayer, but instead of mapping the characteristics of Jesus onto bread, it maps the characteristics of bread onto Jesus: JESUS IS BREAD. Jesus is nourishing; believers hunger after him and are satisfied by him; he is a daily requirement to sustain life.[20]

GETTING MORE PRECISE

At one level, then, the two pieties described above are grounded in a set of metaphors that can be treated as direct opposites: BREAD IS JESUS/JESUS IS BREAD (or, to include the eucharistic cup in the equation, BREAD AND DRINK ARE JESUS/JESUS IS BREAD AND DRINK).[21] The difference in directionality goes far toward explaining the different "feel" of these two strands of eucharistic piety. Yet there is more to be explored here. The frames as stated above are too broad to explain how eucharistic practice and spirituality actually work. It is not *all* bread and drink, for example, that is identified with Jesus in Philoxenus's piety; the metaphor applies only to those particular portions that have been blessed in the eucharistic prayer. And in the piety represented by "We Love the Church Life!" Jesus is not identified simply as *ordinary* bread and drink: eating and drinking Jesus does not simply sustain mortal existence but actually bestows eternal life. To account more fully for how these metaphors function, the frames involved need to be elaborated more specifically.

Barbara Dancygier and Eve Sweetser demonstrate this process of elaboration by examining closely how modern English speakers use the metaphors PEOPLE ARE COMPUTERS and COMPUTERS ARE PEOPLE.[22] Both frequently occur in everyday speech:

My memory banks are scrambled. (PEOPLE ARE COMPUTERS)
My computer is being stubborn and difficult today. (COMPUTERS ARE PEOPLE)

At first glance, the two metaphors appear to be straightforward opposites. On closer inspection, however, they create two different sets of mappings. The first sentence maps the *information-processing capabilities* of a computer onto a human. The second, on the other hand, maps the *emotional moods* of a human onto a computer. The salient features of each frame are different depending on the direction in which the metaphor is invoked. A more precise way to name these two metaphors, Dancygier and Sweetser argue, would be HUMAN COGNITIVE PROCESSING IS COMPUTER INFORMATION PROCESSING and APPARENTLY ERRATIC ASPECTS OF COMPUTER BEHAVIOR ARE EMOTIONAL MOOD-BASED ASPECTS OF HUMAN BEHAVIOR.[23] Both metaphors are useful in their own ways—but they are used in different situations to understand different experiences.The same is true of the two eucharistic metaphors. Exploring each metaphor's roots in the Christian scriptures will help further elaborate the frames involved.

THE SYNOPTIC/PAULINE METAPHOR:
THIS BREAD AND WINE ARE JESUS'S BODY AND BLOOD

The origin of the first metaphor is easy to locate: it comes directly from the well-known Last Supper narrative, which appears in the three Synoptic gospels (Matthew, Mark, Luke) and in Paul's first letter to the Corinthians. Examining Mark's and Paul's versions is sufficient for our purposes, since Matthew's version is only lightly adapted from Mark, while Luke's is a combination of Markan and Pauline language.

Mark

Mark's story of the institution of the eucharist is simple and straightforward:

> While they were eating, after taking a loaf and blessing it, he [Jesus] broke it and gave it to them and said, "Take; this is my body." And after taking a cup and giving thanks, he gave it to them, and they all drank from it. And he said to them, "This is my blood of the covenant, which is poured out for many. Truly, I say to you, I will never again drink from the fruit of the vine until that day when I drink it new in the kingdom of God."[24]

As noted above, conceptual metaphor theory deals not only with sentences expressed explicitly in the form "X is Y" but with the conceptual mappings that underlie any number of different textual formulations. In the case of this passage, however, we do in fact see the form "X is Y," or what linguists call the copula construction.[25] The key clauses are "this is my body" (*touto estin to sōma mou*) and "this is my blood of the covenant" (*touto estin to haima mou tēs diathēkēs*).

What exactly is meant by *this* in the subject of each sentence? In the first case, the referent seems clear: *this* is the broken loaf (*artos*) Jesus is giving to his disciples. The metaphor evoked, then, is linked specifically to one specific loaf: *THIS* BREAD IS JESUS'S BODY.[26] *This* in the second sentence is perhaps somewhat more ambiguous: the only antecedent noun actually to appear in the text is *potērion*, (cup). THIS CUP IS JESUS'S BLOOD is not an attractive metaphor, cognitively speaking. Metaphoric mappings are strongly constrained by a tendency to preserve image-schematic topology from the source into the blend, and so it is difficult to sustain a mapping from a fluid to a solid object like a cup.[27] However, a more promising possibility is available.

Closely related to metaphor—but distinct from it in some important ways—is the phenomenon of *metonymy*. Like metaphor, metonymy is a phenomenon in which a conceptual mapping is created from one concept to another. In metonymy, however, the mapping takes place within a single frame rather than between two separate ones.[28] Referring to a container while intending to indicate its contents, as in "He drank the whole glass," is a common form of metonymy.[29] Here in Mark, then, it is easy and intuitive for a reader to understand *cup* as a metonymic reference to the liquid inside (identified in verse 25 as "the fruit of the vine"). This provides a much more compatible target for the metaphor: THIS WINE IS JESUS'S BLOOD, rather than THIS CUP IS JESUS'S BLOOD. Both blood and wine are liquids, able to be "poured out" (v. 24), and if red wine is in view there is a color correspondence as well.

Paul

Paul, writing to an early Christian community in the city of Corinth, explicitly applies the symbolism of Jesus's body and blood not only to the past event of the Last Supper but also to the ongoing meal practice of Christians in his own time. In 1 Cor 11:27 he warns the Corinthians that "whoever eats the loaf and drinks the cup of the Lord unworthily will be liable for the body and the blood of the Lord," and in 10:16 he asks rhetorically, "The cup of blessing that we bless, is it not the sharing of the blood of Christ? The loaf that we break, is it not the sharing of the body of Christ?" As part of Paul's argument, he retells the Last Supper narrative itself, reporting Jesus's words over the loaf in a format nearly identical to those in Mark: "This is my body that is for you" (*touto mou estin to sōma to huper humōn*).

Paul's version of Jesus's words over the cup, "This cup is the new covenant in my blood" (*touto to potērion hē kainē diathēkē estin en tō emō haimati*), is even more indirect than Mark's in evoking the metaphor THIS WINE IS JESUS'S BLOOD. Instead of Mark's ambiguous "this," the subject is clearly "this cup." Moreover, instead of "my blood of the covenant," the predicate is "the new covenant in my blood." Based on this observation, some commentators have suggested that Jesus's intention in this passage is not to evoke the wine/blood metaphor at all but simply to indicate that the act of drinking the cup is a commemoration of the new covenant soon to be inaugurated by the literal shedding of Jesus's blood on the cross.[30] Such an interpretation represents a choice to recognize the cup as a metonymic pointer to Jesus's shed blood (both occurring as elements within a shared PASSION NARRATIVE frame) while rejecting any metaphoric blend between them.

Yet to constrain the blend in such a way fails to take account of the powerful, metaphor-facilitating effect of the shared image structure between wine and blood. When a well-structured metaphor hovers close at hand, it is likely to arise in the mind of the reader even if implied obliquely.[31] A reader of Paul's letter—even a first-century one who has never seen Mark's version—is still likely to generate THIS WINE IS JESUS'S BLOOD, at least as an implicit cognitive construct, based on image mappings alone.[32] The blends produced by a text are typically not "either/or" but "all-of-the-above." To be sure, it is impossible to reconstruct the historical Jesus's intent beyond what Paul gives us; all we have is the text. But, that being the case, it seems arbitrarily restrictive to place an *a priori* constraint on the range of possible blending that text may evoke in a reasonable reader or hearer.[33]

Diagramming the Synoptic/Pauline Blend

All in all, then, the basic metaphor evoked by the Synoptic and Pauline Last Supper passages can be written more specifically not just as BREAD AND WINE ARE JESUS but as THIS BREAD IS JESUS'S BODY AND THIS WINE IS JESUS'S BLOOD, or in combination, THIS BREAD AND WINE ARE JESUS'S BODY AND BLOOD. Both Mark and Paul apply it specifically to the loaf and cup of wine of the Last Supper, and Paul applies it also to those of later Christian eucharistic meals. This sets up a unidirectional mapping, a single-scope blend, which can be used to think and reason about the target frame. For simplicity's sake, I will diagram only THIS BREAD IS JESUS'S BODY; a similar diagram could be drawn for THIS WINE IS JESUS'S BLOOD, with adjustments for image structure.

The target frame (THIS BREAD) includes basic properties and background knowledge about bread in general as well as about this specific piece of bread, as seen in figure 6.4.

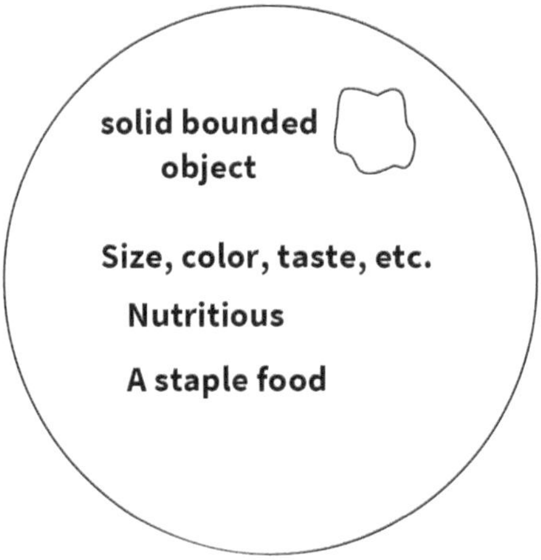

Figure 6.4. Target Frame: BREAD

The source input space harnesses the whole range of an individual reader's or hearer's encyclopedic knowledge about the body of Jesus. As with any human body, we can imagine the source frame including basic physical characteristics: height, hair color, and so on. However, from a believing Christian's point of view, Jesus's body also has certain unique qualities: it has been crucified, buried, and raised into immortal life. Moreover, a person's body *is* that person: Body For Person is a conventional Part for Whole metonymy. Although we commonly think of dimensions of personhood that are conceptually distinguishable from the body—mind, soul, spirit, etc.—to see or touch a person's body is truly to see or touch that person. Philoxenus' prayer shows this metonymy at work in the way it alternates between calling the morsel of bread "the body" and simply calling it "you, Lord." Theologically, Jesus is identified as Lord, Messiah, Son of Man, Son of God, Second Person of the Trinity, and so on, and so all these attributes too pertain to the source frame, as seen in figure 6.5.[34]

The generic space, containing what these two input spaces have in common, is quite minimal in this case. Where the BUTCHERY and SURGERY frames shared several conventional roles (Agent, Implement, Activity, Patient, Purpose) and an abstract but fairly detailed image mapping, the concepts of bread and Jesus's body have less immediately apparent shared structure. Still, there is one important similarity at a very basic, image-schematic level: both a piece of bread and a person's body are solid bounded objects. While this may seem so obvious as to be trivial, this shared structure is in fact critical to the success of the metaphor. Thus

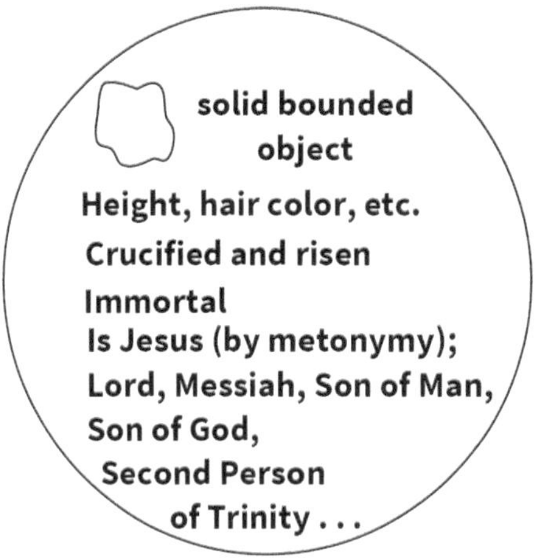

Figure 6.5. Source Frame: JESUS'S BODY

even this very minimal generic space is enough to support the creation of what will prove to be a very richly populated blend.

In that blend, encyclopedic knowledge about Jesus's body is mapped onto the eucharistic bread, as in figure 6.6.

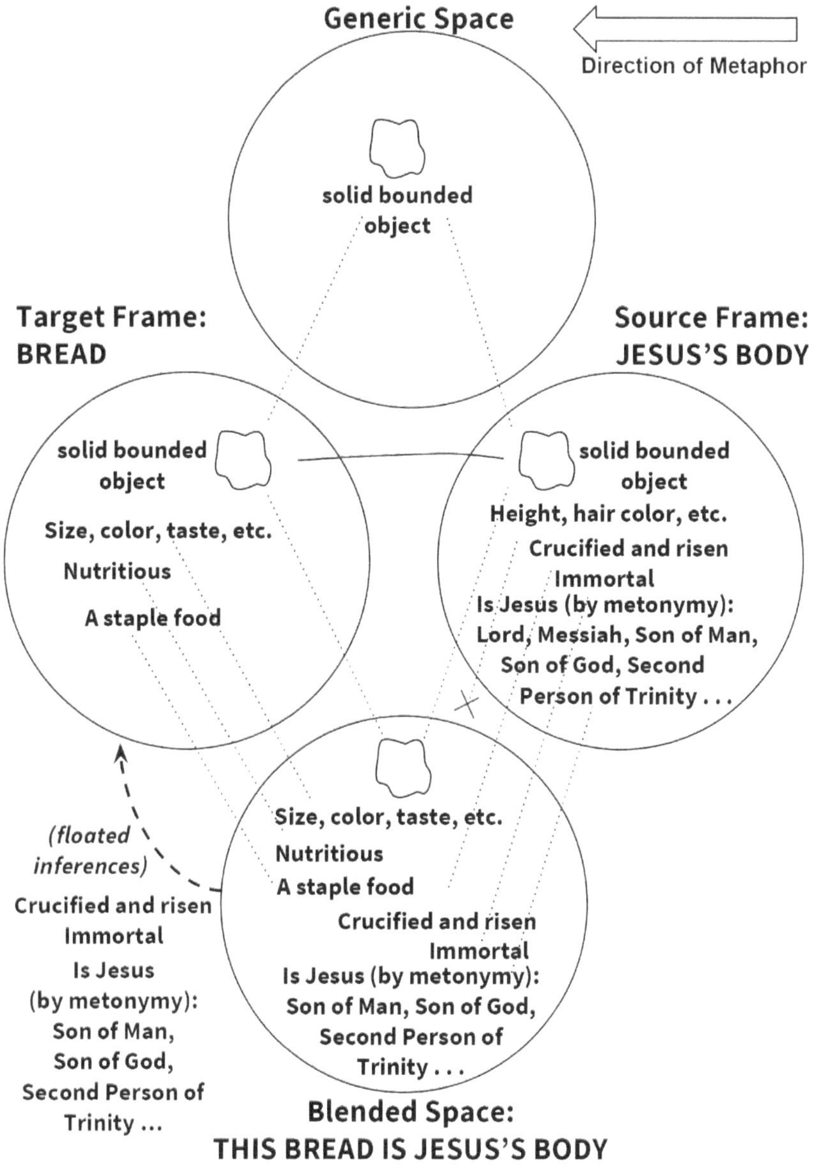

Figure 6.6. THIS BREAD IS JESUS'S BODY

Just as in the surgeon/butcher blends, there is the potential for clashes between target-frame and source-frame structure. In this case, eucharistic bread already has its own sensory characteristics (appearance, taste, size, etc.) and so those of the BODY domain are conventionally simply not mapped into the blend, as shown in the diagram above.[35] On the other hand, the wide range of characteristics for which there are no competing counterparts in the BREAD frame are all available in the blend: immortality, divinity, theological titles and attributes, and so on.

One readily available elaboration of the metaphor THIS BREAD IS JESUS'S BODY draws upon the primary metaphor INTIMACY IS CLOSENESS: the closest a person can possibly get to Jesus is to take Jesus into one's very self. In the blend, eating Jesus is not cannibalism (as it would be in the source frame) but rather an act of intimate communion. Another related elaboration draws upon the common cultural metaphor YOU ARE WHAT YOU EAT: to eat Jesus's immortal body is to become immortal oneself, or perhaps even to become Jesus.[36] Philoxenus's prayer alludes to this elaboration: "Make me worthy . . . to taste the food of your body as a taste of your life."

There is still more going on in this blend, cognitively speaking. As already mentioned above, the Last Supper story (in both its Synoptic and Pauline versions) is embedded within the context of the story of Jesus's passion and death. This familiar story constitutes a PASSION NARRATIVE frame, and within this shared frame the words *body* (*sōma*) and *blood* (*haima*) are used not only in relation to the bread and wine but also in relation to Jesus's physical body (crucified, dead, buried, and raised) and his physical blood (shed on the cross). This creates an almost unavoidable metonymic mapping between the bread and wine and Jesus's body and blood within the shared PASSION NARRATIVE frame, in addition to the metaphoric mappings across the distinct frames BREAD and BODY, WINE and BLOOD. The result is what Fauconnier and Turner call a *megablend*, one which draws from more than just two input spaces.[37] This megablend further strengthens the association between eucharistic bread and Jesus's body, between eucharistic wine and Jesus's blood: not only are they linked by a cross-frame mapping, they can also stand for one another within a single shared frame as well. As I argued above, to restrict the blend to its metonymic aspect alone would be to impose an artificial constraint on the natural possibilities the text evokes. Rather, this megablend includes both metaphoric *and* metonymic mappings at the same time.

Jesper Sørensen has pointed out that the two cognitive operations of metaphor and metonymy lie behind James Frazer's classic typology of ritual magic as governed by two laws of similarity and contagion.[38] An example of similarity (based on image metaphor) would be venerating a saint's image; an example of contagion (based on metonymy) would be venerating a saint's relic. A major part of the enduring cognitive strength of the Synoptic/Pauline eucharistic blend comes from the fact that it partakes of *both* operations.

Figure 6.7 adds this metonymy to the blend (with dashed lines indicating the metonymic connections):

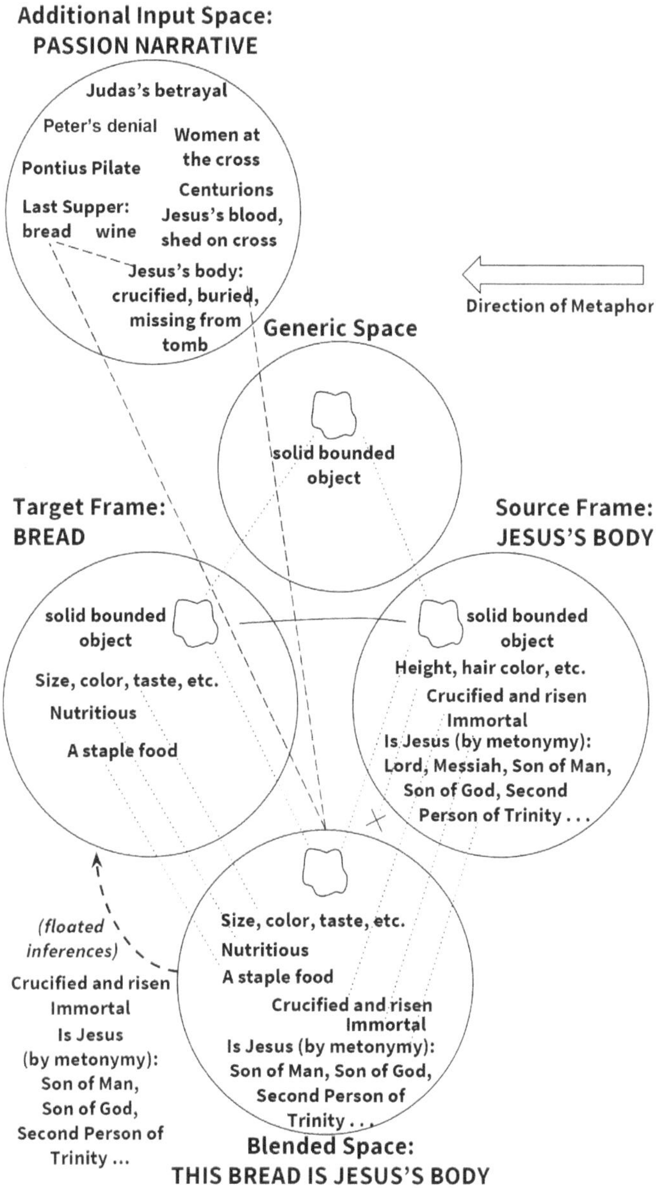

Figure 6.7. THIS BREAD IS JESUS'S BODY with inputs from PASSION NARRATIVE

All in all, the strand of eucharistic piety represented above by the prayer of Philoxenus is grounded in a single-scope blend, or metaphor, strengthened by a concurrent metonymy to create a megablend. In this blend, the most salient attributes of Jesus's body and blood—Jesus's personhood, crucified and risen, immortal, divine—are mapped onto bread and wine, while their metonymic association within the PASSION NARRATIVE frame connects this sacred meal particularly closely with the climactic moments of Jesus's death and resurrection.[39] In a piety grounded in this Synoptic/Pauline metaphor, to receive the eucharist is to feed upon Jesus in a way that is qualitatively unique. Consuming these elements can offer union with Jesus and can bestow Jesus's own risen immortal life.

The Johannine Metaphor: JESUS'S FLESH AND BLOOD ARE HEAVENLY LIFE-GIVING FOOD AND DRINK

The source of the metaphor JESUS IS BREAD AND DRINK lies in the sixth chapter of the Gospel of John. Unlike the three Synoptic gospels, John contains no eucharistic institution narrative. However, it does have a lengthy discourse in which Jesus identifies himself with food and drink. He begins by calling himself "the bread of God . . . that comes from heaven and gives life to the world" and "the bread of life."[40] This discourse clearly establishes the metaphor JESUS IS BREAD—but it is also clear that this is no ordinary bread but a heavenly bread.[41] While reminiscent of the heavenly bread with which God fed the ancient Israelites, it is something more as well: the manna sustained only temporary mortal life, but Jesus as heavenly bread will confer eternal life. "Your forebears ate the manna in the wilderness, and they died. This is the bread that comes down from heaven so that one may eat from it and not die. I am the living bread that has come down from heaven; whoever eats from this bread will live into eternity."[42] So far, then, we have not just JESUS IS BREAD but JESUS IS HEAVENLY LIFE-GIVING BREAD.

At the end of verse 51 Jesus adds more specificity to the metaphor: "And the bread that I will give for the life of the world is my flesh." Now it is not simply Jesus but specifically his flesh that is being identified as bread. In Greek as in English, the Johannine term *flesh* (*sarx*) is a near-synonym of the Synoptic/Pauline term *body* (*sōma*), with the difference that the former is a mass noun (one that refers to a substance) while the latter is a count noun (one that refers to a discrete object.)

Soon Jesus also introduces the idea of his blood as life-giving drink:

> Truly, truly, I say to you, if you do not eat the flesh of the Son of Man and drink his blood, you do not have life in you. Whoever eats my flesh and drinks my blood has eternal life, and I will raise them on the last day. For my flesh is true

> food, and my blood is true drink. Whoever eats my flesh and drinks my blood remains in me, and I in them.[43]

No specific type of drink is named: a reader influenced by the Synoptic and Pauline narratives might presume that wine is in view, but John gives no reason to assume this.[44]

On the whole, then, this discourse from John 6 evokes the metaphors JESUS IS HEAVENLY LIFE-GIVING BREAD and JESUS'S BLOOD IS LIFE-GIVING DRINK, or in combination, JESUS'S FLESH AND BLOOD ARE HEAVENLY LIFE-GIVING BREAD AND DRINK. A diagram of the blend created by the FLESH half of the metaphor is found in figure 6.8; again, a similar diagram could be constructed for JESUS'S BLOOD IS DRINK.

The generic space is again fairly minimal and based on image-schematic compatibility. In this case, the target domain (JESUS'S FLESH) is not a single bounded object but a solid mass substance. This does not present a problem for the mapping, however, since what is in view here is not a specific piece of bread but bread as an imagined heavenly substance. The Greek word *artos* can function either as a count noun (like the English *loaf*) or as a mass noun (like the English *bread*) and works equally well with either image schema.

The blended space represents a mapping of the most salient attributes of the source frame (HEAVENLY BREAD) onto the target (JESUS'S FLESH). Again, some target attributes are retained: the sensory characteristics of heavenly bread would not only clash with those of Jesus but may not be particularly clearly imaginable anyway. In the blend, Jesus's flesh retains all its essential qualities (crucified and risen, immortal, metonymically identified with Jesus himself, etc.); however, it is also (as bread) nutritious, a life-sustaining staple, satisfying to hunger, and so on. Moreover, as the Johannine text stipulates, it sustains not only ordinary life but eternal life. All these attributes are available to be floated back up to the target space as implications about the nature of Jesus.

Vital to the difference between this metaphor and the Synoptic/Pauline one is that no physical food or drink is required by this blend. Instead of functioning as the target frame onto which the properties of Jesus's body and blood are mapped, food and drink function in this metaphor as the source frame, supplying the properties that are mapped onto Jesus's flesh and blood. The implications for piety are enormous. In this blend, *any* act of spiritual union with Jesus can be understood as a metaphorical eating and drinking of this heavenly sustenance. The observance of the Lord's Supper might indeed be an occasion for this spiritual feeding—but it is not the only one, nor even necessarily a privileged one. Prayer itself is a feeding on Jesus, and this can happen at any place and time: "Services but once a week for us will never do. Every day we need the fellowship to take us through."[45]

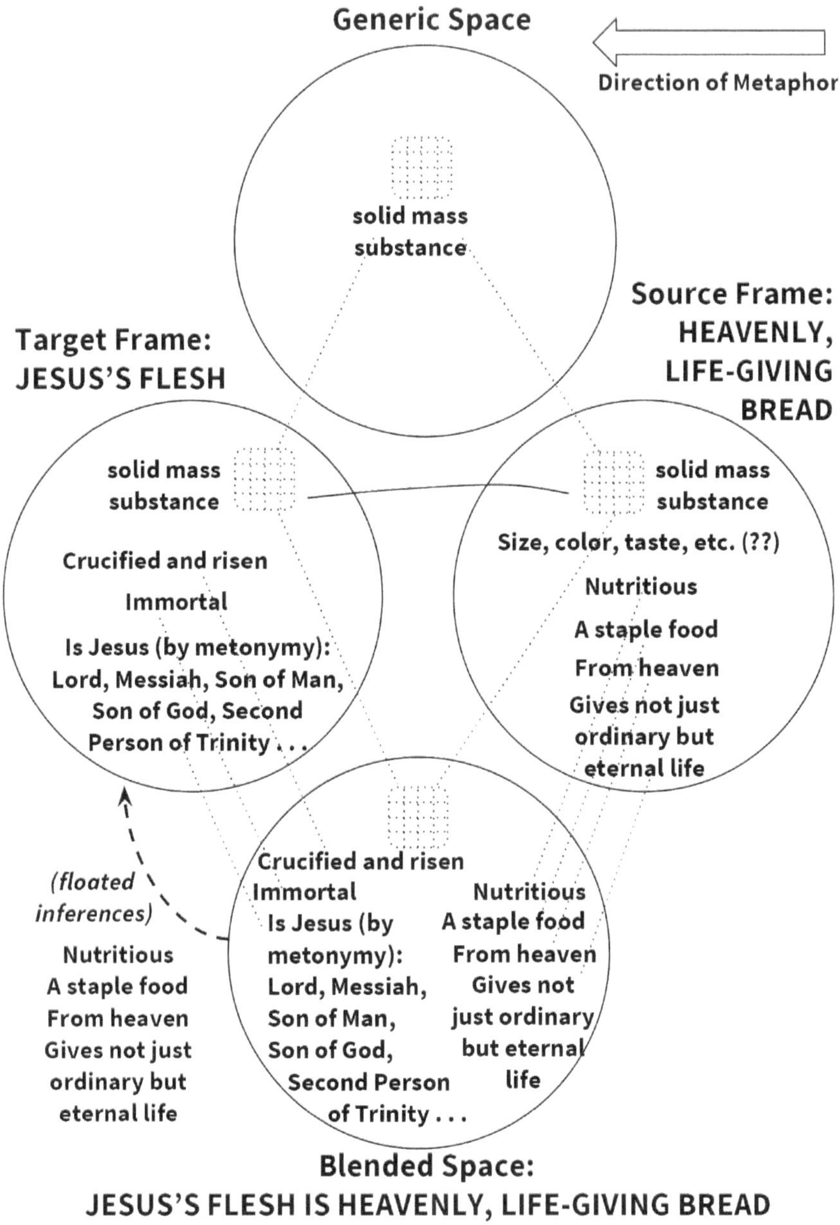

Figure 6.8. JESUS'S FLESH IS HEAVENLY, LIFE-GIVING BREAD

COMBINING THE TWO METAPHORS

Analyzing these two metaphors separately is helpful in illustrating their very different cognitive bases and implications. It can also be misleading, however, because metaphors do not exist in isolation. What we actually experience moment by moment is a rapidly shifting array of megablends combining primary metaphors, cultural assumptions and motifs, past experiences, encyclopedic knowledge about various frames, and so on. It should not be surprising, then, that the Synoptic/Pauline and Johannine metaphors can interact with one another. In particular, it is possible to feed the blended space of the Synoptic/Pauline metaphor (THIS BREAD AND WINE ARE JESUS'S BODY AND BLOOD) *into* the Johannine metaphor (JESUS'S FLESH AND BLOOD ARE HEAVENLY LIFE-GIVING FOOD AND DRINK) as the target frame. Figure 6.9 illustrates how this works.

In this arrangement, the two metaphors (one of which is already a megablend) have been chained together into a more complicated megablend still. The result is that instead of being mapped simply onto the personhood (flesh and blood) of Jesus, the attributes of heavenly, life-giving bread and drink are being mapped onto the eucharistic bread and wine understood as the body and blood of Jesus. In this megablend, it is not simply Jesus in heaven but rather *the eucharistic Jesus in the consecrated gifts* who is the bread of life, food indeed, drink indeed.[46]

The possibility of chaining these metaphors means that one's reading of John 6 can be very different depending on whether or not one comes to the passage with ritual eucharistic practice already in mind. A Christian with a devoutly Johannine piety can read John 6 on its own with no thought given to a ritual meal whatsoever. On the other hand, a Christian with a devoutly Synoptic/Pauline piety may well combine the two metaphors without even thinking about it and read John 6 in such a way that the entire passage is about the eucharistic meal. Context can highlight one reading or the other, of course. When "This is my daily bread" is sung during a service of praise, preaching, and prayer, the Johannine metaphor on its own is likely to dominate.[47] When "My flesh is food indeed and my blood is drink indeed" is sung during a eucharistic liturgy, the combination of the two metaphors will likely prevail.[48]

Chaining the two metaphors can have other surprising implications as well. The Roman Catholic doctrine of transubstantiation, for example, stipulates that the consecrated eucharistic gifts retain none of the *substantia* (essence, reality) of bread and wine but only their *species* (sensory qualities). This theory takes specific account of the clash between the sensory attributes of the source and target frames in the Synoptic/Pauline metaphor and constructs a model to

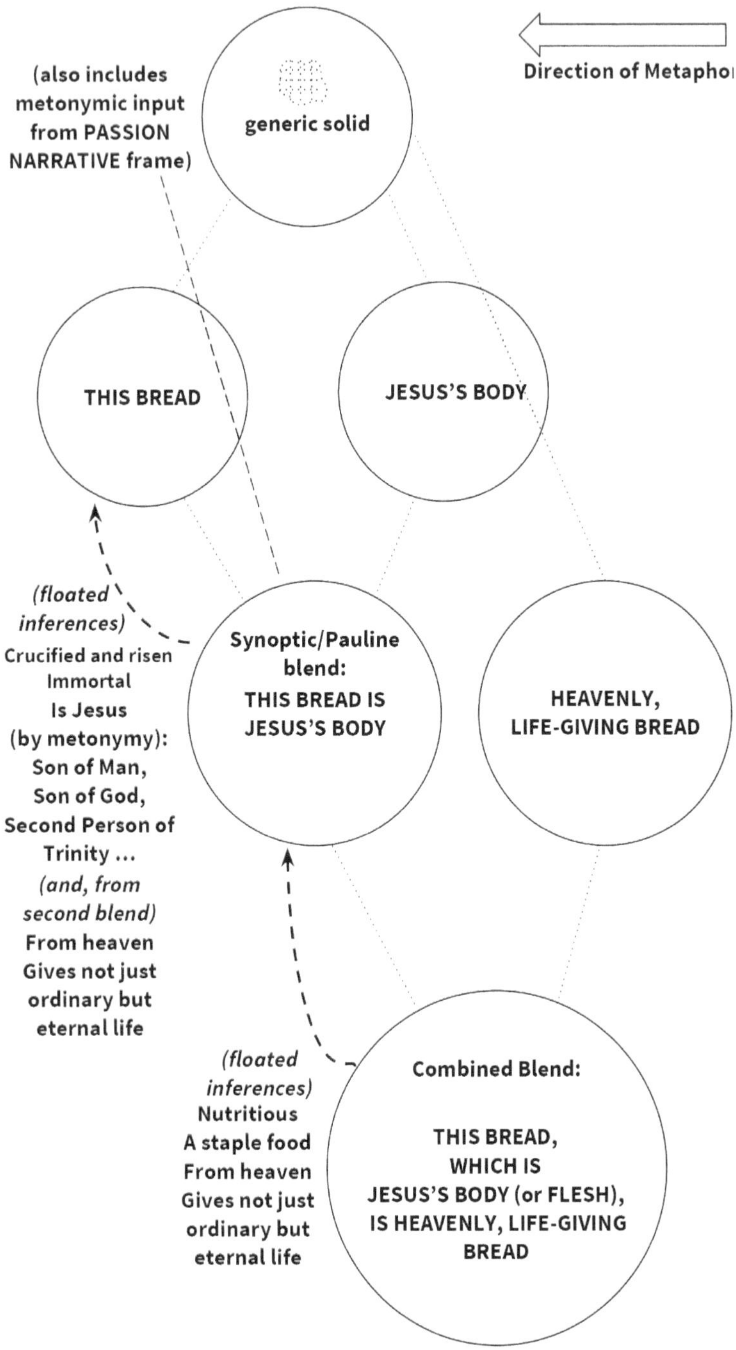

Figure 6.9. Combined Megablend

resolve it, drawing on an Aristotelian form of what George Lakoff and Rafael Nuñez call the "Folk Theory of Essences."[49] One potential complication of this model is that it can raise the question of whether it is still appropriate, strictly speaking, to call the consecrated elements *bread* and *wine.* Since both scripture and many respected ancient authors name them as such, this needs to be accounted for.[50] The thirteenth-century theologian Thomas Aquinas offers two approaches to this question. The first is simply to assert that the *species* retain their previous names despite the change. The second, however, invokes the megablend in which the two metaphors are chained together:

> After the consecration there are two ways in which we can speak of "bread" in this sacrament. First, the species hold onto the name of the original substance. . . . Second, the body of Christ itself can become bread; it is the mystical bread that comes down from heaven.[51]

In the megablend, the eucharistic elements which might (strictly speaking) no longer be considered bread and wine but the body and blood of Christ can nonetheless be identified as *mystical bread, food indeed, drink indeed*, and so on.

The question may arise: can the two metaphors also be combined in the reverse order? At first glance, it might seem as if this should be possible given their opposite directionality: if one can serve as an input to the other, why not the reverse? Yet as we have seen, there are subtle but important differences in the way the input frames are structured in the two metaphors. Chaining them together in one direction works because the source frame of the Synoptic/Pauline metaphor is near-synonymous with the target frame of the Johannine metaphor, and the combined metaphors result in additional meaning, identifying *this* bread and wine with the Johannine heavenly bread and drink, as in figure 6.10.

This is not the case in the opposite direction. The Johannine source frame (HEAVENLY LIFE-GIVING BREAD AND DRINK) is not readily synonymous with the Synoptic target frame (THIS BREAD AND WINE). The Last Supper sayings demand a specific loaf and cup as target rather than the generalized, abstract reality of Jesus-as-metaphorical-heavenly-bread-and-drink. Moreover, even if the two metaphors could be forced into a chain, the result would be tautological (JESUS'S FLESH AND BLOOD ARE JESUS'S BODY AND BLOOD), as in figure 6.11.

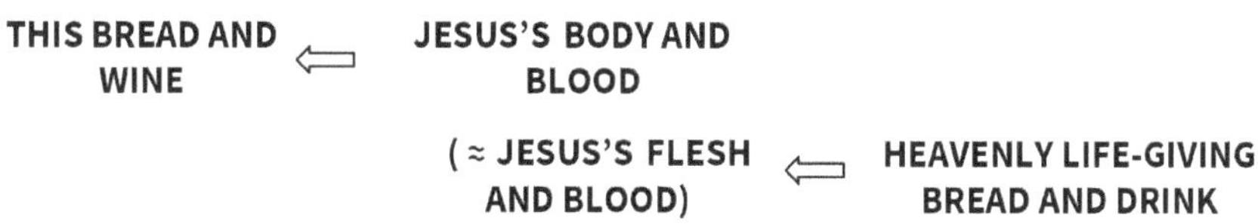

Figure 6.10. THIS BREAD AND WINE ARE HEAVENLY BREAD AND DRINK

JESUS'S FLESH AND BLOOD	⇐	**HEAVENLY LIFE-GIVING BREAD AND DRINK**		
FLESH		**(≠ *THIS* BREAD AND WINE?)**	⇐	**JESUS'S BODY AND BLOOD**

Figure 6.11. JESUS'S FLESH AND BLOOD ARE JESUS'S BODY AND BLOOD

The Synoptic/Pauline and Johannine metaphors can combine, but not in just any way. Their interactions are constrained by the mechanics of the blending process and the particular characteristics of the input frames involved.

CONCLUSION

The proper interpretation of the Synoptic/Pauline institution narratives and John 6 was at the heart of the fierce debate between the sixteenth-century reformers Martin Luther and Huldrych Zwingli. For Luther, Jesus's words "This is my body" and "This is my blood" were a bedrock hermeneutical principle: he famously scrawled them in chalk on the table at the beginning of the two parties' debate at Marburg. Luther took those words to be literal and thus insisted on the real presence of Christ in the eucharistic elements. Zwingli, for his part, took John 6 as his hermeneutical starting point and insisted that feeding on Christ was a spiritual and not a physical act. Zwingli had come to believe that the Synoptic/Pauline words of institution must be figurative—which meant to him that they could be translated into an underlying literal equivalent: "This signifies my body."[52]

Neither Luther nor Zwingli questioned an assumption they both shared: that only literal language is adequate to express proper truth claims. At Marburg, Zwingli's ally Oecolampadius argued that "The Holy Scriptures frequently employ figurative speech, metaphors, metonymies, and the like. In such cases words have a meaning different from what they say." To this Luther rejoined, "There are indeed many metaphors in Holy Scripture. But you have to prove that here, in the words 'This is my body,' a metaphor is contained."[53] Both parties assumed that to agree that the words of institution contained a metaphor would be to agree that they were not, strictly speaking, true, but could rather be translated into an underlying literal equivalent.

Recent advances in linguistic study have challenged this assumption. Contemporary developments in cognitive linguistics suggest that metaphor and metonymy are basic functions without which human thought would be profoundly impoverished, and that there is no clearly distinguishable boundary between literal and figurative language, but rather a continuum from more concrete to more abstract concepts—all of which are ultimately grounded in embodied physical experience. From this point of view, it may be possible to overcome historic impasses with regard to eucharistic theology and to begin to find common ground.

Both the Synoptic/Pauline and Johannine metaphors of eucharistic presence are scriptural. Both make important and irreplaceable contributions to Christian spirituality and practice. An ecumenical theology of eucharistic presence needs to take account of both. Those Christian traditions which have emphasized the Johannine metaphor have much to teach Christians of a high-sacramental piety about feeding on Jesus day by day, living eucharistically in all of life, not only in the ritual meal itself. On the other hand, these traditions have sometimes tended toward a reductionist reading of the Synoptic/Pauline metaphor, such that some Christians would find it difficult to point to the eucharistic bread and simply say "That is the body of Christ"—although they might have no difficulty in pointing to the gathered church community and saying the same thing. Just as Paul's metaphor THE CHURCH IS CHRIST'S BODY expresses a profound truth, one more true than "literal" language can express, so does the Synoptic/Pauline metaphor. An ecumenical theology of the eucharist that honors both metaphors will do well to acknowledge *both* that Christians feed spiritually on Jesus anywhere and everywhere *and* that the eucharistic meal is a particular and unique means of doing so through the bread and wine that Christ calls his body and blood.

Divisions among Christians with regard to the eucharist have been largely based on incompatible interpretations of the Synoptic/Pauline metaphor. Traditions which have emphasized its truth have historically found it difficult to affirm that it is a metaphor, while traditions that have held it to be metaphorical have historically found it difficult to affirm without qualification that it is true. The insights of cognitive linguistics offer a means of transcending this dichotomy in a way that safeguards the legitimate concerns of both high-sacramental traditions on the one side and Reformed and free-church traditions on the other. The Reformed theologian George Hunsinger has argued that "an irreducible minimum" for the reconciliation of ecumenical divisions regarding the eucharist is for all churches to be able to affirm liturgically "that the relation of 'This bread' to 'my body' is actually one of real predication."[54] A cognitively informed ecumenical theology of eucharistic presence could do so while also affirming that it is figurative, since it evokes a complex blend that includes both metaphoric and metonymic mappings.

Such a cognitively informed theology could also do more than that—for Christians through the centuries have developed a rich and varied repertoire of additional ways to speak about their encounter with Christ in the eucharist. Some models rest on image-schematic concepts like the CONTAINER ("Christ's body and blood are *in* the bread and wine") or force-dynamic metaphors like CHANGE IS MOTION ("conversion *from* bread and wine *into* Christ's body and blood"). Others evoke more complex blends: "The bread is the symbol of Christ's body" is not, as Zwingli believed, a simpler translation of "The bread is Christ's body" but rather a prompt for a much more intricate array of mental spaces.[55]

These various models have differing entailments which would make several of them mutually incompatible if understood literally. As metaphors, however, each highlights some aspects of Christians' experience while hiding others.[56] The CONTAINER image, for example, highlights the entailment that when believers receive the elements into themselves they are also receiving Jesus into themselves.[57] But it also has entailments that would be problematic if literalized: Christ is not literally contained in the bread in the sense that he is a prisoner inside it, or is hurt when the bread is broken. The container model makes a distinctive contribution but needs to be complemented and counterbalanced by others with their own different entailments. Each metaphor offers unique insights, even as none is the whole truth.

Recognizing different metaphors of eucharistic presence not as mutually exclusive, but as complementary, may serve as a foundation for an ecumenical understanding of the eucharist that is broader and richer than any single formulation would permit. Such a "multiply metaphorical"[58] way of doing eucharistic theology would move away from the search for a single verbal statement designed to please all parties or to express a precise, objective, viewpoint-independent truth. Instead it would embrace an embodied understanding—we might even say an *incarnational* understanding—that acknowledges the figurative quality of all theological truth claims while insisting that such claims can be real, apt, and true.

NOTES

1. The Roman Catholic Church's 1964 Dogmatic Constitution on the Church (*Lumen gentium*), for example, calls the eucharist "the source and summit of the whole Christian life" (11).

2. From the words of administration in the 1552 service of Holy Communion. See Brian Cummings, ed., *The Book of Common Prayer: The Texts of 1549, 1559, and 1662* (Oxford: Oxford University Press, 2011), 137, 732–33.

3. See, for example, Telford Work, "Communion: A Pentecostal Perspective," in *What Does It Mean to "Do This"?: Supper, Mass, Eucharist*, ed. Michael Root and James J. Buckley (Eugene, OR: Cascade Books, 2014), 121–43.

4. Praise and worship music "not only replaces the service of the Table as a primary ordering liturgical element, it also in some sense functions eucharistically for its participants," Sarah Koenig, "This Is My Daily Bread: Toward a Sacramental Theology of Evangelical Praise and Worship," *Worship* 82, no. 2 (March 2008): 147.

5. Marie Barnett, "Breathe," © 1995 Mercy/Vineyard Publishing, 1995 (admin. in North America by Music Services o/b/o Vineyard Music). All rights reserved. Used by permission. Barnett's song features prominently in Koenig's essay.

6. Mark Stamm recounts several anecdotes illustrating the challenges of very different eucharistic pieties for ecumenical worship in "'What Are We Doing?' Thoughts about a Seminary Chapel Program in an Ecumenical Setting," *Worship* 84, no. 2 (March 1, 2010): 121–37. See also Peter Bouteneff, "What Do We Do with This? Ecumenical Implications of the Handling of the Eucharist," in *What Does It Mean to "Do This"?*, 74–87.

7. The foundational work for conceptual metaphor theory is George Lakoff and Mark Johnson, *Metaphors We Live By* (Chicago: University of Chicago Press, 1980). A good overall introduction is Zoltán Kövecses, *Metaphor: A Practical Introduction* (New York: Oxford University Press, 2002). For epistemological and philosophical implications, see George Lakoff and Mark Johnson, *Philosophy in the Flesh: The Embodied Mind and Its Challenge to Western Thought* (New York: Basic Books, 1999). Following recent work by Karen Sullivan, Barbara Dancygier, and Eve Sweetser, I have chosen to treat metaphors as mappings between frames rather than domains (the terminology used in most earlier literature). See Karen Sullivan, *Frames and Constructions in Metaphoric Language* (Amsterdam: John Benjamins, 2013); Barbara Dancygier and Eve Sweetser, *Figurative Language* (Cambridge: Cambridge University Press, 2014), especially 17–21.

8. In linguistics, an asterisk appearing before an example traditionally indicates an anomalous or unacceptable usage.

9. See the list in Lakoff and Johnson, *Philosophy in the Flesh*, 50–54. Grady's dissertation, which originally developed these examples, is "Foundations of Meaning: Primary Metaphors and Primary Scenes" (PhD diss., University of California, Berkeley, 1997).

10. Various analysts have worked on this particular example. See Joseph E. Grady, Todd Oakley, and Seana Coulson, "Blending and Metaphor," in *Metaphor in Cognitive Linguistics: Selected Papers from the 5th International Cognitive Linguistics Conference, Amsterdam, 1997*, ed. Raymond W. Gibbs and Gerard J. Steen (Amsterdam: John Benjamins Publishing, 1999), 104–6; Kövecses, *Metaphor*, 24–25; George Lakoff, "The Neural Theory of Metaphor," in *The Cambridge Handbook of Metaphor and Thought*, ed. Raymond W. Gibbs (Cambridge: Cambridge University Press, 2008), 32–33.

11. See Gilles Fauconnier and Mark Turner, *The Way We Think: Conceptual Blending and the Mind's Hidden Complexities* (New York: Basic Books, 2002).

12. Fauconnier and Turner, *The Way We Think*, 40.

13. Mary Therese DesCamp, *Metaphor and Ideology: Liber Antiquitatum Biblicarum and Literary Methods through a Cognitive Lens* (Leiden: Brill, 2007), 25.

14. Fauconnier and Turner, *The Way We Think*, 45–46.

15. For the term "float," see Gilles Fauconnier, *Mappings in Thought and Language* (Cambridge: Cambridge University Press, 1997), 61, 112.

16. On image mappings, see George Lakoff and Mark Turner, *More Than Cool Reason: A Field Guide to Poetic Metaphor* (Chicago: University of Chicago Press, 1989), 89–96.

17. Interestingly, Grady, Coulson, and Oakley (see note 12) treat the comment as criticism, while Kövecses and Lakoff treat it as praise.

18. Aelred Cody, "An Instruction of Philoxenus of Mabbug on Gestures and Prayer When One Receives Communion in the Hand, with a History of the Manner of Receiving the Eucharistic Bread in the West Syrian Church," in *Rule of Prayer, Rule of Faith: Essays in Honor of Aidan Kavanagh, OSB*, ed. Nathan Mitchell and John Francis Baldovin (Collegeville, MN: Liturgical Press, 1996), 62–63. The reference to the eucharistic bread as a "fiery coal" is characteristic of Syrian liturgy and derives from Isaiah 6:6-7.

19. "Some, These Days, Would Tell Us That Our Jesus Is Not Food," Hymnal.net, https://www.hymnal.net/en/hymn/ns/192, accessed January 22, 2018. The author of this text is unknown; according to Hymnal.net, it is in the public domain. An online search reveals several locally produced songbooks that include it, often under the title "We Love the Church Life!", as well as a number of video and audio recordings; for one recording, see NYCYPCD, We Love the Church Life!, iTunes track, on I Love thy Kingdom, Lord!, 2012, streaming audio, 2:33, https://itunes.apple.com/us/album/i-love-thy-kingdom-lord!/id513066247, accessed January 22, 2018.

20. Interestingly, both this song and Marie Barnett's "Breathe," cited earlier, add a metaphor—JESUS IS AIR—which further strengthens the believer's dependence on Jesus: not only daily, but every single minute. This metaphor does not appear in scripture but seems to be a creative elaboration of JESUS IS BREAD AND DRINK.

21. DRINK is used instead of the more specific WINE for reasons that will become apparent below.

22. *Figurative Language*, 30–31. These two example sentences are drawn directly from Dancygier and Sweetser's text.

23. Dancygier and Sweetser, *Figurative Language*, 30.

24. Mark 14:22-25. All scripture translations are mine.

25. For an exploration of the role of the copula construction in evoking metaphoric blends, see Sullivan, *Frames and Constructions in Metaphoric Language*.

26. The suggestions occasionally advanced that Jesus is referring not to the bread but to the gathered group of disciples at table, to the meal event as a whole, or simply to his own physical body which is about to be sacrificed, are cognitively unconvincing for the same reasons explored below with regard to the wine. For the first two interpretations, see, e.g., Vernard Eller, *In Place of Sacraments: A Study of Baptism and the Lord's Supper* (Grand Rapids, MI: Eerdmans, 1972), 89–90. The third was the position of the 16th-century radical reformer Andreas Karlstadt: see *The Eucharistic Pamphlets of Andreas Bodenstein von Karlstadt*, trans. and ed. Amy Nelson Burnett (Kirksville, MO: Truman State University Press, 2011).

27. This preservation of schematic topology is known as the Invariance Principle. See George Lakoff, "The Contemporary Theory of Metaphor," in *Metaphor and*

Thought, ed. Andrew Ortony, 2nd ed. (Cambridge: Cambridge University Press, 1993), 215–16. On image schemas as the building blocks for more complex image mappings, see Lakoff and Turner, *More Than Cool Reason*, 97–99. The seminal work on image schemas is Mark Johnson, *The Body in the Mind: The Bodily Basis of Meaning, Imagination, and Reason* (Chicago: University of Chicago Press, 1987).

28. A few common forms of metonymy include Part for Whole ("All hands on deck"), Whole for Part ("I saw a picture of him," when the picture only shows a person's face), Place for Institution ("Scotland Yard is after two suspects"), Institution for Person ("Chevron announces the opening of a new refinery"), and Producer for Product ("Hemingway is fun to read"), Lakoff and Johnson, *Metaphors We Live By*, 35–38.

29. The FrameNet database at the University of California, Berkeley, includes an entry for a CONTAINER frame with a Contents element. In formal terms, then, this can be thought of as a Whole for Part metonymy in which the name of the whole CONTAINER frame is used to indicate the contents alone: https://framenet2.icsi.berkeley.edu/fnReports/data/frameIndex.xml?frame=Containers, accessed June 19, 2017.

30. See Eller, *In Place of Sacraments*, 93–101.

31. Consider André Breton's line "My wife . . . whose waist is an hourglass," analyzed by Lakoff and Turner in *More Than Cool Reason*, 90–95. It is not the entire hourglass, but the *narrow part* of the hourglass, that is mapped onto the woman's waist in this image metaphor. Shared image structure allows readers to process instances like this effortlessly and often even unconsciously.

32. This is even more true in light of the way Paul goes on in verse 27 to make an explicit parallel between "the bread and . . . the cup" and "the body and blood of the Lord."

33. It is interesting to consider the doctrine of concomitance in light of this issue of image compatibility. Concomitance (the teaching that the whole Christ is present in either element) developed in the medieval West as an affirmation of Christ's indivisibility. Over time it came to provide theological support for withholding the chalice from the laity: see Nathan Mitchell, *Cult and Controversy: The Worship of the Eucharist Outside Mass* (New York: Pueblo, 1982), 157–63. Protestant critics often attacked concomitance on what we would call image-schematic grounds. In 1672, for example, the English bishop George Bull wrote, "It is most false that the body and blood of Christ are sacramentally in each element; for it is the bread only that doth sacramentally signify and exhibit the body of Christ, and the wine only that doth sacramentally signify and exhibit the blood of Christ. . . . The effusion and shedding of Christ's blood on the cross . . . is in the Communion only of the bread so far from being perfectly that it is not at all represented but totally obscured." *A Vindication of the Church of England*, quoted in Darwell Stone, *A History of the Doctrine of the Holy Eucharist*, vol. 2 (London: Longmans, Green, and Co., 1909), 444–45.

34. This short overview in fact compresses many other metaphors, metonymies, and blends that are at work: for example, treating Jesus's body as a single entity already represents a blend of Jesus's historical body, his risen body, and his glorified body, which Christian theology treats as continuous but also distinct in certain ways. It also leaves out the ecclesial body of Jesus—that is to say, the church itself, which

Paul also metaphorically identifies with Christ's body (Rom 12:5, 1 Cor 12:12, 27). It is also worth considering the metonymy at work in the fact that not only is the entire loaf identified as the body of Christ, so is each individual morsel broken from it. As the 1549 Prayer Book puts it, members "must not think less to be received in part than in the whole, but in each of them the whole body of our savior Jesus Christ" (Cummings, *The Book of Common Prayer*, 39, spelling modernized). I am grateful to Eve Sweetser for teasing some of these out with me in conversation.

35. The Western doctrine of transubstantiation arose as a response to this clash at the level of academic theology. In popular piety, however, this clash has at times been resolved in the opposite direction, as in the many medieval visions of the consecrated bread as bleeding flesh, the Christ Child, or the Lamb of God. See Miri Rubin, *Corpus Christi: The Eucharist in Late Medieval Culture* (Cambridge: Cambridge University Press, 1991), 108–41.

36. "The essence of Christ, present in the bread, is transformed into a quality of the subject ingesting the bread. . . . [This] is an act in which one container (the subject) absorbs and dissolves another container thereby releasing the essence it contains." Jesper Sørensen, *A Cognitive Theory of Magic* (Lanham, MD: AltaMira, 2007), 105–6. Sørensen notes that this idea of "forward contagion" by which symbolic attributes are gained by ingestion is common across cultures.

37. Fauconnier and Turner, *The Way We Think*, 151ff.

38. Sørensen, *A Cognitive Theory of Magic*, 95–96. See also Sørensen's less detailed but helpful diagram of a blend involved in the theory of transubstantiation, 98-102.

39. Again, the blend can get even more complicated than this. For example, Eve Sweetser recently drew my attention to the fact that the metonymy within the PASSION NARRATIVE frame is reinforced by a metaphoric mapping between Jesus's *giving* the bread and wine to the disciples at the Last Supper and his *giving* up of himself to a sacrificial death.

40. John 6:33, 35, 48, 50, 51.

41. The idea of God's word as heavenly food and drink is in fact already an established blend in the Hebrew Scriptures; see, for example, Ps 42:1-2, Ps 63:1, Jer 15:16, Ezek 3:3. John's gospel identifies Jesus with God's word (1:1–18).

42. John 6:49-51.

43. John 6:53-56.

44. Indeed, some scholars hypothesize that John's gospel may have arisen in a community that used water for its eucharistic meals, at least at some stage of its life. See Margaret Daly-Denton, "Drinking the Water That Jesus Gives: A Feature of the Johannine Eucharist?," in *A Wandering Galilean: Essays in Honour of Seán Freyne*, ed. Zuleika Rodgers, Margaret Daly-Denton, and Anne Fitzpatrick-McKinley (Leiden: Brill, 2009), 343–66, and my own essay "A Eucharistic Origins Story, Part 2: The Body and Blood of Christ," *Worship* 92, no. 4 (July 2018): 298–317.

45. NYCYPCD, *We Love the Church Life!*

46. Note that this arrangement works only because the two different image schemas involved are not actually incompatible. The first blended space, THIS BREAD IS JESUS'S BODY, envisions a bounded object, a specific piece of bread. But because the

interior of that bread is a consistent mass substance, it can easily also be imagined as JESUS'S FLESH and re-blended with HEAVENLY LIFE-GIVING BREAD. The solid object in the blended space is a mass substance which is also bounded.

47. Barnett, "Breathe."

48. Episcopal Church, *The Hymnal 1982: According to the Use of the Episcopal Church* (New York: Church Hymnal Corp., 1985), S168 and S169.

49. This is a common way of modeling the universe in which each thing "has" a substance or essence, a metaphorical reification (IDEAS ARE OBJECTS) of the fundamental category to which it is considered to belong. George Lakoff and Rafael E. Núñez, *Where Mathematics Comes from: How the Embodied Mind Brings Mathematics into Being* (New York: Basic Books, 2000), 107ff.

50. See, for example, Paul in 1 Corinthians 10:16–17, 11:26–28; Justin Martyr, *First Apology* 65; Augustine, *Sermon 272*.

51. *Summa Theologiae* (London: Blackfriars, 1964), 3a.77.6. Aquinas's ninth-century predecessor Paschasius Radbertus expresses this megablend even more clearly: "The substance of the bread and wine is effectually made by an inner change into the flesh and blood of Christ, so that after the consecration it is now believed actually to be the real flesh and blood of Christ, and is regarded by believers as nothing else than Christ the Bread from heaven. . . . It is the flesh of Christ and real flesh, and yet is rightly called the living Bread which came down from heaven, flesh indeed by grace but bread by effect, because, as this earthly bread supplies temporal life, so that heavenly Bread affords eternal and heavenly life." *De corpore et sanguine Domini* 8.2, 15.17, translated in Darwell Stone, *A History of the Doctrine of the Holy Eucharist*, vol. 1 (London: Longmans, Green, and Co., 1909), 220–1, 219–20.

52. "That simple explanation which anyone could understand pleased me: 'This bread signifies my body which is given for you.' . . . The force of the word 'is' undergoes modification and has the value, 'is a signification or representation of.'" Huldrych Zwingli, *Huldrych Zwingli: Writings*, vol. 2, *Letter to Matthew Alber Concerning the Lord's Supper*, trans. H. Wayne Pipkin, (Allison Park, PA: Pickwick Publications, 1984), 357.

53. Hermann Sasse, *This Is My Body: Luther's Contention for the Real Presence in the Sacrament of the Altar* (Minneapolis: Augsburg, 1959), 232. Sasse's reconstruction is based on a synthesis of several accounts of the colloquy. Here Oecolampadius' statement comes from the report of Anonymous, while Luther's retort comes from that of Hedio. Cf. *Luther's Works*, vol. 38, *The Marburg Colloquy and the Marburg Articles* (1529), ed. and trans. Martin E. Lehmann, American ed., (Philadelphia: Fortress Press, 1971), 16–17, 37.

54. George Hunsinger, *The Eucharist and Ecumenism: Let Us Keep the Feast* (New York: Cambridge University Press, 2008), 59–60.

55. See Fauconnier and Turner's discussion of the "X is the Y of Z" construction: *The Way We Think*, 139–54.

56. On highlighting and hiding, see Kövecses, *Metaphor*, 79–83.

57. This quality of CONTAINERS is known as transitivity. "Consider what follows if your car keys are *in* your hand and you then place your hand *in* your pocket. Via the transitive logic of CONTAINMENT, the car keys end up *in* your pocket." Mark Johnson,

"The Philosophical Significance of Image Schemas," in *From Perception to Meaning: Image Schemas in Cognitive Linguistics*, ed. Beate Hampe and Joseph E. Grady (Berlin: Mouton de Gruyter, 2005), 22.

58. "Our most fundamental concepts—time, events, causation, the mind, the self, and morality—are multiply metaphorical." Lakoff and Johnson, *Philosophy in the Flesh*, 128.

BIBLIOGRAPHY

Bouteneff, Peter. "What Do We Do with This? Ecumenical Implications of the Handling of the Eucharist." In *What Does It Mean to "Do This"?: Supper, Mass, Eucharist.* Edited by Michael Root and James J. Buckley, 74–87. Eugene, OR: Cascade Books, 2014.

Burnett, Amy Nelson, ed. *The Eucharistic Pamphlets of Andreas Bodenstein von Karlstadt*. Translated by Amy Nelson Burnett. Kirksville, MO: Truman State University Press, 2011.

Cody, Aelred. "An Instruction of Philoxenus of Mabbug on Gestures and Prayer When One Receives Communion in the Hand, with a History of the Manner of Receiving the Eucharistic Bread in the West Syrian Church." In *Rule of Prayer, Rule of Faith: Essays in Honor of Aidan Kavanagh, OSB*. Edited by Nathan Mitchell and John F. Baldovin, 56–79. Collegeville, MN: Liturgical Press, 1996.

Cummings, Brian, ed. *The Book of Common Prayer: The Texts of 1549, 1559, and 1662*. Oxford: Oxford University Press, 2011.

Daly-Denton, Margaret. "Drinking the Water That Jesus Gives: A Feature of the Johannine Eucharist?" In *A Wandering Galilean: Essays in Honour of Seán Freyne*. Edited by Zuleika Rodgers, Margaret Daly-Denton, and Anne Fitzpatrick-McKinley, 343–66. Leiden: Brill, 2009.

Dancygier, Barbara, and Eve Sweetser. *Figurative Language*. Cambridge: Cambridge University Press, 2014.

DesCamp, Mary Therese. *Metaphor and Ideology: Liber Antiquitatum Biblicarum and Literary Methods through a Cognitive Lens*. Leiden: Brill, 2007.

"Dogmatic Constitution on the Church: *Lumen Gentium*." Vatican City: Holy See, 1965.

Eller, Vernard. *In Place of Sacraments: A Study of Baptism and the Lord's Supper*. Grand Rapids, MI: Eerdmans, 1972.

Fauconnier, Gilles. *Mappings in Thought and Language*. Cambridge: Cambridge University Press, 1997.

Fauconnier, Gilles, and Mark Turner. *The Way We Think: Conceptual Blending and the Mind's Hidden Complexities*. New York: Basic Books, 2002.

Grady, Joseph Edward. "Foundations of Meaning: Primary Metaphors and Primary Scenes." PhD diss., University of California, Berkeley, 1997.

Grady, Joseph E., Todd Oakley, and Seana Coulson. "Blending and Metaphor." In *Metaphor in Cognitive Linguistics: Selected Papers from the 5th International Cognitive Linguistics Conference, Amsterdam, 1997*. Edited by Raymond W.

Gibbs and Gerard J. Steen, 101–24. Amsterdam: John Benjamins Publishing, 1999.

Hunsinger, George. *The Eucharist and Ecumenism: Let Us Keep the Feast*. New York: Cambridge University Press, 2008.

The Hymnal 1982: According to the Use of the Episcopal Church. New York: Church Hymnal Corporation, 1985.

Johnson, Mark. *The Body in the Mind: The Bodily Basis of Meaning, Imagination, and Reason*. Chicago: University of Chicago Press, 1987.

———. "The Philosophical Significance of Image Schemas." In *From Perception to Meaning: Image Schemas in Cognitive Linguistics*. Edited by Beate Hampe and Joseph E. Grady, 15–33. Berlin: Mouton de Gruyter, 2005.

Koenig, Sarah. "This Is My Daily Bread: Toward a Sacramental Theology of Evangelical Praise and Worship." *Worship* 82, no. 2 (March 2008): 141–61.

Kövecses, Zoltán. *Metaphor: A Practical Introduction*. New York: Oxford University Press, 2002.

Lakoff, George. "The Contemporary Theory of Metaphor." In *Metaphor and Thought*. Edited by Andrew Ortony, 2nd ed., 202–51. Cambridge: Cambridge University Press, 1993.

———. "The Neural Theory of Metaphor." In *The Cambridge Handbook of Metaphor and Thought*. Edited by Raymond W. Gibbs, 17–38. Cambridge: Cambridge University Press, 2008.

Lakoff, George, and Mark Johnson. *Metaphors We Live By*. Chicago: University of Chicago Press, 1980.

———. *Philosophy in the Flesh: The Embodied Mind and Its Challenge to Western Thought*. New York: Basic Books, 1999.

Lakoff, George, and Rafael E. Núñez. *Where Mathematics Comes From: How the Embodied Mind Brings Mathematics into Being*. New York: Basic Books, 2000.

Lakoff, George, and Mark Turner. *More than Cool Reason: A Field Guide to Poetic Metaphor*. Chicago: University of Chicago Press, 1989.

Luther, Martin. *Luther's Works*. Vol. 38, *The Marburg Colloquy and the Marburg Articles* (1529). American ed. Edited and Translated by Martin E. Lehman (Philadelphia: Fortress Press, 1971).

Mitchell, Nathan. *Cult and Controversy: The Worship of the Eucharist Outside Mass*. New York: Pueblo, 1982.

Rubin, Miri. *Corpus Christi: The Eucharist in Late Medieval Culture*. Cambridge: Cambridge University Press, 1991.

Sasse, Hermann. *This Is My Body: Luther's Contention for the Real Presence in the Sacrament of the Altar*. Minneapolis: Augsburg, 1959.

Shaver, Stephen R. "A Eucharistic Origins Story, Part 2: The Body and Blood of Christ." *Worship* 92, no. 4 (July 2018): 298–317.

Sørensen, Jesper. *A Cognitive Theory of Magic*. Lanham, MD: AltaMira, 2007.

Stamm, Mark Wesley. "'What Are We Doing?' Thoughts about a Seminary Chapel Program in an Ecumenical Setting." *Worship* 84, no. 2 (March 1, 2010): 121–37.

Stone, Darwell. *A History of the Doctrine of the Holy Eucharist*. 2 vols. London: Longmans, Green, and Co., 1909.

Sullivan, Karen. *Frames and Constructions in Metaphoric Language*. Amsterdam: John Benjamins, 2013.

Work, Telford. "Communion: A Pentecostal Perspective." In *What Does It Mean to "Do This"?: Supper, Mass, Eucharist*. Edited by Michael Root and James J. Buckley, 121–43. Eugene, OR: Cascade Books, 2014.

Zwingli, Huldrych. *Huldrych Zwingli: Writings*. Vol. 2, *Letter to Matthew Alber Concerning the Lord's Supper*. Translated by H. Wayne Pipkin. Allison Park, PA: Pickwick Publications, 1984.

Chapter Seven

Conceptual Mapping and Reception in Ecumenical Theology

Jakob Karl Rinderknecht

Christians confront a divided church. East is divided from West, Catholics from Protestants. This experienced reality is incompatible with both the shared profession of "one holy, catholic, and apostolic church" and the prayer of Jesus "that they might be one."[1] The divisions between Christians represent differences in doctrine, political divides, and the results of particular histories. These cannot merely be wished away or papered over. Any attempt to repair the divisions will require a means of reconciling these differences without merely forgetting about them.

The twentieth century has seen great progress in intra-Christian understanding, but the ecumenical movement still has much work to do. In this chapter, I will be examining one way in which paying attention to conceptual mapping serves the ecumenical project of Christian reconciliation. By focusing on the conceptual blends that structure the ways in which different groups of Christians proclaim the gospel, theologians can help the process of reception (or the broad appropriation) of theological agreements. After describing the problem of ecumenical reception and its relationship to conceptual mapping, I will provide a brief description of blending. I will then show how paying explicit attention to conceptual mapping can help the specialized work of ecumenists to be more broadly received in their churches.

THE PROBLEM OF RECEPTION

The ecumenical project to reconcile the churches has made undeniable progress since its tentative beginnings in the first decade of the twentieth century. When Protestant missionaries gathered in Edinburgh for the World

Missionary Conference of 1910, several participants saw a need to unify the church so that the world might believe.[2] Just two years before, Pope Leo XIII had approved an Octave of Prayer for Christian Unity, although its emphasis was prayer for the return of other Christians to the one true church in communion with the Holy See.[3] An encyclical from the Ecumenical Patriarchate, calling for a permanent "fellowship of churches" lent further momentum to the cause.[4] The World Council of Churches was founded in 1948.[5] In the ensuing years, the landscape has shifted dramatically. Many Protestant groups have come into altar and pulpit fellowship with each other, the World Council of Churches has served as a platform for multilateral conversation and shared mission, and Protestants, Catholics, and Orthodox Christians have actually started working and praying for Christian unity together, instead of separately.

One of the chief bases on which this progress is grounded is bilateral dialogue. Churches have appointed theologians to discuss topics of disagreement and see what new ways forward might be found. After years of conversation, these appointed commissions have declared that there is much more agreement than we once thought, and that many of the remaining differences are not reasons for continued division. Some commissions, like the work of the early International Anglican–Roman Catholic dialogues,[6] or the German Ecumenical Working Group (ÖAK),[7] have declared that astonishing levels of agreement exists on the issues that lie at the very heart of the sixteenth-century divides. The impact of their work on the daily lives of the churches, however, has been limited.

The reception of ecumenical agreement is beset by a common assumption about how theological language works, and therefore what it means for churches to agree on the Gospel. This assumption, called the "idealized conventional view" by Robert Masson, leads theologians to consider matters of meaning and of metaphor, such that:

> reason and concepts are abstract and disembodied. Literal meaning is the default position. Reasoning is primarily about propositions that can be objectively either true or false. The imaginative aspects of cognition—metonymy, metaphor, and mental images—are peripheral and deviations from literal meanings.[8]

If language is primarily literal, then ideas are easy to compare between traditions. Every disagreement is a simple contradiction. When Catholics call the Eucharist a sacrifice and Lutherans do not, there exists a disagreement that can be easily understood and that is itself a reason for the churches to be out of communion with each other.

If, however, both of these statements are meaningful only within a particular system of metaphorically structured discourse, it might be possible for Lutherans and Catholics to discover that their differing blends constitute a *seeming* contradiction rather than a real one. In order to explain why this is the case, it is important to understand the concept of blending and how it helps us to understand how human language, including theological language, works. A blend is "the mental space which results from conceptual integration, giving rise to emergent structure."[9] Because each statement functions metaphorically within a system, it cannot be understood properly without first understanding how it works within that system. Moreover, because these ideas have meaning within their systems, they may not be able to merely be simply transposed into a different system of thought. Doing so might change their meaning, and may even make them false. Consider, for example, the common cross-domain mapping: MORE IS BETTER. In many systems, this is intuitive, obvious and true. More stored food, water, or other necessities make us more secure. Human beings, encountering their own finality, often wish for more. But, it derives its meaning from the metaphoric systems in which it arises, tied to the necessities of life. It cannot simply be applied as a truism in all situations. More water does not help the person who is drowning, more time is not necessarily better for the procrastinator.

This is precisely what often happens in ecumenical questions. One group of Christians reads the writings of another and interprets them wrongly, not because they are misunderstanding the words that the other is saying, but because their language is predicated on different blends. Ecumenists spend years in dialogue precisely because they have to come to learn the language of the other if they are to make true judgments about what is really being said. They have to learn where transposition is possible, and where it is not. When it is not, they have to learn what translations are appropriate and which are not. In learning to do so, they also have to be attentive to areas of real disagreement and ask which of these are *church-dividing* issues, that is, issues where difference requires division, and where they are not.

It is not uncommon that the dialogue members find agreement to exist in places that there had previously seemed to be direct contradiction. What had seemed to be church-dividing is discovered to be a matter of inappropriate transposition. But these discoveries are the fruit of a long and difficult process that is not immediately obvious to those who have not developed familiarity with the specifics of both discourses. When dialogue members present their findings to their own traditions, they are asking them to accept their insights about which differences might be church dividing and which are false transpositions. Figuring out how to help people to recognize these insights without themselves undergoing the long apprenticeship in the others' discourse is the problem of reception.

THE DIFFICULTIES OF ECUMENICAL RECEPTION

The *Eighth Report* of the Joint Working Group between the Catholic Church and the World Council of Churches (JWG) defines reception as:

> the process by which the churches make their own the results of all their encounters with one another, and in a particular way the convergences and agreements reached on issues over which they have historically been divided. As the report of the sixth forum on bilateral dialogues notes: "Reception is an integral part of the movement towards that full communion which is realized when 'all the churches are able to recognize in one another the one, holy, catholic and apostolic Church in its fullness.'" Thus, reception is far more than the official responses to the dialogue results, although official responses are essential.[10]

Bilateral dialogues cannot heal the divisions between churches on their own. Part of the reason for this is structural: they occupy an intermediate position between the churches. Their members speak to one another as members of their respective traditions, but they do not usually speak *for* those traditions. The documents that they produce are therefore the products of the appointed commissions only. They are proposed to "the appropriate church authorities as the outcome of the commission's work . . . for thorough study."[11] This means that any agreements they reach are not final and have no binding force on their respective churches. Dialogue statements rest on their own ability to convince. And to be effective, they must convince both churches equally. In other words, in order to achieve their final goal of overcoming historic theological divisions, these documents must be *received*. If this happens, the agreement in them would then become the new basis on which relationships are built going forward.[12]

In order to describe how this reception happens, it will first be helpful to describe for levels at which reception happens: Official, Academic, Cultural, and Canonical-Institutional.

Official Reception

Reception, as we have said, is complex and operates on several levels. First, and perhaps most obvious, is the reception of dialogue agreements by the churches' official structures. Because the dialogue commissions propose agreements to their respective communities, their proposals must be judged by the appropriate authorities in those communities. The form that that this process takes differs in different communions; it is more or less defined depending on which communions are involved. The Joint Working Group between the World Council of Churches and the Catholic Church studied these various structures in a 2015 document called *Reception: A Key to Ecumenical Progress*.[13] Some churches, like the Roman Catholic Church, have a body that speaks magisterially for the whole.[14] In others, including many Lutherans, some kind of synodal consensus may be reached.[15] Some groups allow smaller units to individually declare that a document is received or not,[16] and some confessions currently have no mechanism for official reception.[17]

The goal of official reception would seem to have been fully accomplished in the 1999 Joint Declaration on the Doctrine of Justification. In it, the churches involved describe the document's task in this way: "The time has therefore come to take stock and to summarize the results of the dialogues on justification so that our churches may be informed about the overall results of this dialogue . . . and thereby be enabled to make binding decisions."[18] The official common statement goes even further:

> On the basis of the agreements reached in the Joint Declaration on the Doctrine of Justification, the Lutheran World Federation and the Catholic Church declare together: "The understanding of the doctrine of justification set forth in this Declaration shows that a consensus in basic truths of the doctrine of justification exists between Lutherans and Catholics" (JD 40). On the basis of this consensus the Lutheran World Federation and the Catholic Church declare together: "The teaching of the Lutheran Churches presented in the Declaration does not fall under the condemnations from the Council of Trent. The condemnations in the Lutheran Confessions do not apply to the teaching of the Roman Catholic Church presented in this Declaration" (JD 41).[19]

But even here, there are difficulties with reception, although not by church authorities. In this case, the difficulty is the reception within the wider church. A number of Lutheran voices, and a few Catholics, have publically rejected the document or denied that it reaches a real consensus, limiting its ability to reconcile the churches in practice.[20]

Academic Reception

This can, perhaps, be dealt with most quickly, as it is the type that most readers will have the most experience of. Ideas in the academy may take off, they may not. Some of them are dispatched by peer review before they get heard by many people at all. Some, like George Lindbeck's *The Nature of Doctrine,* are nearly ignored in the fields they are directed to (in this case, ecumenism), but become very important in others (epistemology).[21]

Over time, consensus can arise, ideas can shape what can and cannot be said. A proposal may found a whole new school of thought, or it may disappear silently into history, or both. Some of the ideas that are received by academics will affect the conversation beyond the academy, sometimes as intended, sometimes not. How exactly this happens is somewhat mysterious, but over time it becomes clear which ideas become canonical, which are respected but optional, and which are rejected.

Ecumenical insights by definition cross communities of discourse. One's own theology is used to describe the gospel in light of someone else's commitments, or their commitments are recognized in light of one's own theology as being the commitments of the gospel itself. This produces a new horizon, that is likely to be the product of a new conceptual integration, based on recognizing that the habitual blends at work in the others' theology are different. As such, it is difficult to promote to those without fluency in all these pieces. Without integrating the structuring insight, a person can have all the data of the dialogues, and not see the integration which is being prompted. Once it is made, however, it can open up new possibilities for thought.

Catherine Clifford explains an aspect of this process using Bernard Lonergan's divisions of the theological task. Dialogue takes place at the intersection between the mediated and mediating phases of theology. This means that the work of the dialogues is to jointly receive the insights of their traditions (mediated phase) and come to a new understanding of them that allows a new possibility for a life in greater communion (mediating phase). This new possibility often arises from the insight into the blends by which the other conceives of something.

In the process, sometimes a new blend is made possible that allows for the integration of insights from both traditions. These new insights need not replace the specificities of the tradition. Instead, the process of learning to receive the history, and to carry it forward together, establishes "a new context within which all these complex questions might be further clarified."[22] It provides a new hermeneutical tool to reinterpret the past and to guide future development so as to not re-rupture the newly-found growth toward koinonia.

Cultural Reception

This leads us to an even more difficult aspect of ecumenical reception. To be effective, reception must be accomplished not only on official levels and in the halls of academe, but needs to become part of the local and day-to-day living out of traditions. We can think of this in two related, but different ways. First, there is the cultural reception that is unofficial but absolutely necessary. Second is what I will call canonical-institutional reception.

A Lutheranism which stands primarily as a rejection of Catholic "[semi-] Pelagianizing tendencies," or a Catholicism that sees itself as the sole locus of the visible, societal church, is unable to recognize truth, or the church, in the other. Reception calls for a re-envisioning not only of the other's positions. My own identity will also change at least insofar as I am no longer defined by my rejection of your position. Often, ingrained theological dichotomies are built into our understandings of the other, of ourselves, and of what divides us.

This is often the most difficult aspect of reception to facilitate and to judge. As the Joint Working Group notes in its Ninth Report, reasons for non-reception can be both theological and non-theological: "The theological conflicts of the past, and the way in which they unfolded in exclusion and persecution, may have left many longstanding and bitter memories that remain unhealed and that can affect responses in the present." Moreover, sociological factors, and a fear of losing influence or power, can interfere with reception.[23] Theological differences can be reinforced by the experience of disunion. The churches' structures and self-understandings are often constituted by their division from one another. In a situation of division, differences are highlighted and become shibboleths.

Martin Luther was quite aware of how concupiscence interferes with systematic truth-telling. In his *Small Catechism*, when considering the eighth commandment, he writes:

> The Eighth Commandment: You shall not give false testimony against your neighbor.
> *What does this mean?* We should fear and love God so that we do not tell lies about our neighbor, betray him, slander him, or hurt his reputation, but defend him, speak well of him, and explain everything in the kindest way.[24]

Luther grounds his interpretation of all of the commandments in love of God—"we are to fear and love God, so that . . ." This is, perhaps, the ecumenical movement encapsulated. We seek not to sell off the truth for the sake of unity, but to seek the truth in Christ. Loving Christ means living, as Luther writes in the first of the ninety-five theses, so that our entire lives are repentance. Such clear-eyed self-evaluaiton and generosity toward the other is the basis of any real reception.

Of course, the lived experience of the churches is not always divisive. Sometimes the common life of Christians testifies to the possibility of reunion in a way that official theologies have been unable to ratify. The experience of intermarriage or friendship between members of separated groups, along with joint political or social work on behalf of the poor, often leads to the sense that the churches are prevented from unity only by the inability of theologians to agree. This impression was voiced even by Pope Francis, who said,

> I believe we are moving forward in our relations with the Orthodox; they have the sacraments and apostolic succession . . . we are moving forward. What are

> we waiting for? For theologians to reach an agreement? That day will never come, I assure you, I'm skeptical. Theologians work well, but remember what Athenagoras said to Paul VI: "Let's put the theologians on an island to discuss among themselves and we'll just get on with things!" I thought that this might not have been true, but Bartholomew told me: "No, it's true, he said that." We mustn't wait.[25]

Some ecumenical theologians might have similar worries about the pace of ecclesiastical reception.[26] This merely shows that both are important, and that church authorities and the official dialogues must work together for the cause of unity.

Canonical–Institutional Reception: Enacting the New Horizon

Of all the kinds of reception, this is the one that is, perhaps, most difficult. It moves beyond the warm feelings of agreement and the friendship of persons into the cold light of corporate action. As just one example of the difference, we might consider the different responses received by (on the one hand) the ELCA's agreements with the Reformed Church of America, United Church of Christ, and Presbyterian Church (USA)[27] which required no structural change, and the one with the Episcopalians, which did.[28] Both were placed before the ELCA Churchwide Assembly in 1999. The one passed overwhelmingly, the other passed by a much slimmer margin, and then saw its implementation unilaterally changed in 2001. At issue was the structural requirement of how pastors are ordained and by whom.

Among Catholics, similar forces are at work. *Unitatis redintegratio*,[29] which is laying out a vision for Catholic ecumenical engagement, is warm and speaks theologically of the Catholic Church's theological relationship all Christians, who, while separated by historical, theological, and political forces, are united by Baptism in one Christ. On the other hand, once the church begins to describe exactly what Catholics should and should not do ecumenically, the *Directory for the Application of the Principles and Norms on Ecumenism* takes a much more clinical tone, and describes the canonical requirements that separation imposes on divided Christians.[30]

Once churches officially recognize consensus to exist and this judgment comes to be broadly received among their members, reception must finally mean the integration of these insights into the lived theology and practice of each church. Unity may begin in doctrinal consensus, but it is made real in the practicalities of church politics. Because the church is made up of flesh-and-blood humans, it must also be a flesh-and-blood community, which means dealing with things that often seem far from the gospel—including pension plans and structures for negotiating disputes that will arise in the future.[31]

These tasks do not seem like ecumenism; but they are truthfully a kind of reception.

Once the divisions are overcome structurally, our common life is that much more likely to persevere — and as much as we care about our theological differences, ask any pastor where the real fights in the parish happen. You are likely to hear stories about carpet, hymnals, and schools. But until we overcome these things, the airy, doctrinal work of the dialogues has not yet been fully received.

RECEPTION AND CONSENSUS

All of these types of reception, however, require that we agree about what it means to agree. Sometimes, in ecumenical dialogue, theologians come to discover that what has been held up as an unbridgeable dichotomy is actually a case of a difference in "language, theological elaboration, and emphasis" to quote the Joint Declaration on the Doctrine of Justification.[32] This document changes several important ways of describing the differences between Lutherans and Catholics, not least of them the diagnosis of a distinction between a merely imputed and an already imparted notion of justification. In this document, Lutherans are able to say that justification changes us, and in some sense, is imparted. Catholics recognize that baptism does not make us over into our finally redeemed selves immediately, and therefore in some sense justification is, for now, imputed.

Such agreements are almost always based on a long-term project of coming to know the other, learning to speak their habitual theological language more fluently, and finally being able to use that language in a way that they would recognize as their own. In this situation, it is possible to recognize what has been called a *differentiated consensus*. In order to understand what this is and how it can be received, this term will require some more attention.

Defining "Consensus"

In talking about how to receive a consensus, we first have to understand what a consensus is: "What does it mean to agree?" Wolfgang Beinert, a German Catholic theologian, distinguishes between three kinds of "consensus": (1) *Übereinstimmung*, (2) *Zustimmung*, and (3) *Übereinkunft*. These can best be translated as (1) the *sensus fidelium*, (2) consent, and (3) healing consensus. The first is the basic agreement that allows a community to make authentic joint decisions, the basis of why we can have a Churchwide Assembly, or a Synod of Bishops, and trust that they will not reject the Gospel. It's also very much the kind of consensus that is discussed above as "academic reception"—people who are well-formed in a tradition can collectively make judgments and speak for it. The second, consent to the community's decisions that can be given or withheld, is what individual representatives are doing when they vote—such as Bishops during a synod. The third Beinert describes as "the taking up again of a broken communication as a result of a discourse. According to the radicality of the break, one can speak of a basic, a partial, or a total consensus."[33]

Most often, people consider ecumenical consensus to most align as the last of these: *Übereinkunft*. This seems like what is indeed happening in ecumenical dialogue—we are finding language to bridge historic divides. Beinert understands this to happen within a process where one side proposes an argument and the other either receives it, or not. Importantly, within Beinert's understanding, the two sides are doing something that properly happens within one language, or even one horizon.

But, this seems inadequate to some of the facts. Listen to another ecumenist, George Lindbeck, describe a common experience in dialogue. Members

> say they have been compelled by the evidence, sometimes against their earlier inclinations, to conclude that positions that were once really opposed are now readily reconcilable, even though these positions remain in a significant sense identical to what they were before. . . . [T]he problem is not with the reality but with the comprehensibility of this strange combination of constancy and change, unity and diversity. The proper response in that case is not to deny the reality on the grounds that it seems impossible, but rather to seek to explain its possibility.[34]

Here we do not have a matter of proposing and accepting arguments on a level playing field. It is more akin to learning to hear differently.

I once spent a week in Austria, and had a terrible time understanding the local dialect of German. One afternoon, however, it occurred to me that it sounded like they were speaking German with an Irish accent. I already had a language filter for understanding Irish English, and I suddenly could understand folks pretty well. The world shifted because I had learned how to listen so that the pieces fell into place. And it happened without the locals changing the way they spoke at all.

When the dialogues discover one of these places where a historic division turns out instead to be a difference of "language, theological elaboration, and emphasis," they describe a "differentiated consensus." These "crystallize over time in the process of working for consensus in the bilateral interconfessional dialogues. They follow from the actual formation of a consensus as its self-reflection."[35] They are often described in three parts: a common statement "articulating the fundamental and essential content of the agreement," and statements explaining how the remaining differences "can be evaluated as admissible and do not call into question the agreement in its fundamental and essential aspects."[36]

Such an agreement often turns out to be a tough sell back home. Not only does it require rethinking the other and myself, it almost always ends up causing a rethinking and a relativizing of cherished theological language. Consider Lutheran and Catholic respondents to the JDDJ who argue that the Joint Declaration and its differentiated consensus is inadequate to their own tradition, or that it cannot be a real agreement because it has not chosen one sixteenth century answer over the other. The Kinki Evangelical Lutheran Church of Japan, for example wrote: "[e]ven if the different doctrinal traditions of the 16th-century did not necessarily condemn each other, as JD[DJ] wants us to believe, they are still different and cannot all be true."[37]

If every difference is a disagreement, then the only ecumenism that is possible is the so-called "return ecumenism" of the nineteenth century, in which everyone either comes back home to Rome or sees their error and converts to the Protestant recovery of the Gospel. Lindbeck's insight is that truth is carried in systems—and formal divergence does not always mean disagreement, let alone a church-dividing disagreement.

The dialogues' official statements encapsulate such insights, often as differentiated consensuses. There are usually three sections. The JDDJ provides a clear example of the form: a common statement that sums up the agreement, a Catholic section that explains why the Catholic position fits with the agreement, and a Lutheran section that does the same for the Lutheran position. These official statements are easy to misread, unless one happens to be a fluent speaker of both theological dialects. Often, readers read the paragraph that engages their own tradition to judge its faithfulness to their beliefs, and pay less attention to the paragraph about the other. Such a way of reading fully reverses the intent of such documents, however. Here, the Catholic paragraph is intended to explain *to Lutherans* why Catholic positions of which Lutherans are skeptical can be reconciled with the consensus paragraph and vice versa.

But this is not the only problem. Differentiated consensus usually rests on an implicit (shared) understanding of two different (and not shared) conceptual mappings by which the shared truth of the Gospel is expressed. Ecumenical documents that express such a consensus prompt for the new integration. But, one can hold all the data—and understand it individually—without having made the leap to the new conceptual mapping that holds it together in tension.

In the case of the JDDJ, for example, §§22–24 argue that justification is *both* "Forgiveness of Sins" (something like imputed justification) and "Making Righteous" (similar to imparted justification). The JDDJ undercuts the traditional distinction by insisting that God's decree forgives sinners, *and* that that very decree has an effect in their lives going forward. The God who creates from nothing changes people by his declaration about them. By holding these seeming incompatible positions together, both traditional Lutheran and Catholic concerns can be expressed. Both ways of speaking are prevented from falling into the distortions that were diagnosed in the sixteenth century by the Council of Trent and the Lutheran Confessions. But, it is possible to read this statement and miss this point. When the Kinki Lutheran Church of Japan rejected the JDDJ, it was in part because the JDDJ did not declare "which of the 16th-century traditions represents the truth."[38] By insisting that the two positions form such an antinomy, the reader assumes that they *share a single framing* and rejects the possibility that they could be held in a productive tension that accepts both.[39] The insights of the dialogue cannot be received, for one must choose between seeing justification as "forgiveness of sins" or as "making righteous." It cannot be both.

Incorporating the insight that the dialogue members built over years of dialogue is itself the condition for the possibility of receiving their work. However one does so, making these mappings and their relation to the shared truth explicit can foster their reception both officially, and within the churches. This was recognized from the very early Lutheran-Catholic dialogues.[40] Indeed, the insights of the JDDJ were initially rejected by a number of Lutherans, and some continue to reject them.[41] Similarly, Roman Catholic authorities, including the Congregation for the Doctrine of the Faith and the Pontifical Council for the Promotion of Christian Unity (PCPCU), called for more clarity on several issues in the text just four months before it was officially signed.[42] The fact that the original document was signed unchanged, but in light of a further document demonstrates the importance of this kind of receptive stance that is structured by receiving central insights of the dialogues.

The difficulty of reading such a statement of differentiated consensus contributes to the problem of reception. If those who are not personally involved in the dialogues cannot come to understand their own insights easily, it is that much more likely that the solutions they propose will be rejected. This is particularly true in situations in which someone can understand all the pieces at play in an argument, but lacking the crucial insight, will miss the conceptual integration that the dialogue is prompting for.

MAPPING AND RECEPTION

In what follows, I will demonstrate how conceptual mapping can serve as a kind of catalyst, lowering the activation energy of the integrations necessary for reception. In order to do this, I will examine one of the early US Lutheran–Roman Catholic Dialogues, *The Eucharist as Sacrifice* (ES). This document provides a good example for several reasons. First, it has been broadly received over the last forty years, so we can trust that it does justice to both the Lutheran and the Catholic position. Second, it deals with a limited number of questions, from which we can draw one clear example to show how a new blend allows its conclusions. Finally, Lutheran and Catholic positions on the Eucharist are sufficiently different to be distinguishable, without being so far apart as to be disconnected. These positions also have the benefit of being generally understood among the theological audience.

Among other questions related to Real Presence, the document engages the seemingly contradictory claims, "The Eucharist *is* a [Propitiatory] Sacrifice" (Roman Catholic) and "The Eucharist *is not* a [Propitiatory] Sacrifice" (Lutheran). While these statements are formally contradictory, the dialogue argued that both statements were attempts to safeguard the one sacrifice of Christ, made present in the Eucharist. On this basis, they were able to conclude that "despite all remaining differences in the ways we speak and think of the Eucharistic sacrifice and of our Lord's presence in his supper, we are no longer able to regard ourselves as divided in the one holy catholic and apostolic faith on these two points."[43]

The Eucharist [Is / Is Not] a Propitiatory Sacrifice

The Lutheran-Roman Catholic Dialogue has been operating simultaneously on both national and international levels since its beginnings. The US dialogue began in 1965, with a conversation about the status of the Nicene Creed.[44] The *Eucharist as Sacrifice* is the third of the US dialogue papers, after a consultation on Baptism in 1966. The 1967 statement is the first of the dialogue statements to investigate a matter regarding which serious differences exist between the two churches. This is evident from its length and format. While the first dialogue produced a two-page statement, the dialogue on baptism concluded with a three-paragraph statement that took less than a page, beginning with the phrase, "We were reasonably certain that the teachings of our respective traditions regarding baptism are in substantial agreement, and this opinion has been confirmed at this meeting."[45]

With the question of the Eucharist, however, the discussion becomes both more difficult and more ecumenically useful. Unlike the previous two dialogues, which concluded their work in one meeting (two days in the case of the first dialogue, three in the case of the second), the dialogue on the Eucharist required multiple meetings held over a year and a half. The statement produced is both more nuanced and more interesting than the previous two, demonstrating a real engagement between the participants.

Whereas their own distance from initial positions to final statements had been bridged through extended dialogue and the growth of mutual understanding, the authors recognized that a real reception would require that their readers receive help to make the same jump. Auxiliary documents were felt to be necessary to translate from the dialogue's agreed statement into the language of each community.[46] Reception has continued to be the most difficult process to foster for every ecumenical dialogue since.

The dialogue had two major questions with which it had to grapple. From the Lutheran side, it wanted to investigate what Catholics mean when they say that the Eucharist is a [propitiatory] sacrifice. From the Catholic side, it asked how Lutherans understand Christ's real presence in the Eucharist.[47]

Our test case for whether conceptual mapping can help bridge the gap for those who have not been active in the dialogue's work will be drawn from the question of sacrifice. The document highlights two concerns about sacrificial language. First, that saying "Calvary was a Propitiatory Sacrifice" might require a particular Anselmian understanding of Christ's saving work; secondly, that to apply the language of "sacrifice" to the Mass could be taken to imply that it "adds to Calvary, is a 're-doing' of Calvary and . . . [thus] that the one sacrifice of Christ is defective and incomplete."[48] We will consider only the second concern in what follows.

The question about whether understanding the Eucharist as a sacrifice diminishes' Christ's work is more complex than it first appears to be. To a large extent, this is because of the emphasis on the question of merit and justification in the reformation. The question gains further weight from the cultural and experiential centrality that the concept has in Catholic circles. I will briefly introduce each of these before showing how the dialogue comes to find its consensus.

Catholic Centrality

On the Catholic side, language about the Eucharist as sacrifice is ubiquitous. It "touches upon the heart of their faith as well as their personal piety and entire worship life."[49] Rejecting the language of Eucharistic sacrifice would change every aspect of Catholic life. But, understanding what that language intends is important, given the role that it played in the disputes about justification in the sixteenth century. If the Eucharist is the central liturgical action of the church, understanding it and how it is "sacrifice" touches on every aspect of the Christian mystery, especially including how it is that Christ saves his people. This centrality leads to some theological dangers, which become clear in understanding the Reformation critique.

Lutheran Concerns

The Apology to the Augsburg Confession, written by Philip Melanchthon in 1530, is one of the confessional documents of most Lutheran churches. It treats of the concept of sacrifice as applied to the Eucharist.[50] Its principle concern is to preserve the unique place of Christ's sacrifice on the cross in order to reject the proposition that sacraments merit grace for those who participate in them. The argument responds to a medieval cultural and theological complex that the Reformers rejected as presuming that salvation must be earned by human works, that is, the heresy of pelagianism or semi-pelagianism.[51]

In this context, an Augustinian term arising from the donatist controversy received a new meaning: *ex opere operato.* In the Apology, Melanchthon rejects that sacraments can merit grace in themselves, because "it is impossible to receive the forgiveness of sins *ex opere operato* on account of our works."[52] The Reform position sees a danger in describing even the sacraments as meriting anything, because that could lead to believers trusting in their own action, rather than in Christ's, for their salvation. Indeed, they are not rejecting a straw man. The mediaeval era saw a flowering of just such a piety.

This terminological shift is made possible by two effects of an earlier controversy about the presence of Christ in the Eucharist. First, there is a strong emphasis on the Eucharistic miracle and the grace given by the making-present of Christ. Second, a de-emphasizing of Christ's presence in the church gathered, and a shift from a sacramental to a societal description of the Church.[53] Together, these lead to an understanding of sacraments as something done by humans which merits grace from God. It should be emphasized that this position was not official teaching, although it does find expression in the writings of some theologians and bishops. But it was prevalent in the cultural practice of sixteenth-century Christianity.

In order to proscribe such an understanding, Melanchthon believes that the language of sacrifice has to be carefully re-defined. He diagnoses an especially strong temptation to understand sacrifices as things that human beings do to affect divine behavior.[54] He therefore sharply distinguishes between two kinds of sacrifice: first, the propitiatory sacrifice of Christ that merits our salvation, and second, the Eucharistic sacrifice, which gives God thanks for the propitiation accomplished by Christ.[55] The connection between sacrificial language and a works-righteousness growing from an "*ex opere operato*" understanding of the sacraments that is forged here largely excises the terminology of sacrifice from the Lutheran Eucharistic vocabulary going forward.[56] We might depict the historic Lutheran blend for sacrifice as in figure 7.1.

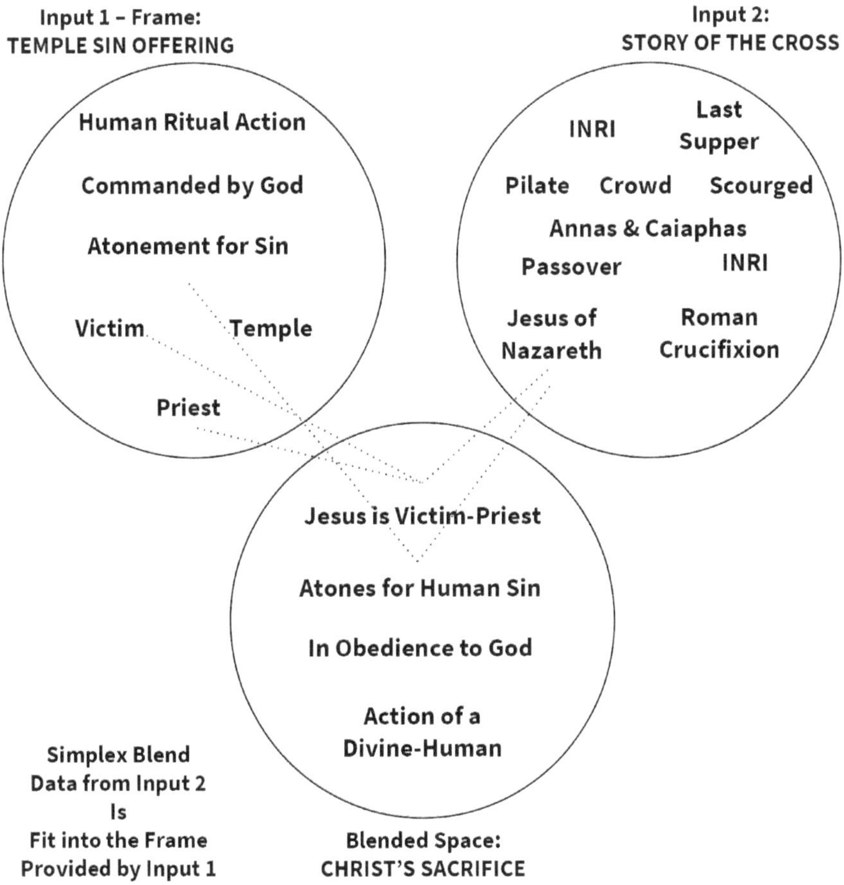

Figure 7.1. Simplex Blend: CHRIST'S SACRIFICE

In Melanchthon's structure, sacrifice is a simplex blend. It takes its primary building blocks from Jewish temple sin offerings, and its particular data from the story of the cross. This means that there is only a single frame, and there is not a major reinterpretation of what that frame means. Sacrifice in the cross remains what it was in the temple, a properly human action. But, humans generally cannot merit their own salvation. Following the logic of Anselm's *Cur Deus Homo,* then, there is only one proper member of the category SACRIFICE for a Christian. This is the sacrifice of the divine-human Jesus on the cross, as described by the Letter to the Hebrews. Jesus is high priest who offers a once-for-all sacrifice on Calvary and enters before the Father in heaven to forever be our mediator and plead for us. Describing any human action as a sacrifice entails ascribing some kind of "merit" to that work, something which Melanchthon is unwilling to do. The Eucharist, understood as a the action of the church, can only be a thanksgiving "sacrifice" to God in response to Christ's work.

The Dialogue's Solution

Both Lutherans and Catholics wish to deny that the Mass is a re-sacrificing of Christ[57] and that the liturgical action completes something that is incomplete in Christ's work.[58] They have, however, historically reached opposite conclusions about the appropriate use of sacrificial language because of this claim.[59]

One important difference between classical Christian language about the Eucharist as sacrifice and the reformation critique is a matter of perspective on who is acting. Where the mediaeval eyes of the Reformers saw a danger in the church acting apart from Christ, the dialogue reclaims a patristic sense that the church is Christ's body, and therefore that in the Eucharist the whole Christ (*totus Christus*) is acting in union with its head.

The dialogue, therefore, insists that the Eucharist is not merely the church's action. In it God acts as trinity, and the assembly is made present to the one sacrifice of Christ offered to the Father at Calvary:

> What God did in the incarnation, life, death, resurrection, and ascension of Christ, he does not do again. The events are unique; they cannot be repeated, or extended or continued. Yet in this memorial we do not only recall past events: God makes them present through the Holy Spirit, thus making us participants in Christ (I Cor 1:9). . . .
>
> The members of the body of Christ are united through Christ with God and with one another in such a way that they become participants in his worship, his self-offering, his sacrifice to the Father. Through this union between Christ and Christians, the eucharistic assembly "offers Christ" by consenting in the Power of the Holy Spirit to be offered by him to the Father.[60]

Thus, if we consider the blend, THE EUCHARIST IS A SACRIFICE from a Roman Catholic perspective (as that theology is accepted by the dialogue), we might picture its most salient aspects as in figure 7.2).

In this example, we see the sacramental action making present the one sacrifice of Christ. It is the action of the church made possible because of its union with Christ, that is, as his body. In this action, the *totus Christus* repeatedly asks the Father's mercy on account of the once-and-for-all action of the Son.[61] The blend is a double-scope blend, meaning that the common space partakes of both inputs. THE EUCHARIST IS A SACRIFICE describes a repeatable event but in a way that maintains the unicity and once-for-all character of Christ's sacrifice on Calvary. It makes the church's action necessary, but

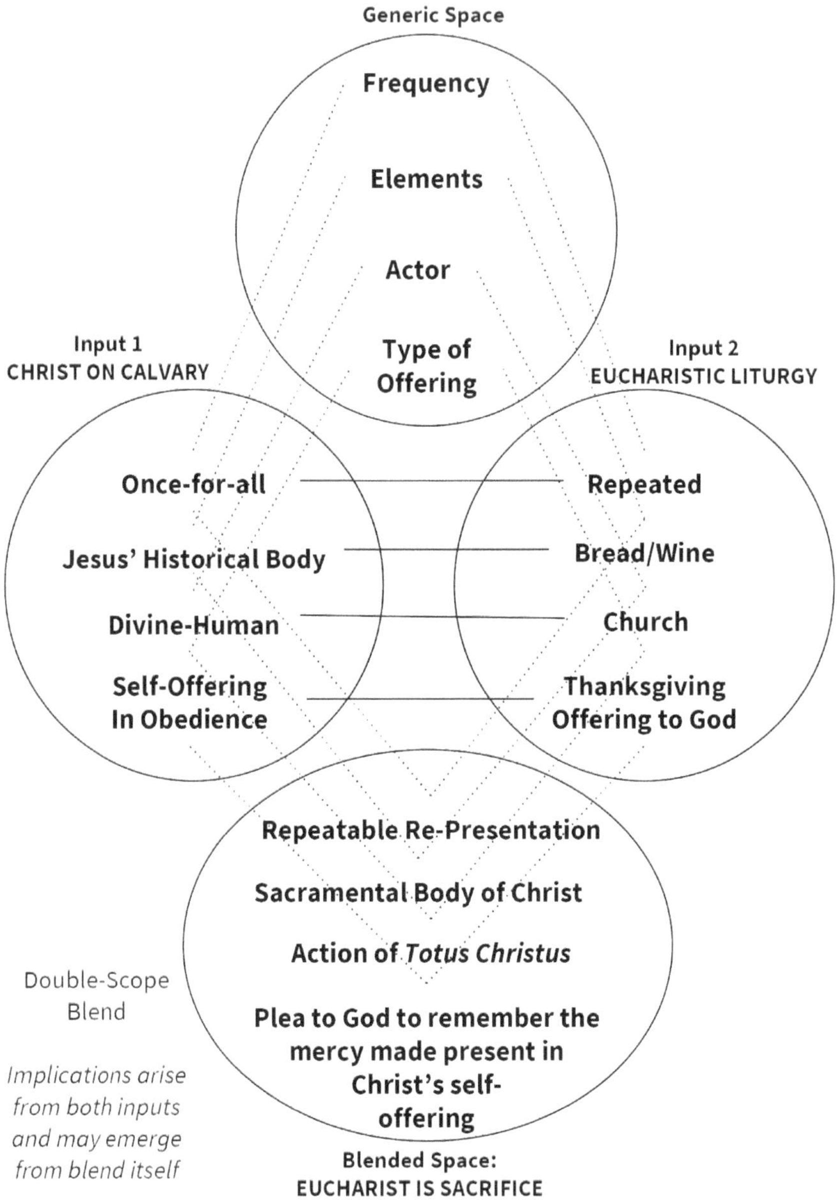

Figure 7.2. Double-Scope Blend: EUCHARIST IS SACRIFICE

in such a way that it remains properly the action of Christ, not an action demanding grace apart from God's work.

Lutherans remain wary of the potential difficulties raised by the Roman Catholic language, but in the dialogue they have been able to acknowledge that these difficulties, although they have historically recurred, are officially proscribed within the Catholic complex. Roman Catholics can recognize the Lutheran hesitancy to use their language not as a denial of the intended meaning, but as a wariness against recurring abuses.

Importantly, this shared blend rests on another habitual tectonic blend that Lutherans and Catholics hold in common, that is, the very complex blend SACRAMENTAL REAL PRESENCE, which allows for both unity and distinction, unicity and multiplicity.[62] "Is" is used in a very particular and technical way when affirming that the consecrated Bread and Wine "is" the Body and Blood of Christ.[63] Because the churches both affirm the real presence of Christ in the eucharist in this way, it can serve as a basis for understanding in what sense the Eucharist is a [propitiatory] sacrifice.

This is indeed a simple mapping, and a simple agreement, now well established among theologians of both churches, but it demonstrates how paying attention to the conceptual blends that are at work in each church's theology can help to make the differentiated consensuses recognized in ecumenical dialogues, and those recognized officially by the churches, more available to readers and thinkers who are not as familiar with the inner workings of the other church's thought.

CONCLUSION: MAPPING AS AN AID TO RECEPTION

The official dialogues between separated churches have long understood that reception poses a difficulty. People are formed as Christians and as theologians in a context of division. We sometimes highlight the differences between Christians and can even promote them in order to not lose our own distinctive identity. Unity can thus become a receding target. Dialogues cannot logistically invite all the members of the separated churches, or even all the theologians, to take part. Some will have to be deputed to speak for their traditions. If in those dialogues new understandings arise, these will likely be the result of new insights that may require new blends. In such cases, it is entirely possible to have all the data and, lacking the formative blend, to mistake what is there.

The difficulty of helping those who did not undergo the longer process of mutual conversion fostered by dialogue can be aided by distilling the central insights of those dialogues through the process of conceptual mapping. Seeing what the blend is that makes the consensus possible can help those who would be likely to misread the dialogues' proposals. It can also help members of the dialogues by concretely "harvesting the fruits" of the dialogues for future dialogues.[64]

In this chapter, in addition to diagnosing the structural problems of reception I have pointed to the central insight of one, very simple agreement drawn from the early Lutheran-Catholic dialogues. This insight has already achieved a wide-spread acceptance among both Lutherans and Catholics. Its reception is broad. But seeing the structure of a simple, accepted agreement demonstrates that this method can have a broader impact on more divisive issues. I have begun some of this more extensive work, specifically related to the Joint Declaration on the Doctrine of Justification.[65] However, the field of ecumenical theology is wide and the workers are few. New tools can be of great aid and conceptual mapping demonstrates a far-reaching potential.

NOTES

1. Nicene Creed; John 17:20–21.
2. Cf. John 17:21
3. See Dagmar Heller, "The Soul of the Ecumenical Movement: The History and Significance of the Week of Prayer for Christian Unity," *The Ecumenical Review* 50, no. 3 (1998): 399–404.
4. Ecumenical Patriarchate, Encyclical "Unto the Churches of Christ Everywhere," 1920. In *The Ecumenical Movement: An Anthology of Key Texts and Voices*, ed. Michael Kinnamon and Brian E. Cope, (Geneva: WCC Publications, 1996), 11–14. It is worth noting that this is a document of the patriarchate, not of the Patriarch, as the patriarchal throne was vacant at the time of its publication. The primary drafter was Archbishop Germanos, later Metropolitan of Thyateira and Exarch of the West, and later president of the WCC. The letter is signed by "Dorotheus, Metropolitan of Brussa, Locum Tenens of the Patriarchal Ecumenical Throne," and by eleven other Metropolitans. See Stephen Charles Neill, "Plans of Union and Reunion 1910–1948," in *A History of the Ecumenical Movement 1517–1948,* 2nd ed., ed. Ruth Rouse and Stephen Charles Neill (Philadelphia: Westminster, 1968), 446.
5. See Jeffrey Gros, Eamon McManus, and Ann Riggs, *Introduction to Ecumenism* (New York: Paulist, 1998), 25–32.
6. The first round of Anglican Roman Catholic dialogue, (the Anglican—Roman Catholic International Commission I or ARCIC I) proposed that a far-reaching consensus existed on major topics, including eucharist, ministry and ordination, with major agreement on authority and primacy. It found convergences on the issues of papal primacy and infallibility. Famously, the Official Roman Response to this document, first given in 1982 in an initial form, and then made public in 1991 in *Origins* 21/28 (Dec. 19, 1991),

441–7. This response rejects much of the consensus proposed by ARCIC as inadequate to Catholic teaching. A collection of the key documents and commentary is available in Jeffrey Gros, E. Rozanne Elder, and Ellen K Wondra, eds., *Common Witness to the Gospel: Documents on Anglican-Roman Catholic Relations 1983–1995* (Washington, DC: United States Catholic Conference, 1997).

7. Karl Lehmann and Wolfhart Pannenberg, *Lehrverurteilungen, Kirchentrennend?*, 4 vols. Dialog der Kirchen, ed. Hermann Kunst and Hermann Volk (Freiburg im Breisgau: Herder, 1986–1994). The key first volume of this study is translated as *The Condemnations of the Reformation Era: Do They Still Divide?* trans. Margaret Kohl (Minneapolis: Fortress Press, 1990).

8. Robert Masson, *Without Metaphor No Saving God: Theology after Cognitive Linguistics* (Leuven: Peeters, 2014), 31.

9. Vyvyan Evans, *A Glossary of Cognitive Linguistics* (Edinburgh: Edinburgh University Press, 2007), 11.

10. Joint Working Group between the Roman Catholic Church and the World Council of Churches (JWG), *Eighth Report: The Nature and Purpose of Ecumenical Dialogue* (Geneva: WCC Publications, 2005), 82–83.

11. International Lutheran-Roman Catholic Commission on Unity, Malta Report, Preface. In Jeffrey Gros, Harding Meyer, William G. Rusch, Thomas F. Best, and Lorelei F. Fuchs, eds., *Growth in Agreement* (Grand Rapids: Eerdmans, 2000), 168. Similarly, *Church and Justification* proposes its work to the churches as furthering the work of earlier dialogues and with them constituting a question to the churches: "whether, taken together, these documents constitute the sufficient consensus which would enable our churches to embark upon concrete steps towards visible unity which have become more and more urgent." JC, Foreword, in Gros, Meyer, Rusch, eds., *Growth in Agreement II* (Grand Rapids: Eerdmans, 2000), 486–87.

12. See Catherine Clifford's treatment of the Joint Declaration, Catherine E. Clifford, "Joint Declaration, Method, and the Hermeneutics of Ecumenical Consensus," *Journal of Ecumenical Studies* 38, no. 1 (2001): 79–91.

13. These processes are described in JWG, *Ninth Report: Receiving One Another in the Name of Christ* (Geneva: WCC Publications, 2015) Section IIB (§§36–53). Also available at https://www.oikoumene.org/en/resources/documents/commissions/jwg-rcc-wcc/ninth-report-of-the-joint-working-group/@@download/file/JWG_9th_Report.pdf

14. See JWG, *Ninth Report*, §39.

15. As, for example, in the Lutheran World Federation, Ibid., §41

16. e.g. the Disciples of Christ. Ibid., §40.

17. e.g. Pentecostals. Ibid., §45.

18. JDDJ, §4.

19. OCS, §1.

20. For a description of these dissenting voices, see chapter 2 of my *Mapping the Differentiated Consensus of the Joint Declaration* (New York: Palgrave, 2015). Also, Pieter de Witte, *Doctrine, Dynamic, and Difference: To the Heart of the Lutheran-Roman Catholic Differentiated Consensus on Justification* (New York: T&T Clark, 2014).

21. See Lindbeck's reflection on this history in the preface to the German edition of *Nature of Doctrine*: "By 1984, ecumenical interests had shifted from overcoming the doctrinal barriers which block Christian unity to co-operating in common struggles for, to use the World Council of Churches' formula, Justice, Peace and the Integrity of Creation (commonly known by the acronym, JPIC). Ecumenists of this new type are not much interested in doctrine, and instead it is systematic and historical theologians, philosophers and sociologists of religion, and even, though to a lesser extent, scriptural scholars who have been the most engaged and frequent participants in discussion of this book. This surprised me. The only fresh aspect of the book, I had supposed was its ecumenical focus." "Foreword to the German Edition of The Nature of Doctrine," in *The Church in a Postliberal Age,* ed. James J. Buckley (Grand Rapids: Eerdmans, 2002), 197.

22. Clifford, "The Joint Declaration, Method, Hermeneutics," 87.

23. Ibid., §128. See also the conclusion of Susan K. Wood and Timothy Wengert, *A Shared Spiritual Journey: Lutherans and Catholics Travelling toward Unity* (Mahwah, NJ: Paulist Press, 2016).

24. Martin Luther, *Small Catechism*, "The 10 Commandments" translation from *Luther's Small Catechism* (St. Louis: Concordia Publishing House, 1986).

25. Pope Francis. In-flight Press Conference of His Holiness Pope Francis from Istanbul to Rome, (Sunday, November 30, 2014). Available at https://w2.vatican.va/content/francesco/en/speeches/2014/november/documents/papa-francesco_20141130_turchia-conferenza-stampa.html. Some ecumenical theologians might say similar things about how ecclesiastical authorities are slow to receive the agreements that they propose. This merely shows that both are important, and that church authorities and the official dialogues must work together for the cause of unity.

26. Catherine E. Clifford points to a wide-spread frustration at the limited reception of the dialogues' work. "The Joint Declaration, Method, Hermeneutics," 79. This is mirrored by a description of a feeling of being overwhelmed by the scale of dialogue documents in JWG, *Ninth Report,* §123.

27. Evangelical Lutheran Church in America, "History–A Formula of Agreement (1997)" ELCA, February 1, 2018, http://www.elca.org/Faith/Ecumenical-and-Inter-Religious-Relations/Full-Communion/History.

28. Ibid. CCM, which also passed, by a narrower margin, and remained more controversial, precisely because it required a change in ELCA practice relating to ordination going forward, while the *Formula of Agreement* only stipulated mutual recognition.

29. Second Vatican Council, Decree on Ecumenism "Unitatis Redintegratio" in *Decrees of the Ecumenical Councils: From Nicaea I to Vatican II*, ed. Norman P. Tanner (Washington, DC: Georgetown University Press, 1990), 2: 908–20. The full text of the Decree is also available through the Vatican website.

30. Pontifical Council for the Promotion of Christian Unity, *Directory for the Application of the Principles and Norms of Ecumenism* (Washington, DC: US Catholic Conference, 1993). The full text of the *Directory* is also available through the Vatican website.

31. A very informative example is found in the Evangelical Lutheran Church in America, which formed from a merger of three Lutheran Churches in 1987. See Edgar R. Trexler, *Anatomy of a Merger: People, Dynamics, and Decisions that Shaped the ELCA* (Minneapolis: Augsburg Fortress, 1991). While many other ecumenical agreements, such as the agreements allowing intercommunion between Catholics and the Assyrian Church or the East, or the full communion agreements among American mainline churches, do not result in mergers, they nevertheless do have their own practicalities that require attention.

32. Lutheran World Federation and the Roman Catholic Church, *Joint Declaration on the Doctrine of Justification* (Grand Rapids: Eerdmans, 2000), §40. Also available at http://www.vatican.va/roman_curia/pontifical_councils/chrstuni/documents/rc_pc_chrstuni_doc_31101999_cath-luth-joint-declaration_en.html

33. "Konsens ist hier die Wiederaufnahme einer abgebrochenen Kommunikation auf Grund eines Diskurses. Je nach der Radikalität des Bruches kann man von einer grundlegenden, einer partiellen oder ein totalen Übereinkunft sprechen." Wolfgang Beinert, "Möglichkeit und Umfang ökumenischer Konsense. Eine historisch – theologische Studie zur 'Grundkonsens'-Problematik," *Catholica* 1989, no 4 (1989): 275.

34. George Lindbeck, *The Nature of Doctrine: Religion and Theology in a Postliberal Age* (Louisville: Westminster John Knox, 1984), 15.

35. Harding Meyer, "Ökumenischer Konsens als 'differenzierter Konsens' Die Prägung einer Formel. Ursprung und Intention," in *Versöhnte Verschiedenheit: Aufsätze zur ökumenischen Theologie III* (Frankfurt/M.: Lembeck, 2009), 41.

36. Harding Meyer, "Consensus in the Doctrine of Justification," trans. William G. Rusch, *Ecumenical Trends* 26, no.11 (1997): 5/165–8/168.

37. Kinki Lutheran Church, "Response to the JDDJ," in *Die Gemeinsame Erkärung zur Rechtfertigungslehre: Dokumentation des Entstehungs und Rezeptionsprozesses*, ed. Friedrich Hauschild, Udo Hahn, and Andreas Siemens (Göttingen: Vandenhoeck & Ruprecht, 2009), Document C.13, §2.

38. Ibid.

39. This kind of productive tension that takes on both framings and allows them to mutually reinterpret each other is called a "double-scope blend" in the cognitive linguistic theory that is being used in this book. Such a blend allows for the emergence of new meaning that is not possible within either of the existing inputs. See Robert Masson, *Without Metaphor*, 96–106; Gilles Fauconnier and Mark Turner, *The Way We Think: Conceptual Blending and the Mind's Hidden Complexities* (New York: Basic Books, 2002), 180–183; Zoltán Kövesces *Language, Mind, and Culture: A Practical Introduction* (New York: Oxford University Press, 2006), 283–87.

40. See discussion below, 173–74.

41. The JDDJ was accepted by the Lutheran World Federation (LWF) after a vote of the member churches. Of the 124 member churches of the LWF, 89 responded to the request for response. 80 accepted the JDDJ, five voted no, and four answers were difficult to categorize. Non-LWF Lutheran Churches, like the Lutheran Church—Missouri Synod in the USA and the Selbständige Evangelisch-Lutherisch Kirche in Germany, are not signatories to the JDDJ. In both Germany and the US, a number of Lutheran theologians have been outspoken critics of the JDDJ. See Pieter de Witte,

Doctrine, Dynamic, Difference: To the Heart of the Joint Declaration on the Doctrine of Justification (New York: T&T Clark, 2012) and Jakob K. Rinderknecht, *Mapping the Differentiated Consensus of the Joint Declaration* (New York: Palgrave, 2016).

42. Roman Catholic Church, "Response of the Catholic Church to the Joint Declaration of the Catholic Church and the Lutheran World Federation on the Doctrine of Justification," http://www.vatican.va/roman_curia/pontifical_councils/chrstuni/documents/rc_pc_chrstuni_doc_01081998_off-answer-catholic_en.html. These difficulties were resolved by the addition of a document named the "Annex" and the JDDJ was signed on October 31, 1999.

43. USA National Committee of Lutheran World Federation and the Bishops' Commission on Ecumenical Affairs, *Lutherans and Catholics in Dialogue III: The Eucharist as Sacrifice* (Washington, DC: National Catholic Welfare Conference Office of Publications, 1967), *Conclusion*. Hereafter, *Eucharist*.

44. The dialogue was announced in a News Release by the Bureau of Information of the National Catholic Welfare Conference on July 4, 1965. It produced a volume called *The Status of the Nicene Creed as Dogma of the Church* (Washington, D.C.: National Catholic Welfare Conference Office of Publications, 1965).

45. T. Austin Murphy and Paul C. Empie, "Joint Statement," in *Lutherans and Catholics in Dialogue II: One Baptism for the Remission of Sins*, ed. Paul C. Empie and William W. Baum (Washington, DC: National Catholic Welfare Conference, 1966), 85.

46. "Due to the extended discussion which surrounded each of the papers the reader may not find it easy to bridge the gap from them to the summary in which the agreements and disagreements are carefully and precisely stated. Two interpretive essays, one by a Lutheran participant and one by a Roman Catholic participant, should help at this point." Paul C. Empie and T. Austin Murphy, foreword to *Eucharist, 3*.

47. Kent S. Knutson, "Introduction: Eucharist as Sacrifice Roman Catholic–Lutheran Dialogue," in *Eucharist,* 7–16.

48. "The Eucharist: A Lutheran–Roman Catholic Joint Statement," in *Eucharist*, §III.3 Hereafter, "Eucharist: Joint Statement."

49. Knutson, "Introduction," 7.

50. Philip Melanchthon, *Apology to the Augsburg Confession*, Article XIV beginning at §9. Robert Kolb and Timothy Wengert, eds. *The Book of Concord: The Confessions of the Evangelical Lutheran Church* (Minneapolis: Fortress, 2000). Hereafter, AAC

51. Pelagianism was officially rejected by the western church after a series of controversies between St. Augustine and a British monk who resided in Rome, named Pelagius. Pelagius argued that God's justice would prevent him from requiring human beings to do something they were unable to do. He therefore reasoned that we were graced by God with the ability to fulfill the law. Jesus showed human beings how to live, and thus to merit salvation. Augustine refuted this position by emphasizing God's gift of grace in Christ.

As theologians continued to consider these positions, a related group of positions were rejected by the Council of Orange in 529. These later came to be called "semipelagianism" although the Reformers did not make careful distinctions between the two. As opposed to pelagianism proper, semi-pelagianism holds a place for divine grace in giving initial faith, but requires that the human being's free will be solely responsible for certain works that contribute to faith, it's growth, and perseverance to salvation.

52. AAC, §11. *Ex opere operato* means "by the work worked." The phrase arises in the controversy about Donatism, in order to answer a quite different question, i.e. whether a sinful minister invalidated the sacrament and prevented its grace. It played quite a central role in the sixteenth-century debates about faith and works. It is important to note that in the Donatist controversy, the phrase implies *ex opere operato Christi* (i.e. from Christ's doing of the work), whereas Melanchthon is rejecting uses that imply *ex opere operato ecclesiae* (by the church's work) or even an interpretation intending the work of the individual receiving the eucharist.

53. The classic description of the shift of Eucharistic terminology that makes this possible is Henri de Lubac, *Corpus Mysticum: The Eucharist and the Church in the Middle Ages—A Historical Survey*, trans. Susan F. Parsons (Notre Dame, IN: University of Notre Dame Press, 2007).

54. While he doesn't make this argument, we might say that the usual cultural integration for sacrifice was made in precisely these terms. Lacking the input of Christ as head of the church and prime actor in the sacraments, the Christian double-scope redefinition is impossible. See below at fig 2.

55. AAC, §19.

56. "Eucharist: Joint Statement," I.2.

57. "Eucharist: Joint Statement," I.1.a. For specifically Catholic support, see Council of Trent, Session 22, Ch 1, DH 1740 and 1743.

58. Council of Trent, Session 22, canon 4, DH 1754.

59. "Lutherans have often understood Roman Catholics to say that the Mass adds to Calvary, is a 're-doing' of Calvary and by this have implied that the one sacrifice of Christ is defective and incomplete. Catholics agree that some of the language used in the 16th century by Catholics could be so interpreted. . . . Now we can agree that this is not what Roman Catholics intend to say. The sacrifice of Christ is complete and unalterable and cannot be supplemented or completed by any subsequent action. Rather, that sacrifice, complete in itself, is made present, made effective and the benefits communicated in the Eucharist." Knutson, "Introduction," 13.

60. "Eucharist: Joint Statement," §I.2.a-b., citing P.C. Rodger, ed., *The Fourth World Conference on Faith and Order* (Montreal, 1963), 73. See also Wood and Wengert, *Shared Spiritual Journey*, 117.

61. It should be pointed out that this blend between "once-for-all" and "repeatedly" is only possible because of the basic Christian assumption that God is eternal (i.e. without time), and therefore eternally present to all time. Christ's one sacrifice in the cross is offered timelessly to the Father, and "after" the ascension made present to all people everywhere and at all times.

62. Masson names blends "tectonic" that are double-scope and allow for new emergent meaning. Such changes are not merely the acquisition of new data, but allow for new possibilities to exist among the old data, reconfiguring the possibilities of what can be thought, said, believed. Masson, *Without Metaphor*, 8, 61–72.

63. Consider, for example, Thomas Aquinas' insistence that Christ is truly present in the transubstantiated matter, but not in such a way that Christ is present in the sacrament "as in a place" or so that he is moved when the paten and chalice are. ST III Q76 A 5–6. See also the discussion in the chapter by Stephen Shaver in this volume.

64. The phrase comes from a call of Walter Cardinal Kasper to the dialogues, to harvest the fruits of fifty years of work to apply them in the Church's common life, and in the ongoing work of theological dialogue. He also published his own book by that title recounting his own account of the dialogues since the council. Walter Cardinal Kasper, *Harvesting the Fruits: Basic Aspects of Christian Faith in Ecumenical Dialogue* (New York: Continuum, 2009).

65. Jakob K. Rinderknecht, *Mapping the Differentiated Consensus of the Joint Declaration* (New York: Palgrave, 2016).

BIBLIOGRAPHY

Church Documents (In Historical Order)

Philip Melanchthon. *Apology to the Augsburg Confession.* In *The Book of Concord: The Confessions of the Evangelical Lutheran Church*, 107–294. Edited by Robert Kolb and Timothy J. Wengert. Minneapolis: Fortress Press, 2002.

The Ecumenical Patriarchate. Encyclical "Unto the Churches of Christ Everywhere," 1920. In *The Ecumenical Movement: An Anthology of Key Texts and Voices*. Edited by Michael Kinnamon and Brian E. Cope, 11–14. Geneva: WCC Publications, 1996.

Second Vatican Council. Decree on Ecumenism "Unitatis Redintegratio." In *Decrees of the Ecumenical Councils: From Nicaea I to Vatican II.* Vol. 2, 908–20. Edited by Norman P. Tanner. Washington, DC: Georgetown University Press, 1990.

USA National Committee of Lutheran World Federation and the Bishops' Commission on Ecumenical Affairs. *Lutherans and Catholics in Dialogue II: One Baptism for the Remission of Sins*, ed. Paul C. Empie and William W. Baum. Washington, D.C.: National Catholic Welfare Conference, 1966.

USA National Committee of Lutheran World Federation and the Bishops' Commission on Ecumenical Affairs. *Lutherans and Catholics in Dialogue III: The Eucharist as Sacrifice*. Washington, DC: United States Catholic Conference, 1967.

Roman Catholic Church. "Response of the Roman Catholic Church to ARCIC I." *Origins* 21/28 (December 19, 1991), 441–7.

Pontifical Council for the Promotion of Christian Unity. *Directory for the Application of the Principles and Norms of Ecumenism.* Washington, DC: US Catholic Conference, 1993.

International Lutheran–Roman Catholic Commission on Unity. *Malta Report*. In Jeffrey Gros, Harding Meyer, William G. Rusch, Thomas F. Best, and Lorelei F. Fuchs, eds., *Growth in Agreement*, 168. Grand Rapids: Eerdmans, 2000.

International Lutheran–Roman Catholic Commission on Unity. *Church and Justification*. In Jeffrey Gros, Harding Meyer, William G. Rusch, eds. *Growth in Agreement II*, 486–87. Grand Rapids: Eerdmans, 2000.

Lutheran World Federation and the Roman Catholic Church, *Joint Declaration on the Doctrine of Justification.* Grand Rapids: Eerdmans, 2000.

Kinki Lutheran Church. "Response to the JDDJ." In *Die Gemeinsame Erkärung zur Rechtfertigungslehre: Dokumentation des Entstehungs und Rezeptionsprozesses*. Edited by Friedrich Hauschild, Udo Hahn, and Andreas Siemens, Document C.13. Göttingen: Vandenhoeck & Ruprecht, 2009.

Roman Catholic Church. "Response of the Catholic Church to the Joint Declaration of the Catholic Church and the Lutheran World Federation on the Doctrine of Justification. In *Die Gemeinsame Erkärung zur Rechtfertigungslehre: Dokumentation des Entstehungs und Rezeptionsprozesses*. Edited by Friedrich Hauschild, Udo Hahn, and Andreas Siemens, Document C.55. Göttingen: Vandenhoeck & Ruprecht, 2009. In English: http://www.vatican.va/roman_curia/pontifical_councils/chrstuni/documents/rc_pc_chrstuni_doc_01081998_off-answer-catholic_en.html.

Joint Working Group between the Roman Catholic Church and the World Council of Churches (JWG), *Eighth Report: The Nature and Purpose of Ecumenical Dialogue.* Geneva: WCC Publications, 2005.

Joint Working Group between the Roman Catholic Church and the World Council of Churches (JWG), *Ninth Report: Receiving One Another in the Name of Christ.* Geneva: WCC Publications, 2005

Evangelical Lutheran Church in America. "History–A Formula of Agreement (1997)." ELCA. February 1, 2018. http://www.elca.org/Faith/Ecumenical-and-Inter-Religious-Relations/Full-Communion/History.

Secondary Literature (Alphabetical by Author)

Beinert, Wolfgang. "Möglichkeit und Umfang ökumenischer Konsense. Eine historisch—theologische Studie zur 'Grundkonsens'-Problematik," *Catholica* 1989, no 4 (1989): 268–94.

Clifford, Catherine E. "Joint Declaration, Method, and the Hermeneutics of Ecumenical Consensus," *Journal of Ecumenical Studies* 38, no. 1 (2001): 79–91.

Evans, Vyvyan. *A Glossary of Cognitive Linguistics*. Edinburgh: Edinburgh University Press, 2007.

Fauconnier, Gilles and Mark Turner. *The Way We Think: Conceptual Blending and the Mind's Hidden Complexities.* New York: Basic Books, 2002.

Francis. Inflight Press Conference. November 30, 2014. Available at: https://w2.vatican.va/content/francesco/en/speeches/2014/november/documents/papa-francesco_20141130_turchia-conferenza-stampa.html

Gros, Jeffrey, Eamon McManus, and Ann Riggs, eds., *Introduction to Ecumenism*. New York: Paulist, 1998.

Gros, Jeffrey, E. Rozanne Elder, and Ellen K Wondra, eds. *Common Witness to the Gospel: Documents on Anglican-Roman Catholic Relations 1983–1995.* Washington, DC: United States Catholic Conference, 1997.

Heller, Dagmar. "The Soul of the Ecumenical Movement: The History and Significance of the Week of Prayer for Christian Unity," *The Ecumenical Review* 50, no. 3 (1998): 399–404.

Kasper, Walter Cardinal. *Harvesting the Fruits: Basic Aspects of Christian Faith in Ecumenical Dialogue*. New York: Continuum, 2009.

Kövesces, Zoltán. *Language, Mind, and Culture: A Practical Introduction.* New York: Oxford University Press, 2006.

Lehmann, Karl and Wolfhart Pannenberg. *Lehrverurteilungen, Kirchentrennend?* 4 vols. Dialog der Kirchen. Edited by Hermann Kunst and Hermann Volk. Freiburg im Breisgau: Herder, 1986–1994.

———. *The Condemnations of the Reformation Era: Do They Still Divide?* Translated by Margaret Kohl. Minneapolis: Fortress Press, 1990.

Lindbeck, George A. *The Nature of Doctrine.* Louisville: Westminster John Knox, 1984.

———. "Foreword to the German Edition of the Nature of Doctrine." In *The Church in a Postliberal Age,* James J. Buckley, ed., 196–200. Grand Rapids, Eerdmans, 2002.

Lubac, Henri de. *Corpus Mysticum: The Eucharist and the Church in the Middle Ages—A Historical Survey*. Translated by Susan F. Parsons. Notre Dame, IN: University of Notre Dame Press, 2007.

Luther, Martin. *Luther's Small Catechism*. St. Louis: Concordia Publishing House, 1986.

Masson, Robert. *Without Metaphor, No Saving God: Theology after Cognitive Linguistics*. Leuven: Peeters, 2014.

Meyer, Harding. "Consensus in the Doctrine of Justification." Translated by William G. Rusch. *Ecumenical Trends* 26, no. 11 (1997): 5/165–8/168.

———. "Ökumenischer Konsens als 'differenzierter Konsens' Die Prägung einer Formel. Ursprung und Intention" in *Versöhnte Verschiedenheit: Aufsätze zur ökumenischen Theologie III*, 41–62. Frankfurt/M.: Lembeck, 2009.

Neill, Charles. "Plans of Union and Reunion 1910–1948." In *A History of the Ecumenical Movement 1517–1948,* 2nd ed. Edited by Ruth Rouse and Stephen Charles Neill, 445–505. Philadelphia: The Westminster Press, 1968.

Rinderknecht, Jakob Karl. *Mapping the Differentiated Consensus of the Joint Declaration*. New York: Palgrave, 2016.

Trexler, Edgar R. *Anatomy of a Merger: People, Dynamics, and Decisions that Shaped the ELCA.* Minneapolis: Augsburg Fortress, 1991.

Witte, Pieter de. *Doctrine, Dynamic, and Difference: To the Heart of the Lutheran-Roman Catholic Differentiated Consensus on Justification*. New York: T&T Clark, 2014.

Wood, Susan K. and Timothy Wengert. *A Shared Spiritual Journey: Lutherans and Catholics Travelling toward Unity*. Mahwah, NJ: Paulist Press, 2016.

Chapter Eight

My Good, Your Good, and the Good

Conceptual Mapping and Altruism

Adam Willows

A sterile ant toils away, providing for other ants with which it will never mate. A ground squirrel sounds the alarm at the sight of a coyote, warning others but drawing attention to itself. A chimpanzee helps an arthritic relative climb a tree. A passer-by rushes into a burning building.

Somewhere along the evolutionary line, altruism seems to appear. This raises two questions. First—*where* does it appear? All of these creatures are caring for others without benefit to themselves. But only some of them are aware that this is the case; and perhaps only one (if that) bases their action on reasoned judgment.

Second—*why* does it appear? All of these creatures are what they are in part because of their evolutionary past. Over time, traits which in their particular environment helped their ancestors reproduce were more likely to proliferate, gradually forming these species into what they are today. So why on earth do we find that some species engage in apparently self-sacrificial behavior? Wouldn't traits that encouraged caring for others like this *damage* that creature's chances of success? After all, the squirrel that sounds the alarm is more likely to get eaten. This has been a perennial question throughout the history of evolutionary science; Darwin identified the existence of sterile ants as "by far the most serious special difficulty, which my theory has encountered."[1]

Evolutionary science is not lacking in solutions for this difficulty, however. One explanation—offered by Darwin—which has proved robust is that altruism arises as a result of group or kin selection. It is not the individual creature *per se* who needs to benefit from altruistic acts in order for such acts to be encouraged by evolutionary pressures, but their genotype. An obvious example is parents who make sacrifices for their children; those children may be more likely to survive, and the tendency to give of oneself for one's offspring will proliferate. But my genome will also proliferate if other relatives of mine do well and the more closely I am related to someone the more my genome may benefit from their advantage. This has been generalized in "Hamilton's law" as follows: "altruism can evolve if *rb>c*; where *b* is the benefit to the recipient of the altruistic act; *c* is the cost to the bearer; and *r* is the degree of relatedness between them."[2]

But kin selection does not seem to give the whole picture, for we are not just charitable toward members of our own extended family. Humans often act altruistically toward complete strangers, or members of another species. Fortunately, evolutionary scientists have a candidate for the missing half of the picture: reciprocity. It is to my advantage to help another in need if by doing so I can ensure (or make more likely) that they help me in the future.[3] In order to encourage reciprocity, we develop systems of trust and ways to detect and punish cheats or free riders who do nor reciprocate.[4] As these systems become more complex they form the network of social norms that we call morality. Although humans exhibit by far the most intricate system of social norms, this system has a fundamental historical dependence on characteristics that are more generally shared across species, such as the ability for empathy. This has led many thinkers to speak of an animal morality that shares a foundation with our own.[5]

Although evolutionary scientists largely agree on this basic account of the evolutionary origins of altruism and morality, this agreement results in two quite different perspectives on our moral natures.

WHAT IS *REAL* ALTRUISM?

During the course of Jane Austen's *Pride and Prejudice*, the protagonist Elizabeth Bennet receives the attentions of three men. One, the charming but villainous Mr. Wickham, does not love her and merely seeks to use her to his own advantage. The next, Mr. Collins, does not love her either; but, being foolish and self-deluding, he persuades himself that he does. Only the last, Mr. Darcy, genuinely loves her.

The difference between Elizabeth's suitors illustrates the concern about evolutionary accounts of altruism like kin selection. There is clearly a difference between Mr. Collins and Mr. Darcy; it is not enough, for Elizabeth or us, that Mr. Collins thinks that he loves her. What matters is whether he *really does* love her; and this goes deeper than Mr. Collins's inadequate self-awareness.

Evolutionary explanations of altruism make it clear that we are not a species of Wickhams; our mutual care is not hiding deliberate schemes and plots, and in this sense altruism is not a facade. But might we be a species of Collinses? If our desire to help one another is simply governed by evolutionary pressures that ultimately increase the fitness of our genotype (if not us individually), then perhaps our belief that we genuinely care for others simply displays ignorance of our true reasons for acting. Just as only *real* love will do for Elizabeth, perhaps only *real* altruism will do for morality.

Here evolutionary scientists are divided into two camps. The first holds that we are indeed like Mr. Collins and that the facts reveal humans to be ultimately self-serving. There is no such thing as true altruism, and what we identify as such is merely a comforting veil cast over our inescapable drive to seek self-advantage. This view is nicely summarized by Jonathan Marks:

> But then came sociobiology, and evolution became meaningful again. . . . Now it was that goodness itself is an illusion, for altruism towards others is either "really" just selfishness towards one's genes (if the altruism is directed at a family member) or towards oneself in the expectation of reciprocation (if the altruism is directed at a non-family member).[6]

In what follows I shall call this group the Pessimists.

The second perspective is that the facts show nothing of the sort; the reports of goodness's demise are greatly exaggerated. Yes, now we know why we became kind, generous, honest and loving. But why should this origin story change anything? What matters is that we *are* those things; the fact that your evolutionary past is responsible for your conscience does not make its imperatives any less real: "we are not hypocritically fooling anyone when we act morally: we are making decisions that flow from social instincts older than our species, even though we add to these the uniquely human complexity of a disinterested concern for others and for society as a whole."[7] In what follows I shall call this group the Optimists.

Part of the problem here is that neither group is especially clear on what they mean by altruism. Both agree on the basic evolutionary facts. They also agree that there is such a thing as *real* altruism and such a thing as *false* altruism; the difference is that the Pessimists believe that the agreed-upon facts indicate that humans only exhibit false altruism, whereas the Optimists believe that they show us to be *really* altruistic. This lack of clarity represents a wider problem; the term *altruism* is used to refer to multiple concepts. The answers to the questions above will vary depending on which concept is in play. A helpful next step, then, is to differentiate between those different concepts, and see what each implies about the scope of altruism and its compatibility with evolutionary theory.

Two Kinds of Altruism

A good starting point is a distinction drawn between *reproductive* and *psychological* altruism. Reproductive altruism is defined as follows: "A behavior is altruistic if it increases other organisms' fitness and permanently decreases the actor's own fitness."[8] Conversely, psychological altruism claims that "An action is altruistic if it results only from motivations directed towards the goal of improving others' interests and welfare."[9]

Here are two very different understandings of what altruism means. The criteria for reproductive altruism are very broad indeed. For one thing, it clearly encompasses many more species than humans; all of the animals mentioned at the start of this chapter would qualify as altruistic by these criteria. But more than this, it broadens the scope of what might count as altruism. This is because whether or not something is altruistic is defined entirely in terms of its effect on the subject—the "other organism" whose fitness is increased. This means that I do not have to mean well in order to be altruistic. If my poor mathematical ability causes me to excessively tip my waiter on a regular basis, I am (or rather my behavior is) altruistic. In fact, it seems that I barely matter at all to the question of whether or not my behavior is altruistic—I am only relevant in the minimal sense that the event involves me and so it is *my* behavior and not someone else's. Suppose Mr. McGregor deliberately cultivates deadly nightshade in his garden because, knowing it to be poisonous to humans, he believes it will eradicate the rabbits he loathes. In fact, the rabbits gobble down the nightshade gratefully with no ill-effect. Mrs. McGregor is unaware of the rabbits or the poisonous nature of the plant; but she also cultivates it because she thinks it pretty. On the definition of reproductive altruism above, the behavior of both the McGregors is altruistic, and it is *only* the effect of their behavior on the rabbits that is relevant to that fact.

To the moral theorist, the scope of this definition may seem nonsensical, since it entails that behavior can be altruistic by accident, or even with the very worst of motives. In fact, it is quite deliberate. In using the term *altruism*, evolutionary biologists are discussing the way in which behavior beneficial to others might become ingrained in a species; and a trait need not be consciously or deliberately exercised to have an impact on evolutionary fitness. Humans, along with many animals and plants, are clearly altruistic in this sense. This use of the term, though, is not suited to moral discourse. The reason for this is that agency plays an almost negligible part in the reproductive definition. It includes a very loose general requirement for an agent, probably best understood in minimal terms—such as a distinct system internally responsible for initiating goal-directed change.[10] On the other hand, morality is almost universally thought to require a much more robust form of agency, for two commonly held reasons. The first is because morality is in some way demanding.[11] The second is that moral responsibility only applies if the agent can at some point control whether or not they meet morality's demands. Taken together, these two lead thinkers to conclude that in order to be a moral agent, one must have the capacity to recognize the demands of morality, in order to act accordingly. This is why internal states such as intention and understanding are relevant even to consequentialist systems which focus on outcomes and external events; the rightness of an act may be evaluated separately from the agent; but that the act is open for evaluation at all still depends on whether or not it issued from a moral agent.

On the reproductive definition, then, humans are *really* altruistic, but this does little to settle the debate between the Optimists and the Pessimists. Instead, the *reproductive* definition of altruism is best understood as a term referencing a concept quite separate from the moral. To the extent that it is applied in moral discourse it will represent a truncated, minimal term.

Unlike reproductive altruism, psychological altruism is focused on the motives of the agent. It therefore seems a more promising candidate for identifying what might count as *really* altruistic. As it stands, though, problems still exist. The requirement that altruistic acts result *only* from motives directed toward improving other's welfare is perhaps too stringent. Could an act not count as altruistic if the relevant motives were the primary or even just sufficient ones for the act? There are obvious parallels here to the criticisms of Kant's claim that acts have moral worth only when done from the motive of duty alone.[12] Opponents point out that in many cases acts arising from other motives appear not just acceptable but desirable. I think the same thing applies here. It is characteristic of a good friendship that each party takes enjoyment in the relationship and each other; were we to find that our friends were *only* motivated to act altruistically toward us because they cared about us and not at all because they liked our company, we might rightly feel that those friendships were diminished.

Although it is not in itself sufficient, I think that the psychological definition of altruism is on the right track. By focusing on motives it connects altruism to our moral natures, and it is here that the disagreement over whether or not humans exhibit *real* altruism is located. In order to narrow down the precise nature of the disagreement, I think it is better to view psychological altruism as a spectrum of positions. I offer a sample below, each more demanding than the last.

Level 1: An act is altruistic if it is motivated by desire for another's well-being.

Level 2: An act is altruistic if it is sufficiently motivated by desire for another's well-being.

Level 3: An act is altruistic if it is primarily motivated by desire for another's well-being.

Level 4: An act is altruistic if it is exclusively motivated by desire for another's well-being.

Level 1 is clearly too weak to be the source of the controversy; both Optimists and Pessimists accept that humans possess motivations to act for the sake of others. Conversely, Level 4 is too strong; neither group claims that the presence of *any* motivation other than care for another renders an act non-altruistic.

We are closing in on the problem; Optimists and Pessimists both accept that humans are motivated by the well-being of others (Level 1), and that altruism does not require that we are not motivated by our own well-being (Level 4). So their difference seems to be not over what motivations we have, but over the relationship between them. In other words, to be altruistic is for the demands of the self and the demands of the other to interact and motivate us in a particular way. Exactly what that particular kind of motivation might be, and whether humans express it, is the topic of the next section.

SELF-REGARDING AND OTHER-REGARDING

So far I have discussed how the development of altruism is explained via evolutionary pressures, notably reciprocity and kin selection. Some claim that *real* altruism in humans is incompatible with this explanation, while others see no conflict. The nature of this disagreement is obscured by the fact that *altruism* is a term with many different definitions. By analyzing some of those, I have narrowed the disagreement to one concerning the relationship between our own well-being and the well-being of others in motivation. In what follows, I argue that this depends on a long-standing disagreement over the nature of morality.

In brief, the disagreement is over the following question: is morality self-regarding or other-regarding? That is, is morality primarily or foundationally concerned with our own good or the good of others? Many ethicists hold that morality is a special realm of action concerned only with how we behave toward others. We may develop bad habits that only affect us, but these are not a moral matter. One argument for this is that morality is to be understood in terms of duties and obligations; and these do not properly apply to the self:

"to have a *duty to oneself* would be to have a *right against oneself*, and this is surely nonsense."[13] Likewise, John Stuart Mill saw a clear division between private and public practice:

> The self-regarding faults . . . are not properly immoralities, and to whatever pitch they may be carried, do not constitute wickedness . . . the term duty to oneself, when it means anything more than prudence, means self-respect or self-development; and for none of these is any one accountable to his fellow creatures.[14]

This in itself is not sufficient to cause any conflict with claims that the evolutionary record shows humans to be *really* altruistic, since it does not claim that self-interested concern is immoral, merely that it is outside the moral realm. It also allows that acts directed toward oneself can be morally relevant insofar as they have an effect on others. However, proponents of this position typically hold that those moral effects are likely to be bad ones. Self-interested motives will lead us astray; morality is *about* others, and although thinking primarily about ourselves may have occasional happy outcomes, in general it is likely to lead to immoral behavior since we fail to give the needs of others their proper motivational place. Thus Mill identifies "the egotism which thinks self and its concerns more important than everything else" as an example of a morally relevant vice.[15]

In theological ethics, this concern appears in discussion of the Love commandment and notably in Anders Nygren's *Agape and Eros*. Nygren argued that the centrality of *agape* (love of other, and most importantly God's love for humanity) to the Christian tradition had been partially usurped and synthesized with the necessarily opposing Hellenistic concept of *eros*, love of the self. He describes the effect of this on our relationship with others as follows:

> Eros does not seek the neighbor for himself. It seeks him in so far as it can utilize him as a means for its own ascent. . . . Agape-love is directed to the neighbor himself, with no further thought in mind and no sidelong glances at anything else. Hence the question arises what grounds there are for this love. What can induce a man to love just simply his neighbor, with no further object in view?[16]

Despite criticism of Nygren's project itself, his perception that there is a fundamental conflict between self-love and other-love continues to be a topic of discussion and concern for theologians, with a significant range of positions, from those which characterize altruism and compassion as an extension and expansion of self-love, to an insistence that it means a radical supplanting of all of our interests with the interests of the other.[17]

Nygren is certainly correct that Hellenistic thought is the primary impetus for the claim that self-love is of central moral importance. In philosophical circles, modern opposition to the claim that morality is fundamentally other-regarding is chiefly aligned with the Neo-Aristotelian renaissance and virtue ethics. One of the primary concerns of the pioneering virtue ethicists such as G. E. M. Anscombe, Philippa Foot, and Bernard Williams was to resist the notion of *obligation* and the idea that morality is somehow confined to a special sphere of action that we pass in and out of on a regular basis.[18] Anscombe and William's rejection of the term *morality* represented not a rejection of the need to live rightly, but of the idea that right and wrong appear in an overriding system distinct from other parts of our lives. Instead, we should be concerned with acting for particular *goods*. Human nature determines in large part what will be good for us; and the moral virtues are inherently desirable because they form part of that good.

This is a *eudaimonistic* system. *Eudaimonia*, the Greek term for happiness, flourishing or well-being, is central to Aristotle's moral theory. A eudaimonistic moral system claims that moral action and virtues are motivating because they direct us toward a good (*eudaimon*) life. Moral goodness is necessary in order to flourish, although it may not be sufficient. In part this is founded on a claim about the nature of motivation. It couples the claim that we always necessarily aim at a perceived good when we act (else we could have no motivation) with the claim that goods are either things that are desirable in, for, and of themselves or otherwise constitute a step on the way toward something that is. Thus the ultimate desire for our own good is necessarily the foundation of every act; if it were not, we would literally be unable to act at all since nothing would motivate us.

This perspective does not deny that the interests of others are often paramount; but this is so because it is not good for us to ignore those interests:

> And it will surely not be denied that there is something wrong with a free-riding wolf, who eats but does not take part in the hunt, as with a member of the species of dancing bees who finds a source of nectar but does not let other bees know where it is. These "free-riding" individuals of a species whose members work together are just as defective as those who have defective hearing, sight, or powers of locomotion. I am therefore, quite seriously, likening the basis of moral evaluation to that of the evaluation of behavior in animals.[19]

One of the criticisms aimed at modern virtue ethics is the same as that directed at evolutionary accounts of morality: it is egoistic, presenting human action as fundamentally directed toward our own needs. As with the evolutionary scientists, virtue ethicists have had little problem dismissing accusations that their theory entails serious disregard for others, since some of the moral virtues—such as justice—are necessarily other-regarding. The paradigmatic example for Aristotelians is the virtue of friendship, which is only truly a virtue when it loves the other simply for themselves.[20] Just as there is something wrong with a friendship only cultivated for the sake of moral duty, there is also something wrong with a friendship only cultivated for the advantage of oneself. Neither is true friendship, and neither will lead to eudaimonia.

But, as with the evolutionary scientists, this is not where the true problem lies for virtue ethicists. Recall that both the Pessimists and the Optimists allow that *some* other-regarding and *some* self-regarding motives are acceptable in *real* altruism. The difficulty is in the relationship between the two. Can our ultimate desire for fulfillment be reconciled with the need to love our friend for their own sake? Can our species's long history of communal care and cooperation avoid being devalued by the discovery of its formation by pressures to increase fitness? In other words—what exactly is the Pessimist's problem? Why is it not enough that we *do*, in fact, love each other with no apparent thought for our own gain?

I think by looking at continuing criticism of virtue ethics on this front it is possible to finally nail down just what it is that the Pessimists are concerned about. One complaint about eudaimonism is that while it may not be selfish, it is self-centered. That is, although the goods of selves and others are both morally valuable, it is the good of the self that is of ultimate value. It is good that I care for others because caring for others is in some way good for *me*, and if it were not good for me it would not be good at all. It does not necessarily matter that we are not always conscious of this; the problem is that on this system, the self is necessarily valued differently to the other. *My* flourishing is of ultimate value, and that of others is not. Addressing what he sees as a problematic relationship between self- and other-value, John Hare writes "Both affections can be responses to what Murdoch calls the pull toward the good. . . . But there is in every person a ranking of the two, and if the affection for advantage is ranked first it will become an improper regard for the self."[21]

I suggest that the real concern of the Pessimists is that evolutionary explanations of altruism and morality indicate that humans are self-centered. To the extent that our moral motives developed because they enhanced the fitness of ourselves or our kin, then our moral motives serve the ultimate (or at least nearer-to-ultimate) purpose of helping ourselves. This does not mean that goodness or morality itself is necessarily self-centered: to make such a claim would be to conflate evolutionary fitness and moral value. Our moral sense may have developed as part of our overall evolution, but that does not imply that moral value supervenes on evolutionary value. Instead, we have the following situation:

Observation: Humans motivation is self-centered.

Optimists: Moral motivation and altruism may be self-centered. Therefore, humans can be altruistic.

Pessimists: Moral motivation and altruism may not be self-centered. Therefore, humans cannot be altruistic.

Mapping GOOD to GOD

We have now narrowed down what it is that the Optimists and Pessimists are fighting about. Whether or not humans are altruistic depends not only on the scientific evidence but on the nature of morality and motivation. Rather than try and identify a victor, I want to suggest that cognitive linguistics and medieval theology offer another way out. In this section, I argue that Aquinas's use of analogy in speaking of God allows a cognitive remapping that breaks the divide between self and other.

My purpose in this section is not to construct a watertight case for Aquinas's position against the Optimist and the Pessimist, but to present it as a viable alternative and an example of the relevance of tectonic mapping to moral and theological thought. Nor do I think that this is a piece only for Thomists. The vital equation between God and The Good explored below is not one exclusive to Aquinas. However, there are good reasons to focus on him here, including the enormous range and influence of his thought, his extensive treatment of analogy, and his repeated appearance in Masson's work.

This chapter is, then, an exercise in mapping in more than one sense. I intend to mark an alternative route through the problem of motivation and altruism. Although it will be clear that I think there is much to recommend this path, I do not claim to offer a complete or watertight case for its superiority here. My intent is simply to show that it is there—a demonstration of the way tectonic mapping can open up new, unexpected avenues of thought. So (for example) the determined Pessimist may, after reading, disagree entirely with Aquinas and go on believing that humans are deeply self-interested—I do not necessarily expect to persuade them otherwise. I do expect to persuade them that the scope of the debate is wider than has appeared so far; in the battle over the deep moral nature of human beings there is more than one front.

Masson identifies Aquinas's thought as a good example of the way religious language can be effectively understood with the concept of tectonic mapping. Aquinas's use of analogy and metaphor to refer to God is, he argues, a "tectonic double-scope conceptual blend."[22] Two different fields of meaning are brought together to create a "blended space" of new meaning that results in a dramatic shift in understanding that entails a new perspective on both of the original fields.[23] This seems to be borne out by Aquinas's account of the need for metaphor when speaking of God.

One especially striking thing that Masson identifies about Aquinas's use of language is the way in which he forces an equivalence between assertion and predication. This is not a blunt tool to allow him to make claims about God in the way we can about creatures, but an elegant way of threading the apophatic/kataphatic needle. It provides a way for Aquinas to express the inexpressible nature of God, for example through the claim that God *is* being itself.[24] His language thus always holds its own inadequacy and the incompleteness of our knowledge of God before the reader: "Aquinas does not reduce an existential assertion to a predicative one. Rather, he extends language—he forces an equivalence between the logic of asserting and the logic of predicating—to display and speak of what is beyond language's grasp."[25]

More generally, all terms of unqualified perfection are properly applied to God, but when perfection is expressed or indicated through creation it can only be applied to God metaphorically:

> Whatever names unqualifiedly designate a perfection without defect are predicated of God and of other things: for example, goodness, wisdom, being, and the like. But when any name expresses such perfections along with a mode that is proper to a creature, it can be said of God only according to likeness and metaphor. According to metaphor, what belongs to one thing is transferred to another, as when we say that a man is a stone because of the hardness of his intellect.[26]

So for Aquinas, God is identified as the thing signified by perfection terms.[27] This tectonic equivalence between God and being, God and goodness, God and truth, etc. runs throughout Aquinas's theology, for it follows from this that the uses of these terms when applied to creatures are only analogical; a wise person, a good meal, a living plant are reflections of the true wisdom, goodness and life that is God. Aquinas thinks that knowledge of a thing must first mean knowledge of its perfection or exemplar, and only secondarily knowledge of particular instantiations of that thing. This is because we know each instantiation only by reference to its perfection. This means that all knowledge is found in God, and all of creation expresses its analogical relation to its true perfection in God: "being absolutely perfect, the divine essence can be taken as the proper exemplar of singulars."[28]

Aquinas's move runs as follows: whenever something is intentionally created, a likeness or image of it pre-exists in the mind of the creator.[29] Suppose I decide to bake you a cake. In order to start baking, or even to come up with the plan, I must have some kind of idea of a cake in my mind that guides my action. So the existence of the cake depends, in a way, on the likeness of it in my mind—for without that likeness it would not be made.

Sadly, I am a terrible baker; the disaster that results is not a good cake at all. Again, this judgment—good cake or bad—depends in a way on the idea in my mind. After all, if I had been *trying* to make a blackened, inedible lump I would have done a good job. As it is, the result of my efforts bears little resemblance to the delicate confection of my imaginings—and it is on that basis that I know I have made a bad cake.

Later, you come upon the charred mess in the kitchen. Curious, you ask me what it is. As I explain, the idea of a cake in my mind once again comes into play; it is from understanding that idea that you understand my intention and can see the mess in the kitchen for what it is—a failed gesture of friendship rather than a deliberate attempt to waste flour and eggs.

God is the creator of all things. In the mind of God, then, there are ideas which are the "exemplars" of all creation. Like the cake, created things depend on these ideas for their existence; they are judged good or bad with reference to them; and they are understood by understanding the ideas from which they are made.

However, this dependence of creation upon God goes much deeper than the dependence of the cake on me. I am not the only thing the cake depends on for existence; and perhaps you could judge and understand the cake by reading a recipe book instead of talking to me. But Aquinas's tectonic shift allows him to say that God *is* being, goodness and truth itself; and so all existence, goodness and knowledge ultimately depend fully on God. "Being, the true, the one, and the good are such that by their very nature they are one in reality. Therefore, no matter where they are found, they are really one."[30]

Thus Aquinas's use of analogy produces a new field of meaning that inextricably weaves God throughout his theology; whether or not God is being explicitly discussed, God is always and absolutely foundational to the understanding and judgment of whatever topic is at hand. "But since the perfect operation of the intellect consists in its knowing the true, that is its good in the sense just mentioned. Hence, since every good and every form is from God, one must say, without any qualification, that every truth is from God."[31]

For Aquinas, the tectonic connection between God and perfection terms means that without God we could quite literally not speak or think at all, for our language depends on the truth and knowledge in the divine ideas—an idea summarized by John O'Callaghan as "No understanding, no words."[32] The role of God in understanding is truly foundational and extends beyond illuminating any particular subject. Aquinas believes that the process of understanding itself is dependent upon the divine ideas.

Analogy in Aquinas is a very extensive topic, and not one to be tackled in its entirety here.[33] I am going to look at one outworking of the mapping of a particular perfection term GOOD to GOD. I think that it offers a new approach to the problem discussed in the first two sections, and a resolution to the disagreement between the Optimist and the Pessimist.

Acting for the Good

Aquinas's ethics and theory of motivation shares much with Aristotle and is essentially eudaimonist. His term for flourishing is *beatitudo*, and unlike Aristotle he divides the good life into two—an imperfect approximation which is the best we can hope for in this life, and true attainment of the good in the life to come. He also agrees with the eudaimonist that all motivation (and all action) is necessarily founded on a desire for our good:

> Man must, of necessity, desire all, whatsoever he desires, for the last end . . . whatever man desires, he desires it under the aspect of good. And if he desire it, not as his perfect good, which is the last end, he must, of necessity, desire it as tending to the perfect good.[34]

So it appears that Aquinas's ethics is inescapably self-centered; all motivation is founded on desire for our own good. Yet, as with the virtue ethicists discussed above, he indicates that there are virtues which require love of the other for their own sake: "Not every love has the character of friendship, but that love which is together with benevolence, when, to wit, we love someone so as to wish good to him. If, however, we do not wish good to what we love, but wish its good for ourselves . . . it is love not of friendship."[35] Aquinas appears to be in the same difficulty as the virtue ethicists; claiming both that we are always foundationally motivated by our own good, and that the good life sometimes involves being motivated by the good of others and not our own.

It is here that Aquinas's mapping of GOOD to GOD comes into play. When GOOD is understood as something ontologically distinct from GOD, then acting for *my* good means a focus on the self. But once the remapping discussed above occurs, I suggest that it enables a further tectonic shift in understanding of the relationship between the self and other. In the debate thus far, LOVE OF SELF and LOVE OF OTHER have been understood as distinct, sometimes opposing goods. After Aquinas's move, all good is understood to be found in God, allowing the two loves to be seen anew as parts of the same love. LOVE OF SELF and LOVE OF OTHER are both understood as LOVE OF GOD. How precisely this occurs is explored below.

Aquinas has already said that we always desire our good when we act; couple this with the understanding that GOD IS GOOD and something dramatic occurs. The desire for GOOD now means a desire for the other (GOD)—because the good of any creature, including myself, is contained in the divine mind, "every creature intends to acquire its own perfection, which is the likeness of the divine perfection and goodness. . . . All things desire God as their end, whether this desire be intellectual, or sensible or natural, i.e. without knowledge; because nothing is good and desirable except forasmuch as it participates in the likeness to God."[36] The conflict between self-love and love of the other is broken because my good is now contained in another: "God alone constitutes man's happiness."[37]

This idea receives its most complete development in Aquinas's discussion of the virtue of charity, the "friendship of man for God" and the greatest virtue of all.[38] Charity is first and foremost our love of God—but, Aquinas says, it is also the means by which we love our neighbors and ourselves. Here is Aquinas's view on love of others:

> Now the aspect under which our neighbor is to be loved, is God, since what we ought to love in our neighbor is that he may be in God. Hence it is clear that it is specifically the same act whereby we love God, and whereby we love our neighbor. Consequently the habit of charity extends not only to the love of God, but also to the love of our neighbor.[39]

And later, on love of the self: "among these other things which he loves out of charity because they pertain to God, he loves also himself out of charity."[40] To love others and to love oneself is the same thing: to love God. Even eudaimonism takes on a new hue; our own good is indeed our ultimate end, but not precisely *because* it is our own good but because it is goodness itself, that is, God.

Return to my unfortunate cake. The Optimist will view my act of friendship as simply altruistic, whereas the Pessimist will argue that beneath the surface are self-centered motives. My ultimate reason for wanting to be your friend, bake you cakes etc. is that being the kind of person that has friends is good *for me*. After Aquinas's tectonic shift, we can say that this is in one sense true—but not the full picture. The good *for me* is to be found in God, who is desirable in and of Godself. Indeed, it is only by loving God that I love myself at all. And this is the case for the rest of creation; it is loved because we love God. So rather than saying I love others because I love myself, it is more accurate to say I love all things—self and other—because I love God.

I take this to be a clear example of the importance of metaphor to theology, one which cognitive linguistics can help us to understand. Aquinas's move exhibits many of the distinctive features of the use of metaphor. It clearly involves the creation of new meaning. Here we see in Aquinas the use of metaphor to develop a new and deeper understanding of love—or rather, to explore that new meaning further, for Aquinas is himself drawing on 1 John 4:16 "Now it is charity that unites us to God, Who is the last end of the human mind, since 'he that abideth in charity abideth in God, and God in him.'"[41]

It also particularly shows the necessity of tectonic mapping in theology and our understanding of God, for this new meaning is also disruptive. It fundamentally breaches the divide between love of self and love of other and blends the two, creating an entirely new understanding of motivation that is directed toward God and so always to the good of *both* the self *and* the other.

This appears to be an example of the "disclosure and revelation" that Masson argues can result from tectonic blends.[42] I also think that it is evidence for another of his particular claims: "Tectonic equivalence and blending are pivotal in the emergence of new understanding in religion, science, culture and the arts, and crucial for comprehending similarities and differences between these fields of meanings."[43] Here, the theological use of metaphor allows a different view of the evolutionary development of our moral natures. In the final section, I explore this further by returning to the problem with which this chapter began.

EVOLUTION AGAIN

I have argued that the disagreement over whether or not humans are altruistic is dependent on a broader discussion on the moral relationship between the self and the other. In particular, it centers on the question of whether or not self-centered motivation can be moral. I showed that Aquinas's remapping of the term GOOD to GOD enables a further tectonic shift in understanding. Love of the self and love of the other are not opposed but in fact part of the same act whereby we love God and cannot occur outside of that act.

What happens when we look back at the struggle between the Optimist and the Pessimist with these new eyes? Consider the question with which I began the previous section: is morality primarily or foundationally concerned with our own good or the good of others? Where before this appeared an essential conflict, the answer is now either "both" or "neither." Both, because our ultimate desire involves a desire for the good of the self *and* the good of the other. Neither, because it is not me or my neighbor on whom the moral life is grounded, but God. The view of the eudaimonists that motivation necessarily demonstrates desire for our own good can remain, but the sting is removed, for it now also demonstrates desire for the good of others. Of course, we do not always appear to desire the good of others (or even ourselves). The eudaimonist's explanation is that such desires are a tragic mistake: we have failed to understand what our good is, or misjudged the value of relative goods, or made some factual error such that our act will not lead to the good that we think it will. So as long as and to the extent that we are not making one of these errors but are actually aiming at our good, we will also be aiming at the good of others.

Aquinas's tectonic shift enables a new theological telling of our evolutionary story. Recall that both the Pessimist and the Optimist agree that humans and other creatures have motivations to help others. The concern of the Pessimist is that we can now trace these motivations to their foundation—their ultimate end. This process is helpfully explored in Anscombe's *Intention*. She observes that there can be multiple levels of reasons for acting, and that each reason may only make sense insofar as it serves a more foundational one, resulting in a series of reasons: "the last term we give in such a series gives the intention with which the act in each of its other descriptions was done, and this intention so to speak swallows up all the preceding intentions."[44]

Return to one of the examples of altruism with which I began: a passer-by rushes into a burning building. Assuming they survive, we might inquire as to their reason for action; *why* did they do it? We might get a response like "I couldn't stand by and do nothing" or "Those people needed help." This evidence of other-regarding motives is enough for the Optimist to say that person acted altruistically. But the Pessimist digs deeper, asking another "why" question: *why* is it that they couldn't stand by and do nothing? Eventually (perhaps after a few more questions), they arrive at what they take to be the terminus of the chain of reasons: because for this person's ancestors it was fitness-enhancing to act for and care about the good of others, by furthering kin selection and reciprocity. Thus the act is taken to be self-centered and so not *really* altruistic.

I think Aquinas's relation of perfection terms to God offers a clear theological response. The Pessimist is right, as far as it goes; but they have not dug deep enough. There is another question to ask: *why* is fitness motivating? By saying that fitness is motivating, I do not mean that organisms are consciously motivated by the desire to improve their fitness, or even that they are conscious of motivation at all. I simply mean that there was a motivation, instinct or drive of some kind that resulted in that organism behaving in a way that enhanced its fitness. Likewise, behaviors that fail to enhance fitness are also initiated by motivations, instincts or drives. Why does this occur?

The answer for the Thomist must be that this is simply the nature of an act. All action, including both fitness-enhancing and fitness-harming acts, result from an apprehension of good on the part of the creature. This is an extension of the eudaimonist view on human motivation to all creation. It occurs in Aquinas because of another tectonic equivalence referred to earlier, one that runs throughout early and medieval Christian thought and can be traced back to Plato: the equation between goodness and being. The existence and the goodness of any creature both depend on the exemplar idea in the mind of God. So Aquinas thinks that everything that exists, simply because it exists, must exhibit some level of goodness. For a thing to exist at all requires that it exhibit some good. "It must needs be that every inclination is to something good… just as the natural appetite tends to good existing in a thing; so the animal or voluntary appetite tends to a good which is apprehended." [45]

So no creaturely action can take place without it being aimed at the good—which is mapped to God. This desire for the good is not just a part of the way humans see the world; it is part of reality itself. That there is ever choice or action—that any creature ever does A rather than B—demonstrates that there is such a thing as desirability; and the most general term for something desirable is *good*. So all acts, including those which enhance fitness, only take place because of the longing of all things for God.[46] *This* is where the "why" questions stop, because they have arrived at something which is desirable in itself—GOODNESS/GOD is an ultimate reason, the answer to its own "why" question. In Aquinas's terms, the "last end" which all things seek.[47]

The theologian can accept that that our surface desires to help others are influenced in part by evolutionary pressures to improve fitness. But this does not imply that all action is foundationally motivated by self-advantage, for the simple reason that evolutionary pressures are not the foundation of motivation or action. Instead, Aquinas's use of analogy brings about a shift in understanding that allows us to see the foundation of all action as desire for God. From this foundation flow both love of the self and love of the other. At different times one or the other may take priority—Aquinas himself holds that the self should be loved more than the other.[48] But the crucial point is that neither is the center or foundation of our moral motivation. This can now be seen simply as an example of the presence of both kinds of motivation (which both the Optimist and the Pessimist acknowledge).

Look again at the disagreement between the Optimist and the Pessimist:
Observation: Human motivation is self-centered.

Optimists: Moral motivation and altruism may be self-centered. Therefore, humans can be altruistic.

Pessimists: Moral motivation and altruism may not be self-centered. Therefore, humans cannot be altruistic.

Whether or not moral motivation or altruism may be self-centered is a worthwhile question to consider for its own sake. But once a tectonic equivalence between GOD and GOOD is made, it is no longer relevant for the question of whether or not humans are altruistic. It does not matter here which of the Optimist and the Pessimist is right; the initial observation is wrong. Human motivation is not self-centered. Our motivations may pass through a desire for our own good, but they stem from love of God, who is goodness itself and the only route by which we can love anything, whether the self or another. In Anscombe's terms, both love for self and love for the other are "swallowed up" by love for God.

CONCLUSION

I began with a look at a question that has exercised evolutionary biologists: how could altruism evolve, given that self-sacrificing individuals are, on the face of it, reducing their fitness? The two most important explanations offered in response to this puzzle are kin selection and reciprocity. It is fitness-enhancing to make sacrifices to help our relatives, most obviously our children; and it is fitness-enhancing to make sacrifices to help other individuals, as long as this makes them more likely to do the same for us.

This account of moral origins leads to a disagreement. Does the fact that our altruistic behavior can be explained in evolutionary terms as an adaption that enhances fitness mean that humans are not *really* altruistic? On one side, the Pessimists say "yes." All of our behavior turns out to be rooted in a drive to benefit ourselves. On the other, the Optimists say "no." Whatever the origins of our motivations, we genuinely care about other people when we act for their sake, and that is what is important.

An Optimist and a Pessimist may look at the same data and draw very different conclusions; but the precise nature of the disagreement is not exactly clear. In a first step toward clarity, I differentiated between two kinds of altruism—reproductive and psychological. Only one of these, psychological altruism, appears to align with moral discourse on altruism, since it holds that motive is an important determinant of altruism. Exactly what motivational conditions must be met for psychological altruism to be present, however, are unclear. I offered four possible definitions, and argued that the debate between the Optimist and the Pessimist must focus on the relation between motivations to act for one's own well-being and motivations to act for the well-being of another.

I then suggested that this debate is a reflection of a larger philosophical and theological discussion on the nature of morality: Is morality other-regarding or self-regarding? There are secular and religious thinkers on both sides, insisting on the primacy of the other and of the self. The disagreement between the Optimist and the Pessimist finally coalesces around whether or not moral or altruistic behavior may be self-centered.

Rather than attempt to argue for one side or another, I suggested that Aquinas's use of analogy produces a tectonic shift in understanding that makes it possible to sidestep the problem entirely. One of the many effects of his mapping of GOOD to GOD is to produce new meaning by blending the concepts of love for the other and love for the self. Rather than being in conflict, both flow from our ultimate desire for goodness, which is God.

The extent of Platonic and Christian thought on the nature of Goodness and Being is vast; and there is simply not enough space here to explore fully the metaphysical reasoning behind Aquinas's position. Instead, my goal was to show how this position enables a new approach to disagreements over the nature of altruism. The connection between God and The Good opens up a third way between the Optimist and the Pessimist.

From this new field of meaning, it is possible to look again at the conflict between the Optimist and the Pessimist and see a new route bridging their divide. Evolutionary accounts of our moral origins do show that self-advantage has played a role in the development of our moral behavior; but it does not play a foundational role. That belongs to our ultimate desire for goodness/God.

The answer offered by Aquinas is that healthy life and offspring are part of the goods of all living species; and this is so because they are part of creaturely perfection, which is itself to be understood as dependent on the true perfection to be found in God. If successful, this tectonic shift allows us to say with confidence that we are not a species of Mr. Collinses. Insofar as we are genuinely motivated by the good of another, we can say that we *really do* love that person, and we are expressing *real* altruism.

NOTES

1. Charles Darwin, *The Origin of Species*, ed. Gillian Beer (Oxford: Oxford University Press, 1996), 197.

2. J. M. Herbers, "Darwin's 'One Special Difficulty': Celebrating Darwin 200", *Biology Letters*, 5, no. 2 (2009): 214–17.

3. E. O. Wilson, *Sociobiology: The New Synthesis* (Cambridge, MA: Harvard University Press, 1975), 120–121.

4. Kim Sterelney, *The Evolved Apprentice: How Evolution Made Humans Unique* (Cambridge, MA: The MIT Press, 2012), 101–123.

5. Marc Bekoff and Jessica Pierce, *Wild Justice: The Moral Lives of Animals* (Chicago: University of Chicago Press, 2009).

6. Jonathan Marks, *Tales of the Ex-Apes: How We Think about Human Evolution* (Oakland: University of California Press, 2015), 46.

7. Frans De Waal, *Primates and Philosophers: How Morality Evolved*, ed. Stephen Macedo and Josiah Ober (Princeton, NJ: Princeton University Press, 2006), 55.

8. Christine Clavien and Michel Chapuisat, "Altruism across Disciplines: One Word, Multiple Meanings," *Biology & Philosophy* 28, no. 1 (2013): 125–40.

9. Clavien and Chapuisat, "Altruism across Disciplines", 127.

10. X. E. Barandiaran, E. Di Paolo, and M. Rohde, "Defining Agency: Individuality, Normativity, Asymmetry, and Spatio-Temporality in Action," *Adaptive Behavior* 17, no. 5 (2009): 367–86.

11. The origin of these demands (social norms, divine law etc.) and their status (hypothetical, categorical) is disputed, but that morality makes some kind of requirement is not.

12. See for example Rosalind Hursthouse, *On Virtue Ethics* (Oxford: Oxford University Press, 1999), 94.

13. Marcus Singer, "On Duties to Oneself," *Ethics* 69, no. 3 (1959): 202–5.

14. John Stuart Mill, *On Liberty*, ed. David Bromwich and George Kateb (New Haven, CT: Yale University Press, 2003), 142.

15. Mill, *On Liberty*, 81.

16. Anders Nygren, *Agape and Eros*, trans. Philip S. Watson (New York: Harper & Row, 1969), 214–215.

17. John P. Reeder, "Empathy, Compassion, and Love of Neighbor," in *Love and Christian Ethics: Tradition, Theory and Society*, ed. Frederick V. Simmons and Brian C. Sorrels (Washington, DC: Georgetown University Press, 2016).

18. G. E. M. Anscombe, "Modern Moral Philosophy," *Philosophy* 33, no. 124 (1958), 1–19; Williams, Bernard, *Ethics and the Limits of Philosophy* (Cambridge, MA: Harvard University Press, 1985).

19. Philippa Foot, "Does Moral Subjectivism Rest on a Mistake?" *Oxford Journal of Legal Studies* 15, no. 1 (1995): 1–14.

20. Aristotle, *Nicomachean Ethics*, trans. by J.A.K. Thomson and Hugh Tredennick (London: Penguin, 2004), 1156a–1156b, p. 35.

21. John Hare, "Scotus on Morality and Nature," *Medieval Philosophy and Theology* 9, no. 1 (2000): 15–38.

22. Robert Masson, *Without Metaphor, No Saving God: Theology After Cognitive Linguistics* (Leuven: Peeters, 2014), 130.

23. Masson, *Without Metaphor*, 74–5, 102–3.

24. Ibid., 142.

25. Robert Masson, "Are Aquinas and Whitehead Metaphorical and Analogical All the Way Down?" *Open Theology* 1, no. 1 (2015): 524–537.

26. Aquinas, *Summa Contra Gentiles*, trans. James F. Anderson et. al., ed. Joseph Kenny (New York: Hanover House, 1955–7), 30.2.

27. Masson, *Without Metaphor, No Saving God*, 134–5.

28. Aquinas, *Summa Contra Gentiles*, 54.4

29. Aquinas, *Summa Theologica*, 1ae 15.1.

30. Thomas Aquinas, *Quaestiones Disputatae de Veritate*, trans. by Robert W. Mulligan, James V. McGlynn, and Robert W. Schmidt (Chicago: Henry Regnery Company, 1952), 1.1.

31. Aquinas, *Quaestiones Disputatae de Veritate*, 1.8.

32. John P. O'Callaghan, *Thomist Realism and the Linguistic Turn: Toward a More Perfect Form of Existence* (Notre Dame, IN: University of Notre Dame Press, 2003), 3.

33. One helpful treatment is Ralph McInerny, *Aquinas and Analogy* (Washington, DC: The Catholic University of America Press, 1996).

34. Aquinas, *Summa Theologica*, 1a2ae 1.7.

35. Ibid., 2a2ae 23.1.

36. Ibid., 1ae 44.4.

37. Ibid., 1a2ae 2.8.

38. Ibid., 2a2ae 23.1.

39. Ibid., 2a2ae 25.1.

40. Ibid., 2a2ae 25.4.

41. Ibid., 2a2ae 184.1.

42. Masson, Without *Metaphor*, 112.

43. Ibid., 114.

44. G. E. M. Anscombe, *Intention* (Oxford: Blackwell, 1957), 46. Italics removed.

45. Aquinas, *Summa Theologica*, 1a2ae 8.1.

46. This does not mean there is a one-to-one correspondence between goodness and fitness. It is easy to think of instances in which securing my genetic heritage would not contribute to a life well lived. In general, though, Aquinas would say that fitness-enhancing acts are likely to be correctly aimed at the goods indicated by natural law, including life, health and the raising of offspring. See Aquinas, *Summa Theologica*, 1a2ae 94.2.

47. Ibid., 1a2ae 1.8.

48. Ibid., 2a2ae 26.4.

BIBLIOGRAPHY

Anscombe, G. E. M., *Intention*. Oxford: Blackwell, 1957.

———. "Modern Moral Philosophy," *Philosophy*, 33, no. 124 (1958): 1–19.

Aquinas, Thomas, *Quaestiones Disputatae de Veritate*. Translated by Robert W. Mulligan, James V. McGlynn, and Robert W. Schmidt. Chicago: Henry Regnery Company, 1952.

———. *Summa Contra Gentiles*. Translated by James F. Anderson, Anton C. Pegis, Vernon J. Bourke, and Charles J. O'Neil. Edited by Joseph Kenny. New York: Hanover House, 1955–7.

———. *Summa Theologica*. Translated by Fathers of the English Dominican Province. Notre Dame, IN: Christian Classics, 1948.

Aristotle, *Nicomachean Ethics*. Trans. by J.A.K. Thomson and Hugh Tredennick. London: Penguin, 2004.

Barandiaran, X. E., E. Di Paolo, and M. Rohde, "Defining Agency: Individuality, Normativity, Asymmetry, and Spatio-Temporality in Action." *Adaptive Behavior* 17, no. 5 (2009): 367–86.

Bekoff, Marc, and Jessica Pierce. *Wild Justice: The Moral Lives of Animals*. Chicago: University of Chicago Press, 2009.

Clavien, Christine and Michel Chapuisat. "Altruism across Disciplines: One Word, Multiple Meanings." *Biology & Philosophy* 28, no. 1 (2013): 125–40.

Darwin, Charles. *The Origin of Species*. Edited by Gillian Beer. Oxford: Oxford University Press, 1996.

De Waal, Frans. *Primates and Philosophers: How Morality Evolved*. Edited by Stephen Macedo and Josiah Ober. Princeton: Princeton University Press, 2006.

Foot, Philippa. "Does Moral Subjectivism Rest on a Mistake?" *Oxford Journal of Legal Studies*, 15, no. 1 (1995): 1–14.

Hare, John, "Scotus on Morality and Nature," *Medieval Philosophy and Theology* 9, no. 1 (2000): 15–38.

Herbers, J. M. "Darwin's 'One Special Difficulty': Celebrating Darwin 200," *Biology Letters* 5, no. 2 (2009): 214–17.

Hursthouse, Rosalind. *On Virtue Ethics*. Oxford: Oxford University Press, 1999.

Lakoff, George and Mark Johnson, *Metaphors We Live By*. Chicago: The University of Chicago Press, 2003.

Marks, Jonathan. *Tales of the Ex-Apes: How We Think about Human Evolution*. Oakland: University of California Press, 2015.

Masson, Robert. *Without Metaphor, No Saving God: Theology after Cognitive Linguistics*. Leuven: Peeters, 2014.

McInerny, Ralph. *Aquinas and Analogy*. Washington, DC: The Catholic University of America Press, 1996.

Mill, John Stuart. *On Liberty*. Edited by David Bromwich and George Kateb. New Haven, CT: Yale University Press, 2003.

Nygren, Anders. *Agape and Eros*. Translated Philip S. Watson. New York: Harper & Row, 1969.

O'Callaghan, John P. *Thomist Realism and the Linguistic Turn: Toward a More Perfect Form of Existence*. Notre Dame, IN: University of Notre Dame Press, 2003.

Reeder, John P. "Empathy, Compassion, and Love of Neighbor." *Love and Christian Ethics: Tradition, Theory and Society*. Edited by Frederick V. Simmons and Brian C. Sorrels. Washington, DC: Georgetown University Press, 2016.

Singer, Marcus. "On Duties to Oneself." *Ethics* 69, no. 3 (1959): 202–5.

Sterelney, Kim. *The Evolved Apprentice: How Evolution Made Humans Unique*. Cambridge, MA: The MIT Press, 2012.
Williams, Bernard. *Ethics and the Limits of Philosophy*. Cambridge, MA: Harvard University Press, 1985.
Wilson, E. O. *Sociobiology: The New Synthesis*. Cambridge, MA: Harvard University Press, 1975.

Chapter Nine

Beyond "Cannot Be Resolved"

Considering Ways Forward for Frozen Embryos

Kathryn Lilla Cox

In 1978, the first human being was born as the result of a pregnancy that began with in-vitro fertilization (IVF) and embryo transfer (ET). Somewhat obscured by this news and the questions regarding the licitness or illicitness of in-vitro fertilization were the ethical questions surrounding the embryos required for IVF. In the succeeding years, what to do with the un-implanted frozen embryos from in-vitro fertilization across the globe has become a pressing concern.[1] A brief survey of literature examining the ethical question of what to do with un-implanted frozen embryos from IVF reveals four possible actions taken by people when they are done having children. The actions include (1) doing nothing and keeping the embryos frozen, (2) destroying the embryos, (3) donating the embryos for research, and (4) giving the embryos to other people for implantation, scientifically called heterologous embryo transfer (HET) and commonly called either embryo donation or embryo adoption.

Within the Catholic theological tradition the question of frozen embryos is situated within the discussion and ethical judgement regarding IVF. In 1987, the Congregation for the Doctrine of the Faith (CDF) in its instruction *Donum Vitae* said that IVF was morally unacceptable.[2] Their rationale included an analysis regarding how the embryo came into existence and what happened to implanted and un-implanted embryos.

John Paul II in 1996 appealed "to the conscience of the world's scientific authorities and in particular to doctors" regarding embryos. He asked "that the production of human embryos be halted, taking into account that there seems to be no morally licit solution regarding the human destiny of the thousands and thousands of 'frozen' embryos which are and remain the subjects of essential rights and should therefore be protected by law as human persons."[3] His language, while negative, seems to leave an opening for the future development of a morally licit solution. One potentially licit theological response was prenatal adoption. In 2004, the Pontifical Academy of Life at their general assembly concluded that the question of prenatal adoption as a response to the concern about "frozen embryos" still needed study.[4] In their 2008 instruction *Dignitas Personae*, however, the CDF deemed that prenatal embryo adoption is an unviable response to frozen embryos.[5] While the CDF acknowledges that prenatal adoption respects human life that is not yet a person, the CDF rejects prenatal adoption because they do not believe it respects marriage and the conjugal act as the place for how new human life comes into existence. The CDF ultimately concludes in *Dignitas Personae* that, "all things considered, it needs to be recognized that the thousands of abandoned embryos represent a *situation of injustice which in fact cannot be resolved.*"[6] These teachings complicate the question for Catholics regarding how to respond ethically to the reality of frozen embryos.[7] Doing nothing means leaving the frozen embryos in a state of suspended animation. Yet responding with one of the other available options, according to the CDF, means participating in unacceptable actions.[8]

Yet, the Catholic moral tradition has long held and recognized that sometimes we need to act in less than ideal situations, finding a way to consider the better of available paths for acting.[9] Therefore, on the one hand, the CDF is correct that the situation of frozen embryos cannot be resolved perfectly and that embryos are human life even as they are not yet persons. On the other hand, the Catholic moral tradition requires us to grapple with what is and find a way forward, even if it is imperfect. This explains why, when the CDF sees no way forward regarding the fate of frozen embryos, others, including some Catholic theologians and philosophers, continue to argue that an ethically valid response exists to the fate of frozen embryos, even if it is imperfect.

This impasse regarding ethical action occurs, however, not just because of different approaches but because we do not yet have the conceptual categories or metaphorical blends to help us grapple with our development, use, and implications of technology to assist with the beginning of human life. Specifically, our theological anthropology and ethical principles are limited in helping us think through the ethical concerns that arise with frozen embryos that, while recognized as new human life, are still only potential human persons. New frameworks or metaphors that might help us reach some moral consensus on a possible solution to what the CDF calls "a situation of injustice that cannot be resolved" have not fully emerged.

Shifting the conversation from an argument regarding licit or illicit actions to a more explicit conversation regarding the conceptual frames used in our consideration of appropriate actions in relationship to frozen embryos reveals the inadequacy of theological and cultural mappings to deal with this particular ethical concern—frozen embryos. This conceptual framework analysis is important because Pope John Paul II, the CDF, theologians, scientists, and other people are imprecise in their language about the embryos' developmental stage.[10] This imprecision develops in part from common usage of the term *embryo* and other cognitive blends where the embryo is referenced as an orphan, a test subject, or a human person. The imprecision and different blends move people into different spaces of meaning, even when theoretically everyone is talking about the *embryo*. As a result, our language and conceptual frameworks fall short; they provide close approximations for defining the new space we are in, but new communal meaning does not arise from current blends.

As a way of proceeding, this chapter will briefly discuss thoughts as a precursor to visible moral action (deeds) to support the claim that an ethical analysis or discernment by Catholics about viable courses of action related to frozen embryos requires more than consideration of the action itself. The second section will briefly discuss the role of conceptual mapping as applied to moral action. The third section will then provide a description of scientific and theological concepts of the embryo. The various understandings of the term *embryo* tap into different conceptual maps that imply different beliefs, values, and commitments. The fourth section maps and examines several conceptual blends influencing courses of action related to frozen embryos. The various conceptual blends used to talk about frozen embryos do not fit completely together, and a new blend has not emerged to resolve the tension of our new reality. Nonetheless, movement is happening. As with the movement of Earth's tectonic plates, what eventually emerges is unpredictable in terms of place and location. Therefore, looking to other possible spaces for emergent blends, such as the Body of Christ, leads to the conclusion that Catholics already have theological resources to construct responses to frozen embryos, which, while they may be imperfect, means Catholics need not see the situation of injustice represented by frozen embryos as unsolvable.

THOUGHTS AS PRECURSORS TO (VISIBLE) MORAL ACTION

Anyone who prays the *Confiteor* confesses their sins "in my thoughts, in my words, in what I have done or failed to do." The confession of sins progresses from an internal forum (thoughts), to a speech act (words), to embodied action (what is done) or a failure to act (what is not done).

Contemporary theological ethicists in various ways and degrees of attention examine all four categories of sin, and advances in neuroscience direct more attention to our cognition and epistemology. Yet, long before neuroscience, the ancient monastics considered the connection between thoughts, actions, and practices.

The early monastics were often single monks who went into the desert as part of their ascetical practices. Once they won their visible struggles with objects or things, fought by abstinence and prayer, monks were left with their struggles of their thoughts, the "invisible struggle."[11] Thoughts, then, are the ground, the soil, that which nurtures the growth of sin or virtue and ultimately affects our actions (deeds). Whereas moderns see the brain and reason as the basis of intelligence, the desert monastics saw the "heart as the seat of intelligence, of the mind." Therefore, it was important to guard the heart, with attentiveness and prayer as the tools for this guarding.[12] This attentiveness and concern was important because it affected the discernment of right actions or ways of behaving in the attempt to follow God/Christ. This teaches us today that attentiveness to thoughts and patterns of thinking is important for the decisions we make; it is not simply a matter of determining the right action to take but also considering the thoughts and conceptual frames that influence our actions.

By focusing on the heart and the way thoughts form the heart toward love or corruption, we retrieve from the ancients the value of approaching our thoughts through a visioning process, that while embodied is not reducible to our brain or mind. This has implications in a scientific age when we risk reducing humanity to a mind, brain, or biochemical processes. In other words, the internal world has external consequences. And for Evagrius, Benedict, and other ancients changing thought patterns also requires changed behavior to reinforce or re-encode new thought patterns, demonstrating that by creating new fields of meaning, we shape our worldviews and actions. Therefore, communal practices and rituals matter for how we think. Attention to our behavior, practices, and conceptual maps of meaning serves as a reminder that any decision by couples or individual persons regarding frozen embryos has communal and societal implications.

Simply stating, however, that changing thoughts leads to changed action remains insufficient. Given the complexity of conceptual frameworks, the meaning attached to language, and the distinction between science and theological terminology in the twenty-first century that did not exist in the ancient world, a brief understanding of conceptual mapping is important before looking at the conceptual blends utilized in responding to the reality of frozen embryos.

MAPPING AND MORAL ACTION: ONE VIEW OF COGNITIVE LINGUISTICS

Cognitive linguists and theologians who utilize cognitive theory study, among other areas, image schemas, cross-domain mapping, conceptual blending, and metaphor to help articulate what is happening in our cognitive processes.[13] This work helps us identify different blends, metaphors, and schemas at work, understand our cognitive processes, and begin to explain how conceptual frameworks influence thoughts and debates about various issues. Robert Masson identifies some blends as tectonic.[14] He defines a tectonic blend as a blend of prior concept fields or ideas that by virtue of their blending and integration generates a new insight that shifts how one sees the world: in other words, a blend from which new meanings emerge.

He points out that any person or community creating the blends or performing the blending might not even realize their subsequent shift in worldview with its emerging meaning. This is similar to what happens when the Earth's tectonic plates move around or collide with each other, changing the Earth's surface; this change may not be noticed for a period of time. Or the collision might be felt, even as the eventual changes are not immediately seen. Nonetheless, change has occurred; likewise in our language, any tectonic shift due to concept blending affects understanding and interpretation of all aspects/terms within the cognitive network and intersecting fields of meaning. For example, the meaning of "the belief that God is and acts" only arises "in the function of the distinctions that have arisen in prayer and lament, narrative and creed, wonder and gratitude, ritual and prophetic action, worship and mysticism."[15] The creed or other doctrines about God are insufficient on their own to create meaning; meaning arises in the interplay of creedal statements, prayer, ritual and worship, and so on.

In other words, understanding a concept in one arena requires understanding the concept in other arenas of meaning as well. This provides what Masson calls a multidimensional or complex network of meaning. Masson's explanation for understanding conceptual shifts of worldview as tectonic actually connects linguistic frameworks and practices. Therefore, his work on tectonic mapping demonstrates how shifting understandings of concepts due to blending, or by bringing different concepts (with their underlying terrain) into interaction with each other, leads to changed beliefs. Changed beliefs often promote changed action even as the language or words stay the same. Thus, Masson provides insight for considering the CDF's claim that there is an irresolvable injustice, as well as disagreement among ethicists and others regarding acceptable responses when we consider frozen embryos. What is at stake includes not just the fate of frozen embryos but also the cultural and theological meaning—not to mention rituals and other communal practices—surrounding marriage, parenthood, kinship, human sexuality, and more. While not using Masson's language, the CDF and ethicists recognize in some way that grappling with the ethical issue of what to do with frozen embryos means we stand on the edge of a potential tectonic and disclosive conceptual blend with accompanying new understandings and meanings related to marriage, parenthood, kinship, human sexuality, and more.

Therefore, understanding the conceptual blends used when trying to resolve the dilemma of what to do with frozen embryos illuminates several things. First, the scientific and theological conceptual frameworks for thinking about the embryo do not necessarily match. Second, frozen embryos are not simply an ethereal concept but rather a human life form requiring actions and interactions; we have theological and cultural practices that signify in some way a relationship with human embryos. As a result, the difficulty regarding what to do with frozen embryos exists partially because we cannot consider frozen embryos isolated from other spheres of meaning. New scientific knowledge about life's beginnings and the dilemma of frozen embryos requires new conceptual blends as we consider how we relate to all human life from conception to natural death.[16]

Thus, Masson's language of *tectonic* is appropriate and evocative; like tectonic plates, our conceptual frameworks slide around or collide with each other as we cannot figure out how to blend our varied theological, scientific, and cultural frameworks for considering the fate of frozen embryos. Where these collisions occur, new blends may arise, providing new frames of meaning and patterns of inference. The ethical questions posed by frozen embryos are one such tectonic zone of potential collision that stretches our current frameworks for discussing human life. Many people recognize the implications of this stretching, even if in halting, tentative, or intuitive manners. Thus, the real collision of blends resulting in tectonic conceptual mappings for comprehending human life takes us into terrain that we cannot yet see clearly but intuitively perceive as a changing landscape.[17]

Complicating this collision is that embryos have a symbolic as well as biological function in our theological imagination. Discussions about frozen embryos primarily revolve around what functionally can be done (action) with the embryos. What the frozen embryo symbolizes is under-examined. Symbols have embedded in themselves frameworks, worldviews, and ways of being. Therefore, symbols function as a type of shorthand for our interactions, past experiences, and beliefs that we bring into a conversation, encounter, or decision-making process. The embryo, while biologically (at the genetic level) is human life, is also still a potential human person. The embryo symbolizes the potentiality for a future human baby; the hopes and dreams of the couple that sought medical help for bringing a new human person into the world, the communal beliefs regarding creation, the proper relationship between God and creature, as well as the mystery, wonder, and awe at the beauty and fragility of human beginnings.[18] Therefore, grappling with the symbolism and ways of conceptualizing the embryo can help provide guidance for determining courses of action connected to people's beliefs, hopes, and dreams when deciding how to handle frozen embryos.

WHAT IS AN EMBRYO? THEOLOGICAL AND SCIENTIFIC CONCEPTIONS

Scientifically, various terms describe the development of the fertilized egg as it progresses from fertilization to birth: for example, zygote, morula, blastocyst, embryo, and fetus.[19] A zygote is defined as "a fertilized egg before it begins to divide."[20] The blastocyst has an inner mass of cells and a cavity from which other structures will emerge, for example, the placenta.[21] In humans, the term *embryo* technically applies after implantation of the organism is complete (approximately fourteen days after fertilization) until eight weeks of development, at which time the developing organism is referred to as a fetus." The fetus is the "unborn offspring from the eighth week after conception to the moment of birth."[22] Technical scientific considerations aside, "the term 'human embryo' commonly refers to the human organism from the time of conception through to eight weeks' gestational age."[23] In other words, the embryo is understood as "an egg that has been fertilized by a sperm and has undergone one or more divisions."[24]

Given these definitions, when it comes to frozen embryos from IVF, they are usually three to five days old, and these embryos are scientifically also referred to as either a zygote, morula, or blastocyst. Frozen embryos have not even reached the time of fourteen days after fertilization, when the term *embryo* more strictly applies. These three- to five-day-old "embryos," however, fit the more common definition of a *donated embryo*: an "embryo that is donated by a patient or couple who previously underwent ART treatment and had extra embryos available."[25]

The scientific community attends to the process of human development from fertilization through birth by defining the structures that arise in a particular order, accounting for differentiation in the form (physical shape) of the human life. Various terms are employed to distinguish the various particular points of prenatal development. Yet, the scientific distinctions based on form and development get lost with the more common usage of the term *embryo*.

The CDF recognizes these scientific distinctions of form and developmental stages when it comes to human zygotes, embryos, and fetuses. The CDF makes no ethical distinction, however, between these stages of human development.[26] The rationale provided for this ethical determination is that science verifies that at conception a new human life has come into existence. This new life is distinctive, unique, and different from other human lives. Therefore, this new life is to be afforded the respect and dignity of human persons.[27] While recognizing that a new human life in its smallest form is not yet a postnatal human being, the CDF nonetheless argues that this new human life be afforded the same respect as a human person.

Throughout both *Donum Vitae* (1987) and *Dignitas Personae* (2008), the CDF uses words and phrases such as "human being," "not yet a person," "human rights," "corpses," "integration of body and soul,"[28] and "orphans" among others when discussing embryos from IVF. The language here highlights the dearth of conceptual frames to consider prenatal human life that (a) we cannot see without the aid of microscopes and (b) is not yet in the form of a human person. With its language of human beings, rights, and orphans and with its rejection that embryos can be test subjects (no to research on embryos), the CDF is moving into a tectonic zone where, with the right combination of inputs, new blends and new meaning could emerge. Likewise, the common use of the term *embryo* in the phrase frozen embryos, instead of blastocysts or the phrase three- to five-day-old embryo, combined with images of prenatal life provide certain inputs and conceptual blends that also move us into a tectonic zone ripe for the emergence of new meaning.

The simplest blends include (1) THE EMBRYO IS A TYPE OF HUMAN LIFE, NOT A PERSON, AND MORE THAN A BALL OF CELLS; (2) THE EMBRYO IS A FETUS; (3) THE BLASTOCYST (EMBRYO) IS TO BE TREATED AS A HUMAN BEING/PERSON CREATED IN THE IMAGE OF GOD; and (4) THE EMBRYO IS HUMAN LIFE (NOT YET A PERSON) AND WORTHY OF PROTECTION/RESPECT. After naming some of the emerging blends, various inputs for the blends are discussed.

The first blend relies on scientific facts that the cells do not simply replicate themselves. Rather, the cells with forty-six human chromosomes will differentiate into specific types of cells and eventually structures as they continue dividing. It also acknowledges the blastocyst's potential to become a human being.

The second blend, THE BLASTOCYST (EMBRYO) IS A FETUS, arises from several inputs. The first input is the linguistic equating of the blastocyst with the embryo, where there is inattention to differences in the form of the prenatal human life. The blastocyst (three to five days after fertilization) looks like a berry and is not implanted in a uterus. Technically, the embryo is at least fourteen days old to eight weeks old, implanted in the uterus, and, depending on its stage of development, looks more like a fetus. The second input into this blend is the various images most people are exposed to of the later embryonic stages where the formation of the nervous system, the eyes, hands, and so forth begin to be visible in this prenatal human life. This exposure comes via ads, billboards, Google searches, and ultrasound images. We might see images from ultrasounds shared by people we know during their pregnancy. Meanwhile, ads and billboard images as part of pro-life campaigns do not carefully distinguish stages of prenatal development. Thus, when the term *embryo* is used to refer to the blastocyst, we often do not visualize prenatal life as the three- to five-day-old group of dividing cells; instead, we might imagine the two-month-old prenatal life (fetus) that is beginning to look like a human being.

The EMBRYO IS A FETUS blend reveals and acknowledges that the blastocyst (embryo) with its forty-six human chromosomes is genetically a human life. The blend conflates and equates different stages of human development, however, effectively leading to the blend THE BLASTOCYST (EMBRYO) IS A FETUS. Therefore, in our imaginations many of us think more of developed prenatal life and babies when the term frozen embryos is employed. Thus, this blend potentially affects us emotionally and intellectually. It also informs, albeit probably unconsciously, the next two blends, in particular THE BLASTOCYST (EMBRYO) IS TO BE TREATED AS A HUMAN BEING/PERSON.

The third and fourth blends, while slightly different, are informed by science and share several theological premises. These theological premises include the following: humans are created in the image and likeness of God; God loved and knew us before we were born; the consistent ethic (or seamless garment) of life, which argues that life should be protected and respected from conception until natural death; and the belief that all life is sacred because life is created by God.

The third blend, THE BLASTOCYST (EMBRYO) IS TO BE TREATED AS A HUMAN BEING/PERSON, has several inputs. The first input is scientific, where science demonstrates that the blastocyst is genetically human, different from other mammals, and still needs a human female body for gestation. The second input is the blend that conflates the embryo with the fetus. The third input is a complex theological mapping. Theology utilizing Sacred Scripture and the theological tradition argues that God knew us before we were born (in the womb), humans are created in the image and likeness of God, all human life is sacred, humans have inherent dignity and are not to be used by others and humans are subjects, not objects. These inputs lend themselves to the blend THE BLASTOCYST (EMBRYO) IS TO BE TREATED AS A HUMAN BEING/PERSON. This means that the blastocyst (embryo) is created in the image and likeness of God, is to be treated with the same respect and dignity as a postnatal child and human being, needs the protection afforded the vulnerable, and is to be seen as a subject, not an object to be used.

What is hidden by this blend with its images of formed human beings (a recognizable shape) is the reality that the blastocyst (embryo) is not the same as a fetus or a postnatal baby, and it ignores the question of whether treatment should really be fully the same. Analogously, we recognize that development matters, and we make distinctions when thinking, discussing, and considering how to interact with at a one-year-old, a twenty-five-year-old, and a seventy-year-old.

The last blend most clearly does not equate the blastocyst (embryo) with a fetus or human person. The blend BLASTOCYST (EMBRYO) IS HUMAN LIFE (NOT YET A PERSON) AND WORTHY OF PROTECTION/RESPECT is the blend that honors scientific distinction while making use of theological frames already in existence for thinking about human beings while moving into the yet undefined space of how we conceive and make sense of new knowledge related to human beginnings. This blend draws on scientific knowledge that new human life is in existence and the theological inputs articulated above regarding how to view human life in its earliest beginnings. As such, there is a tacit acknowledgment that the blastocyst (embryo) is human life and therefore is to be afforded respect and protection and is to be treated as a subject, not an object. Yet, this same blastocyst (embryo) requires different consideration since it is still a potential, not an actual, human being/person.

All four blends are informed by contemporary scientific advances in reproductive knowledge, some by cultural cues, and others theological beliefs. All the blends put frozen embryos in a conceptual map of meanings and set parameters for ethical responses.

MAPPING SEVERAL THEOLOGICAL RESPONSES TO FROZEN EMBRYOS

As a recap, there are four general options for action related to frozen human embryos when people are done having children using IVF: (1) doing nothing and keeping the embryos frozen, (2) destroying the embryos, (3) donating the embryos for research, and (4) giving the embryos to other people for implantation, called either embryo donation or embryo adoption. As noted earlier, the CDF sees all of these possible options as invalid solutions. This section examines the cognitive frameworks, blends, and various assumptions or inputs that inform some, but not all, of the options for the frozen embryos. The examination will not make a judgment about the option for determining the fate of frozen embryos. Rather, the goal is to explore what the language used by others reveals or conceals when discussing the options.

Doing Nothing and Keeping the Embryos Frozen

This option raises several questions related to human dignity, growth, and potential and influences how one views other options. Being frozen for embryos is really a state of deliberate suspended potentiality, intentional suspended development. Life is neither progressing nor regressing. Frozen embryos do not age; they do not develop biologically, emotionally, psychologically, or spiritually. They do not exhibit agency.

Furthermore, considering the term *freezing* illuminates several overlooked features of freezing that are pertinent to the discussion of frozen embryos. Freezing is a way of storing and keeping food or other objects from spoiling, going bad, and needing to be thrown away. It preserves the food for future use and prevents us from wasting food. The frozen food or other objects need to be kept somewhere and thus require certain types of equipment (freezer) at a certain temperature. The food/objects can be thawed and usually used, although sometimes freezer burn renders food unusable.

The language of freezing raises several questions regarding human embryos. How is the language of freezing subtly shaping the way we think about human life? Does IVF and freezing of embryos give the illusion of control and foster a devaluing of life in ways we do not understand yet? Does freezing embryos condition us to see human life as an object? Is it acceptable to freeze human life and see human life as extra, to be held in reserve for future use, like food?

Yet, as a technological intervention, the ability to freeze embryos is different from other technological interventions that the field of health care ethics considers. For example, with humans at the end of their life the concern is the proper time to withdraw or remove technological interventions that are helping sustain life by prolonging the dying process. In keeping embryos frozen, however, we are not providing embryos what they need to sustain life, nor are we permitting embryonic death. Rather, when frozen, embryonic life is suspended.[29] The capacity to successfully freeze and thaw embryos illustrates the difference between prenatal embryonic human life and postnatal human beings. We cannot freeze postnatal human beings without killing them. Thus, the capacity to freeze, halt life's development, and subsequently thaw that human life, permitting it potentially to continue developing, is a new space for understanding what we mean by human life and what is possible for that human life.[30] None of the blends briefly discussed in the section above seemingly account for this difference in pre- and postnatal life.

Destroying the Embryos

This option also raises several questions related to human dignity, growth, and potential. Destruction of embryos occurs for various reasons. During the initial IVF treatment or upon thawing, the embryos may be deemed unviable,[31] the person or couple who commissioned the embryos and were keeping them frozen might stop paying for storage, or the person or couple does not want the embryos anymore and does not like the other options for their embryos. Medically, the embryos constitute disposable biological waste.[32] Just because embryos can be treated as medical waste does not mean that the members of the public, or even medical professionals, see embryos as biological waste. Yet, there are no societal or ecclesial practices or rituals that honor the insight that frozen embryos are a form of human life and not biological waste like phlegm-soaked tissues. Therefore, embryos are treated as waste.

Theologically, the blend that embryos are human life with the rights of human persons and the blend that would equate embryos with fetuses or human persons would not usually foster the deliberate destruction of embryos. Catholic approaches to death and dying forbid the deliberate killing or destroying of another human being. Therefore, since some see the embryos as human beings, persons, or potential human beings, then deliberately killing or destroying embryos is also impermissible.

It is because people do not want to keep embryos frozen or destroy them that the next option becomes a more viable solution, if the people who initially froze the embryos will not implant the embryos. The option about to be discussed is relying on blending some ideas that begin to name aspects of the new reality of human beginnings; yet, the blends do not offer a comprehensive construct for thinking about and providing meaning for this new reality as evidenced by the debate about the option's name.

Embryo Donation or Adoption

Embryo donation or adoption[33] at their core have a similar process: people have embryos from IVF that they will not implant, do not want to keep frozen, and do not want to give to medical researchers. The "donors" will give the embryos away. The givers or donors must sign away rights and obligations to the embryo(s) and resulting child(ren). The recipients may be people desiring embryos to try to have a baby or see themselves as providing a home for needy children similar to adoption. The recipients of the embryos become the ones responsible for and the legal parents of any children born from "donated" or "adopted" embryos. This process of donation or adoption can be closed, partially closed, or open, with various types of contact negotiated between the people donating and those receiving the embryos. This option of donating or adopting embryos illustrates the power of language for shaping ethical reflection as well as revealing and concealing aspects of the same ethical reflection.

This procedure builds on language that the CDF, though not unique to them, uses to describe frozen embryos at one point in *Dignitas Personae*: "orphans." The CDF's use of quotation marks around the term demonstrates its recognition that the particular meanings of the term are not quite a match for frozen embryos. This is one example of how the conceptual frameworks and linguistic tools for considering human life that have worked in the past are stretched in a technological age and their usage pushes us into liminal spaces.

The term *orphan* typically refers to a child whose parents have either died or abandoned them. Like orphans, sometimes, but not usually, the embryo's genetic parents have died. If embryos are abandoned, it is because the genetic parents stop paying storage fees. Unlike orphans or children placed in foster care, embryos do not typically age out of a system due to a biological age and cultural norms for adult agency. "Orphaned embryos" cannot do these things because they are "housed" in canisters, suspended in their development. Even though not all people use the CDF's term *orphans* for frozen embryos, the term does reveal our recognition of the embryos' potentiality to become a human being with agency, evidenced in a growing willingness to "donate" or "give up" the embryos for adoptions. Most embryos are donated or given up because the people commissioning their existence decide that they themselves, for any number of reasons, cannot bring another life into the world. They would prefer the embryos have a chance at life rather than remaining frozen, used for research, or destroyed.[34] This is true whether the language to describe the practice is of donation or adoption. The different language draws our attention, however, to different moral agents and their relationship to the embryos.

Adoption occurs when adults willingly enter into a relationship with another human being, usually a child. The adults will care for the child as they would a biologically related child. Children can be adopted because they are orphaned (parents died), they were abandoned and parental rights are terminated, or their biological/birth parents have signed over parental rights and responsibilities to other people. Decisions to relinquish frozen embryos mirror the adoption of postnatal children in some ways. Therefore, even though an embryo is not physiologically the same as a child, the language of adoption pulls humans into the conceptual framework of adoption and related linguistic concepts about adoption.[35] As a result, embryo adoption becomes a viable response to frozen embryos, especially when the embryo is seen as a human person.[36]

As William Stempsey points out, however, there is a risk in using adoption language. He writes,

> But the risk in using "adoption" in the case of HET [heterologous embryo transfer] is that if we see the adoption of a needy child as good, then assum-

> ing that the embryo is human life can lead to the premature conclusion that HET is just like adoption of a needy child. But that is precisely the moral question to be decided. This is not to deny the inherent human dignity of the embryo. . . . But adoption of a child is quite different from adoption of a human embryo. Having an embryo implanted is to become pregnant and to become pregnant is not the same as rearing a child; prenatal nurturing is not postnatal nurturing. . . . To use adoption as a metaphor for HET is to reinterpret the commonly understood meaning of adoption, embryo implantation, pregnancy, and child-rearing.[37]

Stempsey recognizes that using metaphors shapes our thinking, presets the contours of a moral conversation, and pulls us into webs of meaning that risk being reinterpreted. He is also pointing out that the use of metaphor reveals and conceals aspects of reality.[38] On the one hand, using the language of adoption, with its accompanying image of a postnatal child, attends to the reality that embryos are human life. On the other hand, the metaphor ignores the fact that implanting an embryo and becoming pregnant is different from bringing a postnatal child into one's household to raise and love. Mary B. Mahowald names some of these differences when she articulates that embryo adoption requires the following steps:

> 1. Hormonal treatment of the woman to prepare her body for pregnancy;
> 2. Transfer to her uterus of an embryo formed from another woman's egg that was fertilized in vitro (with sperm from her partner or from someone else);
> 3. Gestation of the embryo until the woman gives birth to a newborn;
> 4. Fulfillment of parental obligations to the child by the woman or couple who agreed to the adoption.[39]

The first three steps for embryo adoption are not the same for postnatal adoption. These differences are precisely what are glossed in the language of adoption, as Stempsey points out.

Furthermore, careful consideration of embryo adoption requires that we not glamorize pregnancy, that we not only recognize the medical risks to women's health due to pregnancy but also examine and analyze the cultural and gender overlays both implicit and explicit that surround pregnancy like a mist we feel but do not always see.[40]

Dislike of the term *embryo adoption* has resulted in the alternative language of embryo donation.[41] The rationale for *embryo donation* rests on several assumptions leading to the EMBRYO CAN BE DONATED blend. First, some women, having had a successful pregnancy and birth as the result of IVF, see the remaining embryos as a potential child and not a collection of cells. Second, donation requires thinking of the needs of others, giving of one's excess, and sharing with others what one has and others need. Third, the donation is sometimes seen as a gift where what one has is freely given with no compensation and further claim.[42] The other person would enjoy and appreciate what is given to them. Fourth, the person donating the embryos has experienced infertility and has some desire to alleviate the suffering of others. Unlike adoption, where the emphasis is on the recipients of the embryos, the language of donation emphasizes the givers of the embryos.

The language of neither adoption nor donation adequately captures the new reality of transferring a human embryo between people. Adoption language obscures the reality that we are discussing prenatal, not postnatal, life. Pregnancy and a birth have not yet happened, and in fact, a live birth might not occur due to a failure of the embryo to implant or a miscarriage at some point during a pregnancy. Donation language pulls us into a matrix of meaning that has arisen around excess objects or the material goods that people need to survive. Donation language has the potential to gloss over the insight that embryos are human life and a potential child, not disposable or transferable objects. The language of gift used by some women corrects this potential gloss.[43]

Yet, given that, when we donate, we typically donate or give away money, clothing, and food, do we really want to consider embryos in the same category of our "excess funds, clothing, food," that which we do not need or are willing to sacrifice for the good of the other? Therefore, is donation truly a helpful category?

Since 1978, we have been struggling to grapple with how technology is stretching and pushing the boundaries of how we understand the connection between biological, gestational, and social mothering, not to mention our lack of understanding how pregnancy is formative of relationships between birth mother and child. The language of embryo donation or adoption continues to confront us with the inability of our metaphorical language to capture the nuances and reality our current technology and knowledge require. The debates over using the language of embryo adoption or donation is evidence that new conceptual blends have not emerged that help us make meaningful sense of our new knowledge related to human beginnings.

Masson argues that certain blends, for example, JESUS IS MESSIAH, result from inputs, which are themselves complex blends. This "not only creates a new conceptual space in which Jesus and the Messiah are equivalent, it also creates space for the emergence of a reconfigured field of meanings (new worldview or higher viewpoint)." The inputs do not change, but the meaning and worldview "transcend the original inputs." This type of complex double scope-blending with tectonic equivalence between the inputs, Jesus and Messiah, are what creates new space and fields of meaning.[44] Masson's conclusion helps us understand what is happening with the inputs and metaphors used to describe both frozen embryos and the options for acting in response to frozen embryos.

What appears to be happening in the conversation about the fate of frozen embryos is that the inputs are not seen as equivalent, thus the resulting blends or new spaces do not result in changed fields of meaning. There is general agreement about what happens in heterologous embryo transfer (HET) but disagreement about how to name the action: HET, donation, adoption, gifting. Different inputs provide insight and illuminate different aspects of the process and practice, but no blends have emerged that adequately help us comprehend the complexities wrought by IVF and frozen embryos. We recognize somewhat that the human embryo is human life, but we have not figured out how to incorporate frozen embryos that are disconnected from but still needing a female body to become a human being into our worldview. Likewise, the languages of adoption or donation focus on the embryo but are inadequate on their own to help us fully comprehend the shifting frameworks for bringing new human life into the world along with its implications for human sexuality, kinship, parenthood, and marriage. In the case where equivalence seems to have happened, for example, for those who see the embryo as a human person, it could be argued that this is a false equivalence because the tectonic shift of meaning has not occurred in the connected conceptual maps related to our understanding of kinship and so forth.

Trying to make a stronger case for embryo adoption as a viable option despite the lack of biological kinship, Darlene Fozard Weaver briefly considers two theological themes within the Christian tradition that subvert biological kinship: baptism into a corporate body and that we are all adopted sons and daughters of God.[45] She argues for a more robust theology of adoption, which she argues will help with the analysis of embryo adoption. Her argument about the subversive theological nature of Christians being adopted sons and daughters of God, while accurate, remains insufficient because she overlooks several things. Baptism is currently reserved for postnatal human beings. Children ready to be baptized into the corporate Body of Christ are different from embryos who occupy the space of the unborn, those who are unable to be baptized. Theologically, in the early church, baptism was primarily for adults and required a switching of identity, religiously and culturally, leaving behind the identity in which one was born, formed, and culturally raised. This switching of identities is still present in our understanding of baptism, but not in the same way. Prenatal adoption of embryos does not have this same feature of identity switching or merging. The embryo has had no familial or cultural formation. The "adopted" embryo will receive, not switch its identity. Therefore, the theological trope of adopted sons and daughters of God does not quite help us make sense of embryo adoption.

Fozard Weaver's observation that more focused theological reflection would enrich consideration of embryo adoption as an option for the fate of frozen embryos, however, applies more broadly. Her observation is also evidence that the metaphors and inputs used to try to explain where embryos fit into our understanding of the continuum of human life are insufficient. There is no equivalence, no helpful blends, to structure and help us understand completely new fields of meaning, and thus we remain in the tectonic zone without tectonic change.

A POSSIBLE WAY FORWARD AND CONCLUSION

As it stands, no option for the frozen embryos is perfect. For many people, deliberately destroying the embryos is seen as taking human life; donating the embryos for research is unacceptable because it also means the nascent human life stops progressing. Likewise, thawing the embryos without implantation is unacceptable because it means frustrating their potential to become a postnatal human being. Letting hundreds of thousands of embryos essentially die is inconceivable for too many people. While many Catholic theologians argue for the validity of embryo adoption or donation, others see this option as unethical. Many conceptual frameworks and blends are utilized to defend or support one option or another, while beginning to wrestle with more foundational questions of belonging, kinship, and so forth. Is there a way forward? If we consider that Masson argues that complex double-scope blends create new meaning, not just intellectually, but because the blends become embedded in rituals, practices, prayers, and so forth—maybe. Considering the fate of frozen embryos' intellectually and in the context of rituals, prayers, and practices, a new frame of meaning might appear.

For example, the blend EMBRYONIC LIFE IS HUMAN LIFE is intellectually supported in the theological claim of protecting and respecting life from conception to death. Using the language of respect for life from conception to death, Catholics are acknowledging a process of living, growth, development, and then decline into death only to be risen into new life. Technology has made it possible to see and follow the process of new human life from conception to birth. Visually, it is clear that while at the chromosomal level a new human life form exists at conception, there is a difference between this early life form and the life form we call a baby. Yet, frozen embryos and what to do with them also seemingly remind us that nascent life exists outside the household of God; the household is not whole. What, then, permits us to incorporate the nascent life into the whole community, into the Body of Christ?[46]

Prayers exist in worship and prayer books for human life in all stages from conception to natural death. Practices differ, however, for pre- and postnatal life. There are practices and rituals to accompany people in dying, including anointing, praying with them, and ultimately burying them. In other words, religious rituals exist for life in particular forms after birth, when human life can fit into rituals already constructed and formalized. Yet, as a church we have very little in the way of ritual practices for miscarriages, stillbirths, or even abortions.[47] Therefore, we intellectually acknowledge nascent embryonic life in our theologizing, but not ritually in its smallest, most nascent form. Prenatal life is to be respected, prayed for, and advocated for in a legal framework, but widespread ritual practices incorporating the prenatal human life in all its forms, from invisible embryonic human life that looks more like a berry to a fetus looking more like a baby, are almost nonexistent. In other words, when human life is not in the form of a postnatal human baby, child, or adult, we have difficulty understanding both the essence of embryonic life and its place in our community. Lacking conceptual frameworks, language, or ritual practice makes it harder to think about grappling with the reality of frozen embryos resulting from IVF and all possible options for not keeping them in suspended animation. Right now, adoptive language is the closest comprehensible field of meaning we have theologically and societally that has some rites of passage or practices associated with it.

The CDF argues, however, that this new human life is to be afforded the same respect as a human person, and this begs the question: How is suspended animation a form of respect? Would it be more respectful to let the embryos die with some form of accompaniment? Theologically, there is an intellectual tradition as well as rites for the dying. There are few, if any, rituals to accompany the loss of prenatal life. As a result, resistance to thawing and letting the embryos die might be intuitively pointing to the need for rituals. If embryos are a form of human life to be respected as human persons, it is insufficient to let embryos die in a lab dish unaccompanied and then be disposed of as biological waste. Can we consider rituals, use the sacraments already present in the Catholic Church, and develop a theological understanding of death that can be applied to frozen/thawed embryos? Can we develop theological guidelines for "allowing the embryo" to die its natural death, analogous to what we have for the human life form we call a person? How can we accompany the embryos in dying?

The answers to these questions might mean developing a new ritual or shifting how we think about baptism to incorporate forms of human life that do not look like a baby, child, or adult into the Body of Christ. Fozard Weaver begins this shifting but does not adequately account for the differences in the pre- and postnatal life. For example, baptism is for the living human being who breathes, cries, eats—not the dead or not yet born. Can we expand the notion of living to include the embryo, a human life but in a different form and a human life that does not breathe, cry, or eat? Incorporating embryos into the community by baptism or another ritual would mean expanding who is considered a member of the Body of Christ.

The Body of Christ metaphor can be expanded, however, without necessitating baptism. Typically, individuals or communities are associated with the visible body parts—eyes, ears, hands, feet. Yet, the body has visible (what we can see with the naked eye) and invisible (what we can see with a microscope) parts. Expanding the Body of Christ metaphor to include prenatal life, including embryos, requires acknowledging both what is visible and invisible in the human body. As it is, the Body of Christ already includes those alive and those no longer with us, the dead (communion of saints). Embryos, seen as members of the Body of Christ, invisible, with us and not yet with us, opens new possibilities for wrestling with the fate of frozen embryos. This is a necessity since, even if one believes that embryo donation or adoption is the most ethical response for frozen embryos, given the number of frozen embryos, donation or adoption on its own is insufficient. Therefore, a way needs to be found to incorporate other options into a meaningful narrative, even if it means death.

The Body of Christ metaphor has embedded within it a recognition of connectedness to community, our reliance on each other, and our inability to live fully into the reign of God. After all, it is only God who can bring about the fullness of life. As a result, we strive to live well with the imperfect and various responses to the ethical dilemmas of our lives. Therefore, while the CDF says the reality of frozen embryos is an irresolvable situation of injustice, it is only irresolvable if we are seeking a perfect solution. What is resolvable is that the Christian tradition has resources for thinking about death, dying, and a God who accompanies the community. We have rituals for the liminal spaces in human experience. If we bring embryonic life into the Body of Christ, it fosters, and pushes us toward, a relational, ritual framework, which potentially enables varied responses to the tragedy that is hundreds of thousands of nascent human life in suspended animation. It potentially provides further consideration for HET/embryo adoption/donation. Moreover, the Body of Christ metaphor in all its complexity, when combined with other aspects of the moral tradition, provides a way for making sense of one option that leads to embryonic death, thawing to let them die. While embryonic death is undesired, unwanted, and lamentable, it is at least another feasible response to frozen embryos when considered within the theological framework of the Body of Christ and the Paschal Mystery.

NOTES

1. The US Department of Health and Human Services reports that there are approximately 600,000 cryo-preserved (frozen) embryos in the United States, of which 60,000 could be available for embryo transfer into a woman who is not the woman originally trying to get pregnant and bring a child to term. See Health and Human Services, "Embryo Adoption," last modified August 3, 2007, https://www.hhs.gov/opa/about-opa/embryo-adoption/index.html.

2. The CDF evaluated both homologous IVF, which used the spouses' own gametes (eggs and sperm), and heterologous IVF, which used gametes from "donors," as morally illicit. The 1994 English version of the *Catechism of the Catholic Church*, while following this instruction, does say that artificial reproductive techniques that use spousal gametes are "perhaps less reprehensible, yet remain morally unacceptable" (par. 2377).

3. Congregation for the Doctrine of the Faith, *Instruction on Certain Bioethical Questions (Dignitas Personae)*, art. 19, last modified December 18, 2008, http://www.vatican.va/roman_curia/congregations/cfaith/documents/rc_con_cfaith_doc_20081208_dignitas-personae_en.html, citing John Paul II, Address to the Participants in the Symposium on "*Evangelium vitae* and Law" and the Eleventh International Colloquium on Roman and Canon Law (24 May 1996), 6, in *Acta Apostolicae Sedis* 88 (1996), 943–44.

4. Pontifical Academy of Life, *Final Communique on "The Dignity of Human Procreation and Reproductive Technologies: Anthropological and Ethical Aspects,"* last modified February 2004, http://www.vatican.va/roman_curia/pontifical_academies/acdlife/documents/rc_pont-acd_life_doc_20040316_x-gen-assembly-final_en.html; for an excellent overview of the debates regarding embryo adoption, see Sarah-Vaughan Brakman and Darlene Fozard Weaver, eds., *The Ethics of Embryo Adoption and the Catholic Tradition: Moral Arguments, Economic Reality, and Social Analysis* (New York: Springer, 2007).

5. *Dignitas Personae* affirmed the 1987 instruction *Donum Vitae*, which prohibited artificial insemination, in-vitro fertilization, and surrogacy while advocating for the proper use of technology to correct underlying reasons for infertility. *Dignitas Personae* clarified or nuanced some 1987 positions of the CDF in light of additional information and argumentation from theologians and philosophers, while also addressing new questions that had emerged since 1987 in bioethics and reproductive technologies.

6. *Dignitas Personae*, art. 19. Emphasis in the original.

7. For purposes of clarity in this essay, when using the term "Catholics," I am referencing the Roman Rite. This complication exists for Catholics who have used IVF and have to grapple with their own frozen embryos, as well as Catholics who do not use IVF but are concerned about and see a moral obligation to engage with the reality of the number of frozen embryos that in the Catholic tradition are on the continuum of human life.

8. Both before and after the CDF published *Dignitas Personae*, Catholic theologians have argued for the validity of embryo adoption. See, for example, Glenn Breed, "The Only Moral Option Is Embryo Adoption," *The National Catholic Bioethics Quarterly* 14, no. 3 (2014): 441–47; Mary Jo Iozzio, "It Is Time to Support

Embryo Adoption," *The National Catholic Bioethics Quarterly* 2, no. 4 (2002): 585–93.

9. Principles have been developed to guide these types of decisions. These principles include the principle of double effect, the principle of cooperation, just war theory meant to guide decisions of going to war, and the principle of gradualism.

10. See the websites listed in fn. 19 for images of the embryo's developmental stages.

11. Tomáš Spidlík, *The Spirituality of the Christian East* (Collegeville, MN: Liturgical Press, 2008), 237.

12. Ibid., 242–43.

13. See Robert Masson, *Without Metaphor, No Saving God: Theology after Cognitive Linguistics* (Leuven: Peeters, 2014). He provides an overview of the cognitive linguistics in the first half of the book and applies the insights to theological debates in the second.

14. Ibid., 249.

15. Ibid.

16. This language of "conception to natural death" is used in theological scholarship and prayer.

17. Brakman and Fozard Weaver, "Introduction," in *The Ethics of Embryo Adoption*, 3–24, at 18. Brakman and Fozard Weaver argue that frozen embryos and the debates around embryo adoption touch on questions of belonging, kinship, embodiment, personhood, etc. See also Darlene Fozard Weaver, "Embryo Adoption: Expanding the Terms of the Debate," in *Applied Ethics in a World Church*, ed. Linda Hogan (Maryknoll, NY: Orbis Books, 2008), 199–207, at 205.

18. Additionally, in the United States embryos have a symbolic political place whereby one's attitude toward embryos become a stand-in for other viewpoints and are code for other political differences in the country.

19. Françoise Baylis, "Embryo Research," in *The International Encyclopedia of Ethics*, ed. Hugh LaFollette (Malden: MA: Wiley-Blackwell, 2013), 3:1579–85. For images of these various stages please see: M.A. Hill, "Embryonic Development," last modified August 2, 2016, https://embryology.med.unsw.edu.au/embryology/index.php/Embryonic_Development.

20. Centers for Disease Control and Prevention, American Society for Reproductive Medicine, Society for Assisted Reproductive Technology, *2013 Assisted Reproductive Technology National Summary Report* (Atlanta, GA: US Department of Health and Human Services, 2015), 63.

21. *Encyclopedia Britannica*, s.v. "Blastocyst," last accessed February 21, 2018, https://www.britannica.com/science/blastocyst.

22. CDC, *2013 Assisted Reproductive Technology National Summary Report*, 62.

23. Baylis, "Embryo Research," 1579.

24. CDC, *2013 Assisted Reproductive Technology National Summary Report*, 61.

25. Ibid., 61.

26. Congregation for the Doctrine of the Faith, foreword to *Donum Vitae*, last accessed January 1, 2018, http://www.vatican.va/roman_curia/congregations/cfaith/documents/rc_con_cfaith_doc_19870222_respect-for-human-life_en.html.

27. *Donum Vitae*, 1.1.

28. The Catholic Church teaches that it is unknown when exactly the soul enters the body, but given the belief in the unity of the body and soul, respecting this unity means respecting the prenatal human life in the same way as a postnatal human being.

29. Thank you to my philosophy colleague Jean Keller, who helped me clarify this distinction.

30. Not all embryos successfully survive the thawing and freezing process.

31. "Unviable" is a clinical term meaning the three- to five-day-old embryo for any number of reasons has stopped developing or has enough wrong at the chromosomal level that it will stop developing soon. As such, it is an accurate description even as it is distancing. During embodied conception, three- to five-day-old embryos that will not continue to develop will not implant in the uterine lining, and the woman will have her menstrual cycle on schedule or possibly a little late. In either case, she might not even realize she had conceived.

32. Legally, the embryos are often treated as property (secular world), governed by law and the CDC, which all affect what the doctors can and cannot do.

33. Even within the Catholic moral theology world there is debate regarding whether to use the language of adoption, donation, rescue, or heterologous embryo transfer (HET). "Heterologous" means that the embryo is genetically unrelated to the woman who will have the embryo transferred into her uterus. HET is the scientific language for the process. See Brakman and Fozard Weaver, "Introduction," in *The Ethics of Embryo Adoption and the Catholic Tradition*, for their rationale for using adoption language. See William E. Stempsey, "Heterologous Embryo Transfer: Metaphor and Morality," 25–42, in the same book for his rationale for using HET. For language on rescue, see Kent Lasnoski, "Setting the Captives Free: Precedence for Embryo Adoption in Scripture and the Catholic Tradition," *The Josephinum Journal of Theology* 20, no. 1 (Winter–Spring 2013): 88–112. For information on embryo adoption facilitated by a Christian agency, see the Nightlight Christian Adoptions "Snowflake" program at http://www.embryoadoption.org/ and https://www.nightlight.org/snowflakes-embryo-adoption-donation/, last accessed February 21, 2018.

34. This decision is complicated for many reasons, among them couples not thinking ahead to the possibility of unimplanted embryos, as well as how one thinks about the embryos—biologic material, potential child, et cetera. For an example of these studies, see Robert D. Nachtigall, Gay Becker, Carrie Friese, Anneliese Butler, Kirstin MacDougall, "Parents' Conceptualization of Their Frozen Embryos Complicates the Disposition Decision," *Fertility and Sterility* 84, no. 2 (2005): 431–34.

35. See Stempsey, "Heterologous Embryo Transfer," 25–42 for both literature on embryo adoption and an analysis of this metaphor.

36. See John Stanmeyer, "An Embryo Adoptive Father's Perspective," 231–36, and Suzanne Stanmeyer, "An Embryo Adoptive Mother's Perspective," 237–49, both in Brakman and Fozard Weaver, *The Ethics of Embryo Adoption and the Catholic Tradition*.

37. Stempsey, "Heterologous Embryo Transfer," 29.

38. Exploring more in depth what is concealed would require considering what has been compressed in this blending of adoption with the embryo as a human being/person. This is beyond the scope of this project. For more on compression, see Raymond W. Gibbs, *The Cambridge Handbook of Metaphor and Thought* (Cambridge: Cambridge University Press, 2008), 53–54; Gilles Fauconnier and Mark Turner, *The Way We Think: Conceptual Blending and the Mind's Hidden Complexities* (New York: Basic Books, 2002), 113–35. Fauconnier, Gilles, and Mark Turner. *The Way We Think: Conceptual Blending and the Mind's Hidden Complexities*. New York: Basic Books, 2002

39. Mary B. Mahowald, "Embryo *Adoption*? An Egalitarian Perspective," in Brakman and Fozard Weaver, *The Ethics of Embryo Adoption and the Catholic Tradition*, 175–84, at 181.

40. See Mahowald, "Embryo *Adoption*?," who begins this conversation. Darlene Fozard Weaver has also noted the need for this analysis. See her articles cited elsewhere.

41. Lucy Frith and Eric Blyth, "They Can't Have My Embryo: The Ethics of Conditional Embryo Donation," *Bioethics* 27, no. 6 (2013): 317–24.

42. Masae Kato, "Giving a Gift to the Gift: Women's Experiences of Embryo Donation in Japan," *Anthropological Forum* 24, no. 4 (2014): 351–63. The article raises questions about the role culture plays in the donation/adoption frames, which is beyond the scope of this essay.

43. Ibid.

44. Masson, *Without Metaphor*, 107–9.

45. Darlene Fozard Weaver, "Embryo Adoption Theologically Considered: Bodies, Adoption, and the Common Good," in Brakman and Fozard Weaver, *The Ethics of Embryo Adoption and the Catholic Tradition*, 141–59, at 152–56.

46. Thank you to Fr. Dale Launderville, OSB, for asking this question about the household during a robust discussion of a much earlier draft of this essay. Thank you also to all my theology colleagues at the College of Saint Benedict, Saint John's University, and the School of Theology/Seminary who participated in that and subsequent discussions with me. As well as the graduate students who asked about the language of "orphans" in *Dignitatis Personae* which informed that section of this essay.

47. There are programs that exist and pastoral practices that some individual churches have incorporated into their communal life. Nevertheless, as a worldwide community, the Roman Catholic Church does not have a rite or ritual practices that are drawn on in the event of a miscarriage, abortion, or stillbirth—all forms of prenatal loss. Yet, there are funeral rites for those who die after being born, and there is a practice of anointing the sick.

BIBLIOGRAPHY

Baylis, Françoise. "Embryo Research." In *The International Encyclopedia of Ethics*, edited by Hugh LaFollette, 3:1579–85. Malden, MA: Wiley-Blackwell, 2013.

Brakman, Sarah-Vaughan, and Darlene Fozard Weaver, eds. *The Ethics of Embryo Adoption and the Catholic Tradition: Moral Arguments, Economic Reality, and Social Analysis*. New York: Springer, 2007.

———. *The Ethics of Embryo Adoption and the Catholic Tradition: Moral Arguments, Economic Reality, and Social Analysis*. Philosophy and Medicine ; Catholic Studies in Bioethics, 95. V. 6. New York?: Springer, 2007.

Breed, Glenn. "The Only Moral Option Is Embryo Adoption." *The National Catholic Bioethics Quarterly* 14, no. 3 (2014): 441–47.

Catechism of the Catholic Church. 2nd ed. Washington, DC: United States Catholic Conference, Inc.—Libreria Editrice Vaticana, 1994.

Centers for Disease Control and Prevention, American Society for Reproductive Medicine, Society for Assisted Reproductive Technology. *2013 Assisted Reproductive Technology National Summary Report*. Atlanta, GA: US Department of Health and Human Services, 2015.

Congregation for the Doctrine of the Faith. *Donum Vitae*. Last modified February 22, 1987. http://www.vatican.va/roman_curia/congregations/cfaith/documents/rc_con_cfaith_doc_19870222_respect-for-human-life_en.html.

———. *Instruction on Certain Bioethical Questions (Dignitas Personae)*. Last modified December 18, 2008. http://www.vatican.va/roman_curia/congregations/cfaith/documents/rc_con_cfaith_doc_20081208_dignitas-personae_en.html.

Fauconnier, Gilles, and Mark Turner. *The Way We Think: Conceptual Blending and the Mind's Hidden Complexities*. New York: Basic Books, 2002.

Fozard Weaver, Darlene. "Embryo Adoption: Expanding the Terms of the Debate." In *Applied Ethics in a World Church*, edited by Linda Hogan, 199–207. Maryknoll, NY: Orbis Books, 2008.

———. "Embryo Adoption Theologically Considered: Bodies, Adoption, and the Common Good." In Brakman and Fozard Weaver, *The Ethics of Embryo Adoption and the Catholic Tradition*, 141–59.

Frith, Lucy, and Eric Blyth. "They Can't Have My Embryo: The Ethics of Conditional Embryo Donation." *Bioethics* 27, no. 6 (2013): 317–24.

Gibbs, Raymond W. *The Cambridge Handbook of Metaphor and Thought*. Cambridge: Cambridge University Press, 2008.

Health and Human Services, Office of Population Affairs. "Embryo Adoption." Last modified August 3, 2017. https://www.hhs.gov/opa/about-opa/embryo-adoption/index.html.

Hill, M. A. "Embryonic Development." Last modified August 2, 2016. https://embryology.med.unsw.edu.au/embryology/index.php/Embryonic_Development.

Iozzio, Mary Jo. "It Is Time to Support Embryo Adoption." *The National Catholic Bioethics Quarterly* 2, no. 4 (2002): 585–93.

John Paul II. Address to the Participants in the Symposium on "*Evangelium vitae* and Law" and the Eleventh International Colloquium on Roman and Canon Law (24 May 1996), in *Acta Apostolicae Sedis* 88 (1996): 943–44.

Kato, Masae. "Giving a Gift to the Gift: Women's Experiences of Embryo Donation in Japan." *Anthropological Forum* 24, no. 4 (2014): 351–63.

Lasnoski, Kent. "Setting the Captives Free: Precedence for Embryo Adoption in Scripture and the Catholic Tradition." *The Josephinum Journal of Theology* 20, no. 1 (Winter–Spring 2013): 88–112.

Mahowald, Mary B. "Embryo *Adoption*? An Egalitarian Perspective." In Brakman and Fozard Weaver, *The Ethics of Embryo Adoption and the Catholic Tradition*, 175–84.

Masson, Robert. *Without Metaphor, No Saving God: Theology after Cognitive Linguistics*. Leuven: Peeters, 2014.

Nachtigall, Robert D., Gay Becker, Carrie Friese, Anneliese Butler, and Kirstin MacDougall. "Parents' Conceptualization of Their Frozen Embryos Complicates the Disposition Decision." *Fertility and Sterility* 84, no. 2 (2005): 431–34.

Pontifical Academy of Life. *Final Communique on "The Dignity of Human Procreation and Reproductive Technologies: Anthropological and Ethical Aspects."* Last modified February 2004. http://www.vatican.va/roman_curia/pontifical_academies/acdlife/documents/rc_pont-acd_life_doc_20040316_x-gen-assembly-final_en.html.

Spidlík, Tomáš. *The Spirituality of the Christian East*. Collegeville, MN: Liturgical Press, 2008.

Index

About the Contributors

Kathryn Lilla Cox has taught at Saint John's School of Theology and Seminary and in the undergraduate Department of Theology of the College of Saint Benedict and Saint John's University since 2007. She teaches courses in fundamental moral theology and applied ethics. Her research explores the theology of infertility, the role of emotions in the moral life, conscience, and the intersection of science and theology. Her book *Water Shaping Stone: Faith, Relationships, and Conscience Formation* was published in December 2015 and received a Catholic Press Association award in June of 2016. She is currently researching the ethics of speech, and the potential of neuroscientific insights for understanding moral formation.

Julia Feder is assistant professor of theology at Creighton University in Omaha, Nebraska. She specializes in systematic theology, with a particular focus on theological anthropology, suffering, and salvation. Her forthcoming book, *Trauma and Salvation: A Theology of Healing*, draws on the writings of Spanish mystic Teresa of Avila and Flemish political theologian Edward Schillebeeckx to construct healing from sexual trauma as a mystical-political practice. Before joining the faculty at Creighton, she was a research fellow at the Center for Theology, Science, and Human Flourishing at the University of Notre Dame where she examined the centrality of symbol-making in the human niche. She continues to think and write theologically about human evolution, drawing connections between Edward Schillebeeckx's understanding of human experience and imagination (particularly the role of "negative contrast experiences") and biological anthropologists' understanding of human symbolic behavior and cognition. Her articles appear in *Philosophy, Theology, and the Sciences*, the *Journal of Religion and Society*, and *Theological Studies*.

Christopher M. Hadley, SJ is assistant professor of systematic theology at the Jesuit School of Theology of Santa Clara University, a member school of the Graduate Theological Union in Berkeley, California. His research interests lie in Christology, Trinitarian theology, and Christian ecumenism. He is the director of the Masters in Divinity program at the school and teaches core courses on fundamental theology and the theology of priesthood in that program. He also teaches introductory and advanced courses in Trinitarian theology, theological aesthetics, pneumatology, and eschatology. Fr. Hadley serves as a priest in the Diocese of Oakland and in the Melkite and Ukrainian Greek Catholic churches of the San Francisco Bay Area and Silicon Valley.

Erin Kidd is assistant professor in the Department of Theology and Religious Studies at St. John's University (Queens, New York) where she teaches courses in systematic theology and gender studies. Her research focuses on the body, particularly as it informs and intersects with topics in theological anthropology, theological method, God-talk, feminist theology, and science and religion. She is currently working on a book titled *Doing Theology from the Gut: Body, Method, and God* (Lexington Press/Fortress Academic), which draws on insights from a number of disciplines (cognitive science, trauma studies, and affect theory) to develop a feminist theological account of the body.

Robert L. Masson is professor emeritus of theology at Marquette University and author of *Without Metaphor, No Saving God: Theology after Cognitive Linguistics* (Leuven: Peeters Press, 2014). He specializes in systematic and philosophical theology. The focus of his current research is the role of metaphor, analogy, and symbol in religious understanding and theological argumentation, particularly in light of recent research in cognitive linguistics. He has served as president of the College Theology Society (2004–2005) and coordinator of the Karl Rahner Society (1995–1998).

Jakob Karl Rinderknecht is the director of the Pastoral Institute at the University of the Incarnate Word in San Antonio, Texas. His recent research considers the implications of embodiment for theology, especially in the areas of ecumenism, intercultural engagement, and sacramental theology. He recently published *Mapping the Differentiated Consensus of the Joint Declaration* (Palgrave, 2016), which examines Lutheran-Catholic agreement on Justification. His articles appear in *Horizons, Open Theology*, and *American Benedictine Review*, as well as several edited collections.

Jason P. Roberts is member of the Department of Religion faculty at the University of Georgia. As a lecturer of Christian theology, his main teaching responsibilities include introducing students to the Abrahamic faith traditions, as well as deepening students' engagement with Roman Catholic scholarship, religiosity, and history. Beyond these general areas, his teaching and research interests focus on topics and figures at the intersections of theology, Christian anthropology, ethics, hermeneutics, and the natural sciences.

Stephen R. Shaver is a priest in the Episcopal Church and completed a PhD in liturgical studies in 2017 at the Graduate Theological Union in Berkeley, California. His current research focuses on the intersection between liturgical theology and cognitive linguistics. He is author of *Eucharistic Sacrifice as a Contested Category: A Cognitive Linguistics Approach*, Alcuin/GROW Joint Liturgical Studies 85 (Norwich: Hymns Ancient and Modern, 2018).

Adam M. Willows is a research fellow at the University of Leeds. He specializes in philosophical theology, with particular interests in normative ethics, virtue, free will theory, and philosophy of religion. His work so far emphasizes the potential for philosophical and theological traditions to interact, often to mutual benefit. Before working at Leeds, he completed his doctorate at the University of Durham (2015) and was a postdoctoral researcher in theology at the University of Notre Dame (2015–2017).

www.ingramcontent.com/pod-product-compliance
Ingram Content Group UK Ltd.
Pitfield, Milton Keynes, MK11 3LW, UK
UKHW041913130926
475466UK00001B/3

9 781978 703964